MOON

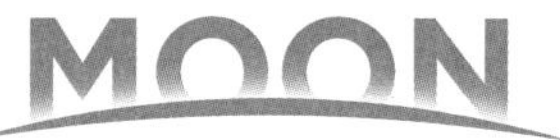

SAN JUAN, VIEQUES & CULEBRA

SUZANNE VAN ATTEN

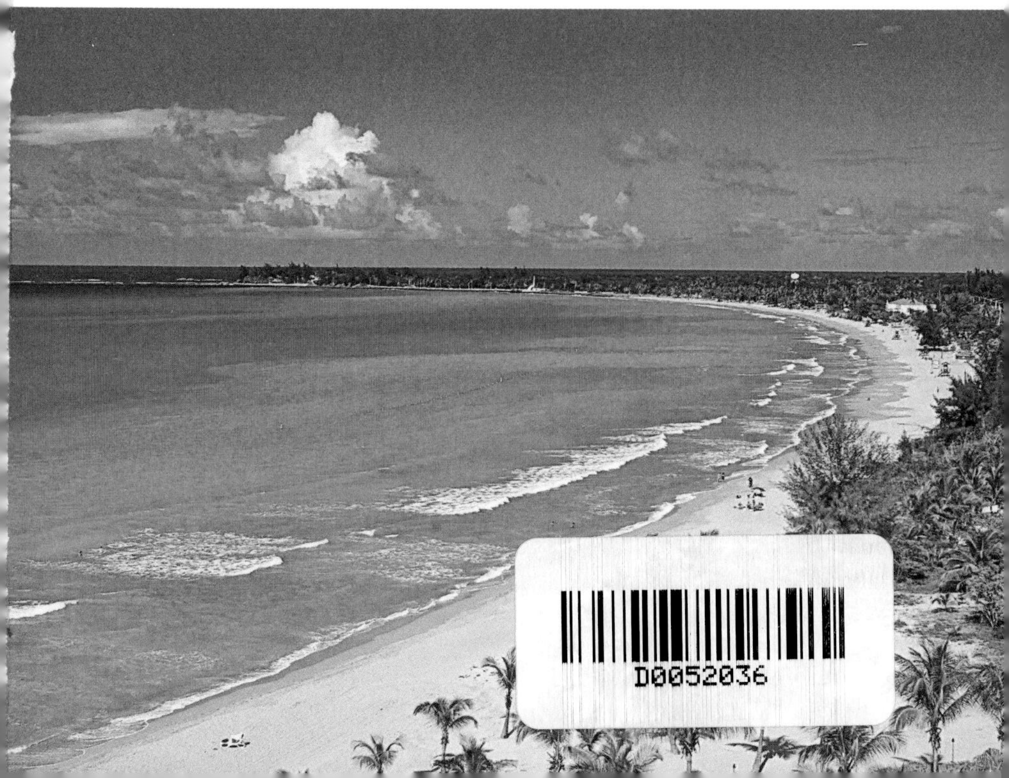

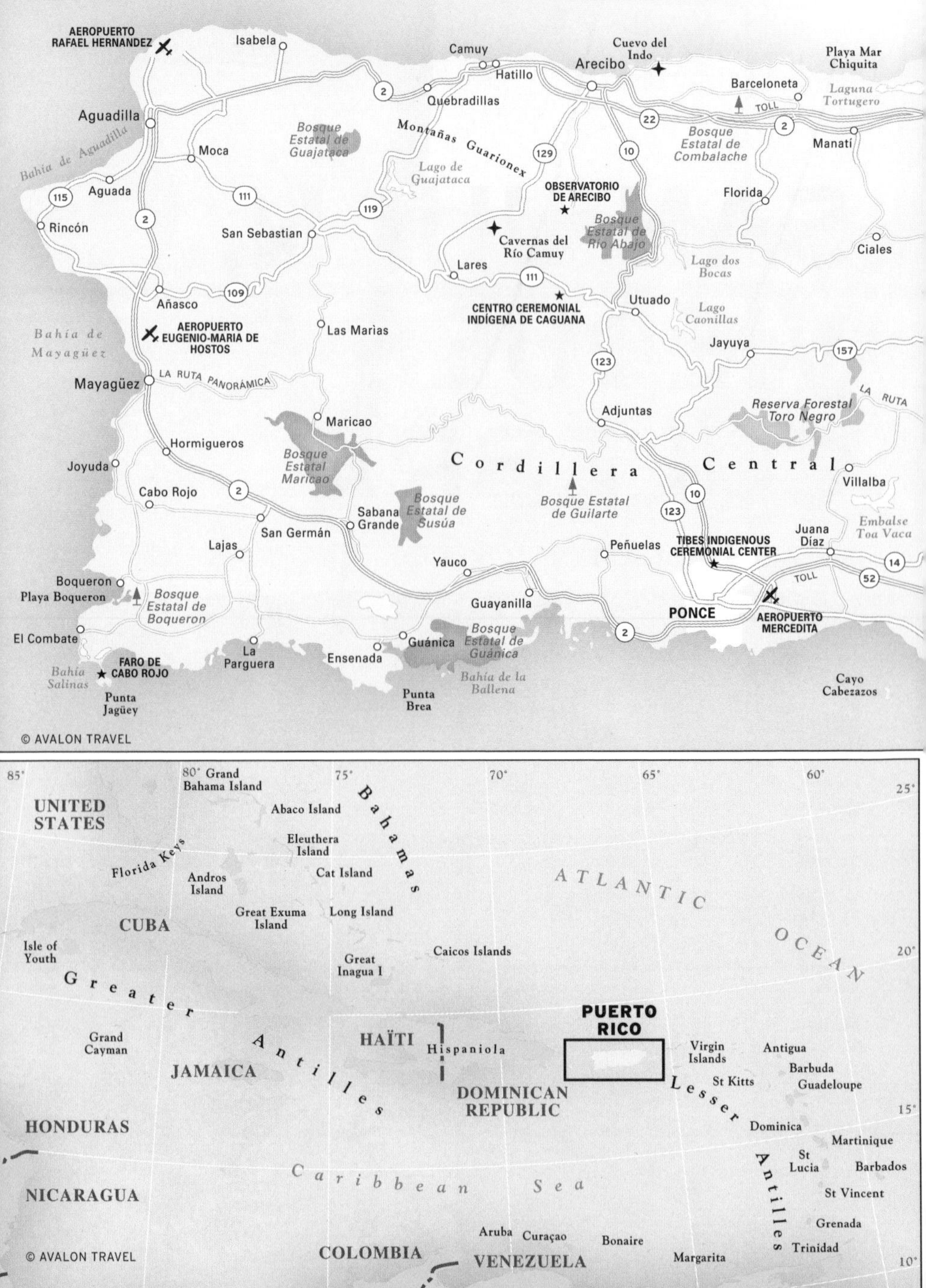
AEROPUERTO RAFAEL HERNANDEZ
Isabela
Camuy
Cuevo del Indo
Playa Mar Chiquita
Hatillo
Arecibo
Barceloneta
Laguna Tortugero
Quebradillas
TOLL
Aguadilla
Bosque Estatal de Guajataca
Montañas Guarionex
Bosque Estatal de Combalache
Manatí
Bahía de Aguadilla
Moca
Lago de Guajataca
OBSERVATORIO DE ARECIBO
Aguada
Florida
Rincón
San Sebastian
Cavernas del Río Camuy
Bosque Estatal de Río Abajo
Ciales
Lares
Lago dos Bocas
Añasco
CENTRO CEREMONIAL INDÍGENA DE CAGUANA
Utuado
Lago Caonillas
Bahía de Mayagüez
AEROPUERTO EUGENIO-MARIA DE HOSTOS
Las Marìas
Jayuya
Mayagüez
LA RUTA PANORÁMICA
Adjuntas
Reserva Forestal Toro Negro
LA RUTA
Maricao
Hormigueros
Bosque Estatal Maricao
Cordillera Central
Joyuda
Villalba
Cabo Rojo
Bosque Estatal de Guilarte
Sabana Grande
Bosque Estatal de Susúa
San Germán
Juana Díaz
Embalse Toa Vaca
Lajas
Peñuelas
TIBES INDIGENOUS CEREMONIAL CENTER
Yauco
Boqueron
Playa Boqueron
Bosque Estatal de Boqueron
Guayanilla
PONCE
AEROPUERTO MERCEDITA
El Combate
La Parguera
Ensenada
Guánica
Bosque Estatal de Guánica
Bahía Salinas
FARO DE CABO ROJO
Bahía de la Ballena
Punta Jagüey
Punta Brea
Cayo Cabezazos
© AVALON TRAVEL
85°
80°
75°
70°
65°
60°
25°
20°
15°
10°
Grand Bahama Island
UNITED STATES
Abaco Island
Bahamas
Eleuthera Island
Florida Keys
Andros Island
Cat Island
ATLANTIC OCEAN
Great Exuma Island
Long Island
CUBA
Isle of Youth
Caicos Islands
Great Inagua I
Greater Antilles
PUERTO RICO
Grand Cayman
HAÏTI
Hispaniola
Virgin Islands
Antigua
JAMAICA
Barbuda
St Kitts
Guadeloupe
DOMINICAN REPUBLIC
Lesser Antilles
HONDURAS
Dominica
Martinique
St Lucia
Barbados
Caribbean Sea
NICARAGUA
St Vincent
Grenada
Aruba
Curaçao
Bonaire
Trinidad
COLOMBIA
VENEZUELA
Margarita
© AVALON TRAVEL

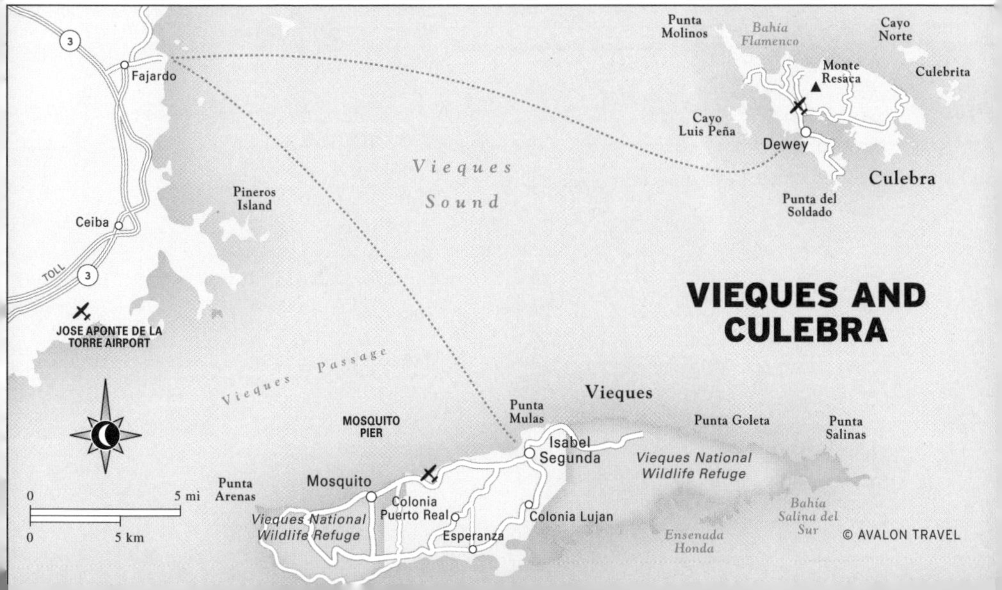

PUERTO RICO

Punta Cerro Gordo
Punta Salinas
OLD SAN JUAN
AEROPUERTO INTERNACIONAL LUIS MUÑOZ MARIN
Bosque Estatal de Piñones
Vega Baja
Dorado
Toa Baja
Cataño
Santurce
22
26
Vega Alta
Carolina
Loíza
Río Piedras
188
187
Playa Luquillo
Laguna Grande
Cayo Icacos
Toa Alta
Bayamón
Canóvanas
Luquillo
SAN JUAN
3
Río Grande
Las Croabas
66
Las Cabezas de San Juan Nature Reserve
Corozal
Guaynabo
Trujillo Alto
185
52
167
El Yunque Caribbean National Forest
Fajardo
Morovis
1
Embalse Río Grande de Loiza
Naranjito
Montañas de Corazol
Pineros Island
Aguas Buenas
Gurabo
Ceiba
156
Caguas
Orocovis
Juncos
TOLL
31
Comerío
Naguabo
JOSE APONTE DE LA TORRE AIRPORT
Barranquitas
30
Las Piedras
53
PANORÁMICA
SAN CRISTÓBAL CAÑON
Cidra
TOLL
San Lorenzo
Humacao
3
Vieques Passage
Aibonito
Cayey
Vieques
Reserva Forestal Carite
LA RUTA PANORÁMICA
Palmas del Mar
Coamo
52
Sierra de Cayey
Yabucoa
Baños de Coamo
Patillas
Maunabo
Salinas
Guayama
53
1
3
Punta Tuna
Santa Isabel
Arroyo
0
10 mi
Cayos Caribes
Cayos de Barca
Bahía de Jobos
0
10 km

VIEQUES AND CULEBRA

3
Fajardo
Punta Molinos
Bahía Flamenco
Cayo Norte
Monte Resaca
Culebrita
Cayo Luis Peña
Dewey
Culebra
Vieques Sound
Pineros Island
Punta del Soldado
Ceiba
TOLL
3
JOSE APONTE DE LA TORRE AIRPORT
Vieques Passage
Vieques
MOSQUITO PIER
Punta Mulas
Punta Goleta
Punta Salinas
Isabel Segunda
Vieques National Wildlife Refuge
Punta Arenas
Mosquito
Colonia Puerto Real
Colonia Lujan
Vieques National Wildlife Refuge
Esperanza
Bahía Salina del Sur
Ensenada Honda
0
5 mi
0
5 km

Contents

DISCOVER

San Juan, Vieques & Culebra

Like any major metropolitan city, San Juan is many things to many people. To historians it is blue cobblestone streets and 17th-century fortresses that harken back to the birth of Spanish colonialism. To foodies it is the taste of celebrity chefs pushing the boundaries of Caribbean cuisine and mom-and-pop restaurants that are preserving the traditional flavors of *criolla cocina* (Puerto Rican cuisine). To culture buffs it is world-class museums and heritage festivals. To the party crowd, it is enjoying the glitzy casinos, rooftop lounges, cozy bars, and frenetic nightclubs thumping with the beat of salsa, techno, or reggaetón. To outdoor enthusiasts, it is thrill-a-minute action spent swimming, sailing, surfing, snorkeling, paddleboarding, horseback riding, ziplining, and deep-sea fishing. And to sun worshippers it is wide sandy beaches, shady palm trees, tropical breezes, and a cooling dip in the surf.

But if your idea of an island getaway doesn't involve glitz and glam or some of the attendant woes of city life, like traffic and crowds, then the solution is a short plane or ferry ride away. Vieques and Culebra are the antithesis of San Juan. Located off the east coast of the main island and accessible by plane or ferry, they are sometimes referred to as the Spanish Virgin Islands or "the way Puerto Rico

Clockwise from top left: La Concha Resort; La Fortaleza; *vejigante* mask; Playa Flamenco in Culebra; calabash tree gourds; Laguna del Condado.

used to be." Sleepy, rustic, and predominantly undeveloped, they boast miles of deserted beaches, diving and fishing spots galore, and a low-key ambiance designed for rest and relaxation.

Vieques is the largest of the islets and the most populated. Aside from the free-range horses that roam the place, its biggest claim to fame is Mosquito Bay, Puerto Rico's most dramatic bioluminescent lagoon. Culebra is smaller and even sleepier than Vieques, and it is famous for having one of the most magnificent beaches in the Caribbean—Playa Flamenco, a mile-long crescent where the water is clear as glass and the sand is blindingly white.

Between San Juan, Vieques, and Culebra, it is possible to experience everything Puerto Rico has to offer, from the sophisticated to the sublime.

Clockwise from top left: boats dock in Culebra; cobblestone street in Old San Juan; sunset in Vieques; the eastern shore of Culebra, across from Playa Flamenco.

Planning Your Time

Where to Go

San Juan

Situated on the northeast coast, sophisticated, fast-paced San Juan is Puerto Rico's capital and largest city. Its heart is **Old San Juan,** the original walled city founded by Spanish settlers in 1521, home to two fortresses: **Castillo San Felipe del Morro** and **Castillo de San Cristóbal.** Other significant neighborhoods include **Isla Verde,** with the city's best beaches and most exclusive hotels, and **Condado,** considered the tourist district, where you'll find high-rise hotels, high-end shops, and casinos. In nearby **Santurce** is a burgeoning arts district, home to galleries, studios, and **Museo de Arte de Puerto Rico.**

Land-and-air vacation packages are available at resorts and hotels in Condado and Isla Verde. Because the island is only 111 miles by 36 miles, you can take a **day trip** to anywhere in Puerto Rico from San Juan; popular ones include El Yunque Caribbean National Forest in Río Grande, the beach and *kioskos* in Luquillo, and the colonial city of Ponce.

Vieques and Culebra

Vieques and Culebra are two small islands off the main island's east coast. Both offer some of the best wilderness beaches to be found in Puerto Rico—if not the entire Caribbean. **Balneario Sun Bay** in Vieques is a mile-long sandy crescent on crystal-blue waters. **Playa Flamenco** on Culebra is considered one of the best beaches in the United States. Both islands are renowned for their spectacular diving and snorkeling. Vieques is also the site of **Mosquito Bay,** Puerto Rico's most outstanding

Castillo San Felipe del Morro

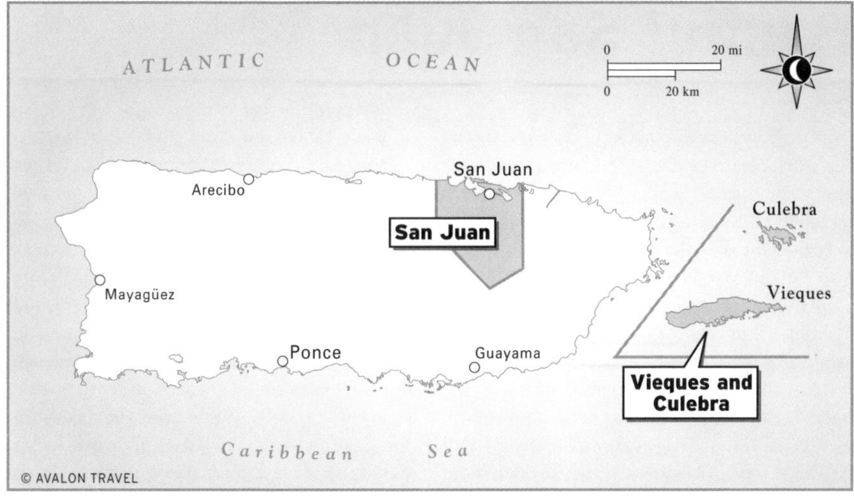

bioluminescent bay, where the water glows an electric blue at night. If you need a history fix, Vieques is home to **El Fortín Conde de Mirasol,** the last fort built by colonial Spain, which now holds the **Vieques Museum of Art and History.**

When to Go

The climate in Puerto Rico is classified as tropical marine, which means it is sunny, hot, and humid year-round. The average year-round temperature ranges from 80°F on the coast to 68°F in the mountains.

Puerto Rico has two seasons. **Dry season** is January-April. This is when humidity is the lowest, and temperatures hit an average high of 84°F and an average low of 71°F. It should be noted that rain does occur during dry season, but at a much lower rate than in summer and fall. Airline tickets and hotel room rates tend to be higher during dry season. From December through the end of dry season is **high season** for the tourist industry throughout much of the island, including San Juan and Vieques.

Rainy season is May-November, when an average of 4-6 inches of rain falls each month. The island's hottest months are June-September, when temperatures average 89°F, but it can spike as high as 97°F on the coast. The rainy season is also hurricane season. Airline ticket prices and hotel room rates are often reduced during rainy season.

In some parts of the island, particularly areas that cater primarily to Puerto Rican tourists, high season coincides with summer, when children are out of school.

Best of San Juan

Day 1

First-time visitors should begin their stay in Old San Juan. Start the day with a toasted *mallorca* pastry and *café con leche* at **Cafeteria Mallorca,** and then take a self-guided walking tour of one or both of the island's two Spanish forts, **Castillo San Felipe del Morro** and **Castillo de San Cristóbal.** Lunch on traditional Puerto Rican dishes such as *chuleta can can* (pork chops) or *arroz con pollo* (chicken and rice) at **Restaurante Raíces** and then escape the heat of the afternoon exploring the island's history and culture in some of Old San Juan's many museums, including **Museo de las Americas,** which features an outstanding collection of Latin American folk art. Dine on creative Caribbean cuisine at the casually elegant **Bodega Chic** and try out your salsa moves on the dance floor at **Nuyorican Café.** End the evening with a nightcap at the bar at **Marmalade.**

Day 2

Time to hit the beach. Rent a car for the day and head east toward **Isla Verde,** along the way stopping first at Walgreens for a Styrofoam cooler and some sunscreen, and then at **Kasalta Bakery** for a quick breakfast of *quesitos* (cheese pastries) or egg sandwiches. While you're there, pick up picnic provisions: a hunk of cheese, a loaf of *pan de agua* (water bread), a tub of ceviche, Medalla beer, bottles of water, and a bag of ice. Continue eastward to **El Alambique Beach** in Isla Verde, where you can rent lounge chairs and umbrellas and supplement your picnic with *piraguas* (snow cones) and *frituras* (fritters) from beachside vendors. While away the day swimming, riding Jet Skis, parasailing, surfing, or just soaking up the rays. Return to the hotel to shower off the sand, and then take a taxi to **La Placita** party district in Santurce. Put your name on the list for a late-night dinner at **Jose Enrique** and stroll the area, people-watch, dance to salsa, and have a pre-dinner cocktail or two while you wait for the cell phone call alerting you that your table is ready.

Day 3

Start the day with pancakes banana flambé at

Capilla del Cristo chapel

Dance the Night Away

If you want to hear live music, you're in luck. There are festivals nearly every weekend throughout the island, and music is always a major component. On weekends and holidays, parks and plazas are filled with the sounds of salsa, *bomba,* and *plena* music. To make an evening of it, try these popular hot spots.

- **Brava** (page 47): Salsa is often on the menu at this upscale club at El San Juan Resort & Casino in Isla Verde.
- **Downtown Bar & Restaurant** (page 48): Located in Hato Rey, San Juan's business district, this large, chic music venue hosts live performances by national and local Latin bands.
- **La Respuesta** (page 47): At night, it's where the hip crowd in Santurce goes to listen to DJs, live bands, hip-hop, rock, R&B, metal, and Latin jazz. Wednesday is Noche de Cine, featuring film screenings.
- **Libraría Libros AC Barra & Bistro** (page 48): This large, modern bookstore in Santurce is also a popular music venue for local rock, jazz, and Latin Bands.
- **Nuyorican Café** (page 45): In Old San Juan, this is the island's premier nightclub for live contemporary salsa music. The place gets packed with tourists and locals alike, and the dance floor is always smoking.

Caficultura and spend the morning shopping for local crafts, designer clothes, Indonesian imports, cigars, and fine jewelry in **Old San Juan.** Along the way, walk to the end of Calle Cristo and check out **Capilla del Cristo** chapel and feed the pigeons at **Parque de Palomas.** For lunch, nosh on empanadas (meat turnovers) and *pinchos* (grilled kabobs) from food trucks and street vendors at **Plaza de Hostos.** In the afternoon, go snorkeling at **Balneario El Escambrón** or learn how to stand-up paddleboard at **Laguna del Condado** with the instructors from **Velauno.** In the evening dine on traditional Puerto Rican cuisine at **Casa Lola Criolla Kitchen** in Condado, and hit the gaming tables at the **Caribe Hilton** casino. While you're there, try a piña colada; the hotel claims to have invented it in 1954.

Day 4

Head to **Santurce** and start the day with a Caprese omelet or Nutella-stuffed croissant at **Abracadabra Counter Café.** Spend the day exploring the extensive collection of Puerto Rican artwork at **Museo de Arte de Puerto Rico.** For lunch, cross the street and dine at **Bistro de Paris;** on weekends brunch is served from 11am to 4pm. In the afternoon, bet on the horses at the **Hipódromo Camarero** racetrack. In the evening, dine on *nueva criolla* cuisine at **Bodega Chic** and stroll along **Calle San Sebastián,** which turns into a street party at night, and hit a few of the bars along the way.

Day 5

For a day of adventure, pick up a rental car and head to Isla Verde, stopping at **Mi Casita** in La Plazoleta de Isla Verde shopping center for a cheap, filling breakfast. Continue eastward to **Hacienda Campo Rico,** where you can spend the morning horseback riding, kayaking, ATV riding, and ziplining. For lunch go to **Boca de Cangrejos** and dine on an assortment of fritters from one of the many roadside vendors, and then find a patch of sand where you can spend the afternoon. Be sure to leave before dusk, when the sand fleas attack. For dinner, go to **Budatai,** an upscale restaurant in Condado that serves Asian-Puerto Rican fusion cuisine. Afterwards head to the upstairs lounge at **Di Zucchero Lavazza Restaurant & Lounge** and dance the night away to techno music.

Options

If you want to spend the rest of your time in

Parque de Palomas

Puerto Rico on the beach or enjoying water sports, fly or take a ferry to Vieques and spend one to three days exploring the deserted beaches at **Refugio Nacional de Vida Silvestre de Vieques** wildlife refuge, the bioluminescent **Mosquito Bay,** and **El Fortín Conde de Mirasol.** Fly or take a ferry to Culebra and spend one to two days swimming and sunbathing at **Playa Flamenco** and exploring the underwater world of **Cayo Luis Peña.**

Best of Vieques and Culebra

Some people go to Vieques or Culebra for the day, just long enough to take in a water sport and have a meal. A few hop back and forth between the two. But most people stay a week or more, soaking up the slow-paced, do-nothing vibe. Vieques is the most diverse in terms of accommodations, restaurants, and water sports. Culebra is the sleepier, less-developed of the two. Both islands are rustic and boast spectacular stretches of pristine coastline and clean, clear waters.

Vieques

Visitors to Vieques must **fly into San Juan first.** If they plan to take a plane to Vieques, they can fly right out again from Luis Muñoz Marín International Airport. This is preferable as the ferry to Vieques is unreliable, and requires travelers to secure transportation via rental car, *público,* or van transport to Fajardo, 30 miles east (allow one hour).

DAY 1

Pick up your rental car and head straight to **Balneario Sun Bay** to spend the early part of the day swimming and sunbathing. Nosh on pizza and fritters from beachside vendors for lunch. In the afternoon, explore the island's history at **El Fortín Conde de Mirasol** and check out **El Faro Punta Mulas** lighthouse. In the evening, dine on seafood at **Trade Winds Restaurant,** overlooking the ***malecón* (sea walk)** in **Esperanza.** Afterwards, sing karaoke and have a nightcap at **Al's Mar Azul.**

DAY 2

Start the day with banana pancakes at **Belly Buttons** and take a half-day tour fishing for amberjack and tarpon with **Caribbean Fly Fishing** or take a paddleboard tour of the bay with **Vieques Paddleboarding.** Go to **Orquideas**

Best Beaches

- **Balneario El Escambrón** (page 40): This publicly maintained beach in the San Juan neighborhood of Puerta de Tierra features a small crescent beach on a protected cove. On the ocean floor is a collapsed bridge that provides an excellent site for underwater exploration.
- **Balneario Sun Bay** (page 97): The long white crescent and calm waters of Balneario Sun Bay make this the crown jewel of beaches in Vieques. The herd of horses grazing here adds to its charm.
- **Culebrita** (page 112): It requires a boat ride to get there, but Culebrita, a *cayo* (caye) off the coast of Culebra, is the place to go if you really want to get away from it all. In addition to multiple beaches perfect for swimming or shore snorkeling, there are several tidal pools and a lovely, abandoned lighthouse. To get there, either rent a boat or catch a water taxi at the docks in Dewey.
- **El Alambique Beach** (page 41): Located in Isla Verde, El Alambique Beach is a great spot for novice surfers to master the sport. Wow Surfing School & Water Sports rents boards and offers instruction.
- **Playa Carlos Rosario** (page 112): For easy access to a site rich in marine life with good visibility, visit this narrow beach in Culebra flanked by boulders and a protruding coral reef.

Playa Flamenco in Culebra

- **Playa Flamenco** (page 112): In Culebra, the wide, mile-long, horseshoe-shaped beach boasts fine white sand and calm, aquamarine water. Playa Flamenco is home to two hotels—Villa Flamenco Beach and Culebra Beach Villas (the latter operates Coconuts Beach Grill, serving sandwiches and beverages to beachgoers).

in Esperanza for a light lunch of sandwiches and salads. Afterwards, stroll along the *malecón* and hit some of the shops, including **Sol Creation.** In the afternoon, explore the **Sugar Mill Ruins** and then drive to **Isabel Segunda** and dine on fajitas and margaritas at **Cantina La Reina.** Once the sun goes down, take a kayak tour of the bioluminescent **Mosquito Bay.**

DAY 3

Grab a breakfast sandwich at **El Resuelve** and then take a two-hour guided tour of the island atop a Paso Fino horse with **Esperanza Riding Company.** For lunch, dine on burgers and crab cakes while overlooking the *malecón* at **Duffy's Esperanza,** and then spend the afternoon exploring the deserted beaches at **Refugio Nacional de Vida Silvestre de Vieques** wildlife refuge. For dinner, hit **El Quenepo** and dine on *nueva criolla* cuisine. Afterwards, hit the bars that line the *malecón* in Esperanza, including **Bananas Guesthouse, Beach Bar & Grill.**

Culebra

Visitors to Culebra must first **fly into San Juan.** To fly into Culebra, travelers must take a taxi to the regional Isla Grande Airport in Miramar. If they plan to take the ferry, they will need to secure transportation via rental car, *público*, or van transport to Fajardo, 30 miles east (allow one hour).

DAY 1

Hit **Pandeli Bakery** in Dewey for a breakfast sandwich or pastry and stock up on sunscreen before heading to **Playa Flamenco,** where you'll want to rent lounge chairs and umbrellas and spend the day swimming, sunbathing, and walking the mile-long crescent of pristine beach. When hunger pangs strike, visit one of the beachside kiosks and lunch on pizza, empanadas, *pinchos,* and fried seafood. In the afternoon, go for a challenging hike through a mangrove and boulder forest to **Playa Resaca,** a coral reef beach ill-suited for swimming but an important nesting site for sea turtles. For dinner, enjoy home-style *criolla* cuisine on the front porch at **Barbara Rosa.** Afterwards, have a Bushwhacker nightcap on the outdoor patio at **Mamacita's Restaurant.**

DAY 2

To fully appreciate all Culebra has to offer, visitors need to get underwater and explore the rich sea life, so take a one-tank dive with **Culebra Divers** or take a snorkel kayak tour with **Aquafari Culebra.** Afterwards, enjoy a late lunch of seafood tacos and fresh fruit margaritas at **Zaco's Tacos.** In the afternoon take a drive around the island and visit the **Museo Histórico de Culebra El Polvorin.** For dinner, dine on creative Caribbean cuisine at **Susie's Restaurant** and end the evening with a nightcap at **The Sandbar.**

Options

If you want to add on a few days to your Vieques or Culebra trip, spend some time in **San Juan** exploring the historic sights and museums, the world-class shopping, and the trendy nightclubs and restaurants. To plan your visit to San Juan, refer to the *Best of San Juan* itinerary.

Romantic Getaway

Whether celebrating the start of a new relationship or rekindling a long-running one, nothing says *amor* like the sun-kissed sights, sensual flavors, and sizzling sounds of San Juan, Vieques, and Culebra. Perhaps that's why they are all popular honeymoon destinations.

Day 1

Because romance loves luxury, plan to stay in one of the lavish hotels and resorts in Isla Verde. If your style is classic, stay at **El San Juan Resort & Casino.** If you're looking for a hip accommodation, stay at **San Juan Water Beach Club Hotel.** Start the day with a breakfast sandwich at **Piu Bello,** then spend the early afternoon at the lagoon-style pool at El San Juan Resort or lounging on the beach. At San Juan Water Beach Club, you can cool off and sun yourself at the petite rooftop pool. Share a black olive and blue cheese pizza for lunch at the Argentine-Italian restaurant **Ferrari Gourmet,** and then stroll through El San Juan's mini-mall of high-end shops, including David Yurman jewelry and Godiva chocolates. In the afternoon, get in a workout at the hotel gym before having dinner at one of the eight restaurants at El San Juan. Afterwards, stroll over to **The Ritz-Carlton San Juan Hotel** and gamble the night away at the island's largest casino. End the evening with a nightcap at **Mist,** the rooftop lounge at San Juan Water Beach Club.

Day 2

Eat breakfast at **Don Jose Restaurant and Bar** in Isla Verde and then hit the waves with the instructors of **Wow Surfing & Water Sports.** Afterwards, take a taxi or bus to **Condado** and wander through lovely **Ventana al Mar.** Grab a savory Belgian waffle at **Waffler Avenue** and dine al fresco before strolling the promenade. In the evening, order sea bass and lobster risotto at

Perla, an elegant clamshell-shaped restaurant at La Concha Resort, also in Condado. Afterwards, go to the alfresco lounge **La Terraza Condado** for an after-dinner drink.

Day 3

Start the day in Old San Juan people-watching in **Plaza de Armas** while having a breakfast of *café con leche* and *quesitos* (cheese pastries) at the plaza kiosk. Wander the cobblestone streets, shopping for local crafts, designer labels, and imports. After lunch at **Café La Princesa,** indulge with facials, massages, and pedicures at **Eden Spa.** In the evening, dine on tapas and risottos at **Carli's Fine Bistro & Piano** and enjoy the piano bar late into the evening.

Day 4

Catch a flight to Culebra, grab a muffin or breakfast sandwich from the airport café, pick up your rental car, and check in at the secluded **Club Seabourne.** Drive to the remote deserted beach at **Playa Zoni** and admire the outstanding views of Culebrita, Cayo Norte, and St. Thomas. Lunch on the popular hummus and feta burger at **The Spot.** In the afternoon, rent bikes and explore the off-road terrain of Culebra, ending your day watching the sunset at **Playa Flamenco.** In the evening, dine on Caribbean-American cuisine and local seafood at **Mamacita's Restaurant.** If you really want to just relax on remote beaches, you can spend another day or two in Culebra before heading home. Otherwise, you can check out Vieques the following day for water-sport fun and island nightlife.

Day 5

Fly to Vieques, pick up your rental car, and check into the **Inn on the Blue Horizon.** Head over to **Esperanza** and rent Jet Skis from **Fun Brothers Hut.** Have a light lunch at **Bananas Guesthouse, Beach Bar & Grill,** and in the afternoon check out some of the private beaches past **Balneario Sun Bay,** like **Media Luna** and **Navio Beach.** That night take a kayak tour of **Mosquito Bay,** and have a late dinner overlooking the *malecón* in Esperanza at **El Quenepo.** Afterwards, drop by the **Living Room Bar,** a chic oceanfront lounge at **W Retreat & Spa,** for a nightcap.

a beautiful sunset in the Isla Verde section of San Juan

San Juan

San Juan, Puerto Rico, is arguably the most cosmopolitan city in the Caribbean.

The second-oldest European settlement in the Americas, it is a place where world-class restaurants and luxury hotels compete for space alongside glitzy nightclubs and casinos; where Spanish colonial and neoclassical buildings line cobblestone streets; where designer stores and import shops beckon spend-happy tourists; where art, music, and dance thrive in its theaters, museums, and festivals; and where you're never very far from wide strips of sand and surf, ideal for sailing, sunbathing, and swimming.

Situated on the northeastern coast of Puerto Rico, San Juan stretches along 25 miles of coastline and 10 miles inland. It spans 30,000 acres of coastal plain, encompassing rivers, bays, and lagoons, and is home to 1.1 million residents in the greater San Juan area. Established by Spain as the island's capital in 1521, the city's early role as a military stronghold is evident in its 16th- and 17th-century fortresses and a nearly 400-year-old city wall erected around the oldest part of the city to protect it from foreign attacks.

The heart of the city is historic Old San Juan, a 45-block grid of blue cobblestone streets lined with pastel 16th- to 18th-century buildings trimmed with ornamental ironwork and hanging balconies. By day its streets crawl with tourists shopping for souvenirs and designer duds. At night it throbs with locals and tourists alike, both partaking of some of the city's finest restaurants and nightclubs.

But Old San Juan is only the tip of the city. Travel eastward to Puerta de Tierra, a small, shady neighborhood with a lovely park, a small stadium, a classic hotel, and the closest public beach to Old San Juan. Continue eastward along the coast to Condado, considered the city's tourist district. High-rise hotels, condos, and apartment buildings overlook the Atlantic Ocean. High-end shops line the main thoroughfare, Avenida Ashford, and many fine restaurants and casinos serve night crawlers.

Farther eastward is Ocean Park, a fine stretch of beach with a stately residential community and a handful of guesthouses and restaurants. Beside it is Isla Verde, where the city's best beaches and most exclusive hotels are, along with fast-food restaurants and a cockfight arena.

Previous: Isla Verde boasts the widest beaches in San Juan, Castillo San Felipe del Morro; **Above:** Palm trees line Ocean Park Beach.

Look for ★ to find recommended sights, activities, dining, and lodging.

Highlights

★ **Castillo San Felipe del Morro:** Established in 1539, this imposing Spanish colonial fortress was designed so sentries could spot enemies entering San Juan Bay. That's what makes it such an exceptional place to admire the views (page 26).

★ **Castillo de San Cristóbal:** Built to protect San Juan from attack by land, San Cristóbal was begun in 1634 and eventually encompassed 27 acres, making it the largest fort on the island. It provides stunning views of the city (page 26).

★ **Catedral de San Juan Bautista:** Established in 1521, the cathedral lays claim to being the oldest existing church in the western hemisphere. The current structure dates from the 1800s and contains the tomb of Juan Ponce de León (page 32).

★ **Museo de Arte de Puerto Rico:** This impressive museum showcases Puerto Rican art from the 17th century to the present, from classical portraiture to politically charged conceptual art (page 37).

★ **Ocean Park Beach:** Easy access and pristine sand make Ocean Park Beach an excellent place to spend the day in the sun. On weekends, lounge chairs are available for rent and street vendors patrol the area selling snacks and beverages (page 40).

★ **Nuyorican Café:** The casual Old San Juan nightclub is where locals go to dance the night away on the tiny dance floor. Get there early if you want a seat (page 45).

★ **La Placita and Plaza del Mercado:** By day, it's a popular farmers market selling fruits, veggies, and meats. By night, it is the apex of a roving street party as revelers stroll from bar to bar, restaurant to restaurant, leaving a festive atmosphere in their wake (page 48).

San Juan

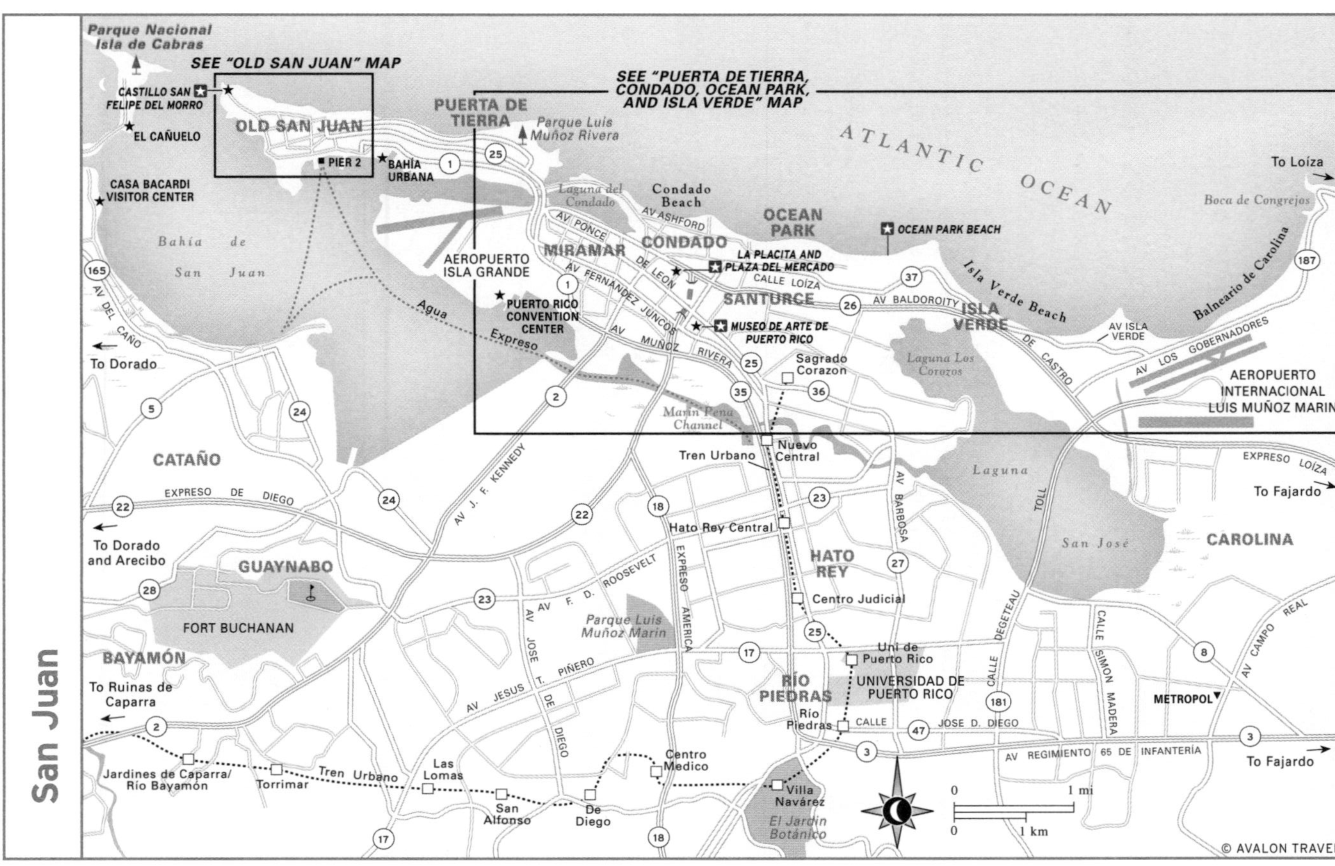
Parque Nacional Isla de Cabras
SEE "OLD SAN JUAN" MAP
CASTILLO SAN FELIPE DEL MORRO
EL CAÑUELO
OLD SAN JUAN
PIER 2
BAHÍA URBANA
CASA BACARDI VISITOR CENTER
Bahía de San Juan
AV DEL CAÑO
To Dorado
SEE "PUERTA DE TIERRA, CONDADO, OCEAN PARK, AND ISLA VERDE" MAP
PUERTA DE TIERRA
Parque Luis Muñoz Rivera
ATLANTIC OCEAN
To Loíza
Boca de Congrejos
Laguna del Condado
Condado Beach
AV ASHFORD
AV PONCE DE LEON
OCEAN PARK
OCEAN PARK BEACH
CONDADO
MIRAMAR
AEROPUERTO ISLA GRANDE
LA PLACITA AND PLAZA DEL MERCADO
CALLE LOÍZA
AV FERNANDEZ JUNCOS
SANTURCE
AV BALDOROITY DE CASTRO
ISLA VERDE
Isla Verde Beach
Balneario de Carolina
PUERTO RICO CONVENTION CENTER
MUSEO DE ARTE DE PUERTO RICO
Agua Expreso
AV MUÑOZ RIVERA
AV ISLA VERDE
AV LOS GOBERNADORES
Sagrado Corazon
Laguna Los Corozos
AEROPUERTO INTERNACIONAL LUIS MUÑOZ MARIN
Marin Peña Channel
Nuevo Central
Tren Urbano
CATAÑO
AV J. F. KENNEDY
Laguna
EXPRESO LOÍZA
To Fajardo
EXPRESO DE DIEGO
AV BARBOSA
TOLL
Hato Rey Central
To Dorado and Arecibo
GUAYNABO
HATO REY
San José
CAROLINA
AV F. D. ROOSEVELT
EXPRESO AMERICA
Centro Judicial
Parque Luis Muñoz Marín
FORT BUCHANAN
CALLE DEGETEAU
CALLE SIMON MADERA
AV CAMPO REAL
BAYAMÓN
Uni de Puerto Rico
UNIVERSIDAD DE PUERTO RICO
RÍO PIEDRAS
AV JESUS T. PIÑERO
AV JOSE DE DIEGO
To Ruinas de Caparra
METROPOL
Río Piedras
CALLE JOSE D. DIEGO
AV REGIMIENTO 65 DE INFANTERÍA
To Fajardo
Jardines de Caparra/ Río Bayamón
Torrimar
Tren Urbano
Las Lomas
Centro Medico
Villa Navárez
El Jardín Botánico
San Alfonso
De Diego
0 1 mi
0 1 km
© AVALON TRAVEL

Though it may seem so, San Juan isn't all beachfront property. Condado is the seaside strip of a sprawling, working-class sector called Santurce, which has in recent years transformed into a vital contemporary arts district accompanied by a profusion of hip new restaurants, bars, and shops.

Across the Condado lagoon is the neighborhood of Miramar, a high-rise residential community and home of the Puerto Rico Convention Center, the largest of its kind in the Caribbean. Travel inland for a locals-only experience in Hato Rey, San Juan's commercial district; Río Piedras, home of the Universidad de Puerto Rico; and Bayamón, a bedroom community.

As in any large city, all is not paradise. San Juan is a densely populated metropolis thick with automobile traffic. A heavy cruise-ship trade dumps thousands of tourists in the city several days a week, and the number of trinket shops catering to day-trippers has proliferated. Burger Kings and Pizza Huts are not an uncommon sight. Neither are pockets of poor neighborhoods, some of whose residents contribute to a petty street-crime problem.

But despite its big-city ways, San Juan's natural beauty is apparent in its miles of sandy beaches, its shady plazas, and its beloved coqui, a tiny tree frog whose "co-QUI" song fills the night air. Puerto Rico is a commonwealth of the United States, and American influence is clearly present, but San Juan proudly maintains its Spanish heritage in its language, its culture, and its customs. And although the city is firmly planted in the 21st century, San Juan's rich history endures in its carefully preserved architecture, its stately fortresses, and the hearts of its inhabitants.

PLANNING YOUR TIME

It's possible to hit San Juan's highlights in one whirlwind **long weekend,** but it's equally possible to spend a whole month here and not see all the city has to offer.

Six municipalities make up greater San Juan. They include San Juan, Cataño, Bayamón, Guaynabo, Trujillo Alto, and Carolina. The six sectors visitors gravitate to are Old San Juan, Puerta de Tierra, Condado, Santurce, and Ocean Park in San Juan and Isla Verde in Carolina. Not surprisingly, five of those areas are along the coast, and they are all within about 20 minutes of one another by car, taxi, or bus.

Several spectacular day trips are less than an hour's drive east of San Juan, the most popular being **El Yunque Caribbean National Forest,** the rainforest, and **Balneario La Monserrate (Luquillo Beach),** considered one of Puerto Rico's most beautiful beaches.

ORIENTATION

Old San Juan

Old San Juan is the cultural center of Puerto Rico. The 500-year-old walled city is filled with beautiful pastel-colored colonial buildings, Spanish forts, art and history museums, plazas, restaurants, bars, shops, and ship docks. Visitors could easily spend a couple of days wandering the cobblestone streets, exploring the city's history and culture. The downsides are that there is no beach in Old San Juan and hordes of tourists sometimes clog the sidewalks, especially when the cruise ships dock. But the town's copious charms are undeniable.

Many of the island's must-see sites are located in Old San Juan. They include two Spanish fortresses, **Castillo San Felipe del Morro** and **Castillo de San Cristóbal;** the historic churches **Catedral de San Juan Bautista** and **Capilla del Cristo;** and a couple of terrific museums, including **Museo de las Americas.**

The best way to see Old San Juan is by foot. The roads are drivable, but they're narrow and one-way, and only residents' automobiles are permitted inside at night. Just be sure to wear flat, sturdy shoes; it's easy to turn an ankle on those cobblestones.

If walking gets to be too much, there is a free trolley service that runs throughout the town. Getting into and out of Old San Juan is easy. The main public bus terminal is near the cruise-ship piers on Calle de Marina, just south of Plaza de Colón, and there are taxi stands at Plaza de las Armas and south of Plaza del Colón at Calle Tetuán and Calle Recinto Sur.

Puerta de Tierra

Geographically this small spit of land is part of Old San Juan, but it's located outside the walled city and lacks the cobblestone streets and pastel-colored colonial buildings that distinguish that part of town. Nevertheless, despite its size (little more than half a square mile), it packs in a diversity of sights.

Puerta de Tierra is the home of many government buildings, including **El Capitolio,** a neoclassical structure built in the 1920s. But it's also the site of two classic hotels, the Caribe Hilton Hotel and the Normandie; **Fuerte San Jeronimo,** a diminutive fort; **Parque Luis Muñoz Rivera,** a lovely 27-acre park; **Balneario El Escambrón,** the closest public beach to Old San Juan; and **Sixto Escobar Stadium.**

Condado

The strip of beachfront real estate that stretches between Old San Juan and Ocean Park has undergone more facelifts than an aging Hollywood star. From its heady, glamorous days starting in the late 1950s to a period of decline in the 1980s to a new era of burgeoning prosperity in the 2000s, Condado has seen some ups and downs. The good news is its current renaissance seems to be on the ascent and gathering momentum.

Condado is home to some of San Juan's flashiest resorts—The Condado Plaza and La Concha Resort—as well as the grand Condado Vanderbilt Hotel, a 323-room Spanish Revival hotel built in 1919, which reopened in 2014 after a multimillion-dollar renovation. And where fancy resorts can be found, splashy restaurants can't be too far away. Some of San Juan's highest profile restaurants are located in Condado, including *Iron Chef* competitor Roberto Treviño's Budatai and Casa Lola Criolla Kitchen, and *Top Chef Masters* competitor Wilo Benet's Pikayo. Naturally it follows that the area is home to shops selling the world's most exclusive designs, from Cartier and Louis Vuitton to Prada and Manolo Blahnik. Condado is not referred to as the tourist district for nothing.

There's more to Condado than commerce, of course, most notably that long, wide stretch of beach that attracted visitors in the first place. The waves can be big, especially in the winter, and the sand is coarse, but that suits the tourists who flock here just fine. The neighborhood is pedestrian friendly with its wide, well-maintained sidewalks and strategically placed parks, such as **Ventana al Mar** (Windows to the Sea), which features seaside picnic shelters, a promenade, and several installations of contemporary public art. The area is also home to **Laguna del Condado,** a small, natural lagoon where fishing and kayaking are permitted and a wide boardwalk provides a place for runners and bicyclists to exercise.

Transportation in Condado is a breeze thanks to the reliable and comfortable bus system that serves the area and the constant flow of taxis. There are also a couple of car rental agencies in the vicinity if you want to explore outside San Juan.

Condado has more of a Miami vibe than a traditional Puerto Rican one, but visitors who stay here enjoy the creature comforts the area provides, not to mention the central location, which makes it a great home base for exploring other parts of the island.

Ocean Park

Ocean Park is a small community between Condado and Isla Verde comprising a cluster of modest shops, restaurants, and guesthouses that have cropped up around an upscale residential neighborhood of the same name. The neighborhood features wide, leafy streets and well-maintained homes built during the first half of the 1900s, and it includes some terrific examples of Caribbean-style midcentury modernist architecture. Enter the neighborhood via Calle Santa Ana, just off Calle McLeary. Visitors are free to come and go during the day, but after 6pm a guard checks visitors' identification, and on weekends, car traffic is limited to residents and patrons of the neighborhood's restaurants and guesthouses.

For visitors, the best thing about Ocean Park is its long, wide strip of beach, which is free from the domination of high-rise buildings and resort hotels. Instead, the sunny strip of sand and surf is lined with a wide, paved boardwalk, populated by an assortment of food vendors on weekends. The beach is called Ultimo Trolley by locals, because when the island's electric trolley system ceased to operate in 1946, the last trolley car was converted into a snack bar and placed in Parque Balboa, across the street from the beach. Speaking of **Parque Barbosa,** the park features several sports fields as well as a trail for biking, walking, and running. It also has a small parking lot, conveniently located across the street from the beach.

Ocean Park is home to Kasalta Bakery, a large, popular spot for picking up freshly baked breads, cheesecakes, and pastries, as well as dining on outstanding *criolla* fare, from *cubano* sandwiches to empanadas to *carne guisada*. Traffic getting in out and of the bakery's small parking lot is always congested. Parking in general is limited and challenging in Ocean Park. Walking or taking a taxi is recommended if you want to spend time exploring the area.

Isla Verde

Isla Verde is renowned for its long, wide beaches, its luxury resorts, and some pretty spectacular nightclubs and casinos. When you're catching some rays on the beach or partying the night away in a glitzy hot spot, it can feel as glamorous as a mini-South Beach. Unfortunately, except for one entrance at the end of Calle Tatak, the only way to actually see Isla Verde's gorgeous coast is from one of the high-rise hotels and condominiums that line every inch of the way. And the traffic-choked main thoroughfare, Avenida Isla Verde, is a chaotic jumble of fast-food restaurants, pizzerias, and souvenir shops. The best way to enjoy Isla Verde is to ensconce oneself in one of the community's cushy seaside resorts and stay there. The community is also home to the Luis Muñoz Marín International Airport.

Santurce

Santurce is one of the most densely populated districts on the island, and it has something of a split personality. On the one hand it is

oceanfront promenade at Ventana al Mar park in Condado

home to Condado, the oceanfront tourist district thick with hotels, high-end restaurants, bars, and shops that cater to vacationers. But the inland part of Santurce is, for all practical purposes, its own separate neighborhood. For years it has endured a reputation as a somewhat gritty, occasionally crime-ridden, working-class neighborhood densely populated with mom-and-pop businesses and discount chain stores.

But in recent years Santurce has undergone a dramatic renaissance to become the epicenter of the island's exploding contemporary arts scene.

The transformation began with the opening in 2000 of the **Museo de Arte de Puerto Rico,** an institution built upon the permanent collection of works by Puerto Rican artists from the 17th century to the present. Santurce is also home to **Centro de Bellas Artes Luis A. Ferré,** a fine arts performance center and a number of contemporary galleries, art collectives, and design centers. In 2010, a group of artists started Santurce es Ley, an annual arts festival in August that emphasizes community. In addition to gallery tours and musical performances, elaborate murals are painted throughout the neighborhood, which has transformed the streetscape into a 24-hour gallery.

And naturally, where artists go, hip restaurants, bars, and boutiques soon follow. Calle Loíza has exploded with trendy new restaurants, vintage clothing stores, tattoo parlors, and artisanal bakeries that attract a youthful clientele. Santurce is also the site of **La Placita and Plaza del Mercado,** a thriving farmers market by day, which provides the backdrop for nightly street parties on the weekends, when the surrounding restaurants and bars beckon revelers.

Miramar

Located south of Condado, on the opposite side of **Laguna del Condado,** Miramar has long been home to the city's prosperous middle class, but it has suffered an economic decline over the years. The neighborhood's main, one-way thoroughfares—Avenida Ponce de León and Avenida Fernández Juncos—run parallel from one tip of the community to the other, and a drive along either one reveals the spotty character of the neighborhood. Modern high-rise apartment buildings and classic colonial homes abut boarded-up storefronts and abandoned buildings scrawled with graffiti. Most intersections contain at least one panhandler going from car to car seeking a handout.

In 2000, millions of dollars in public and corporate funds began pouring into the former site of a naval base on the western tip of Miramar along San Juan Bay for the development of the Puerto Rico Convention Center District. At the center is the **Puerto Rico Convention Center,** a modern, 580,000-square-foot facility. Next door a Sheraton Convention Center Hotel & Casino was built. Future plans include a second hotel, office buildings, and high-rise residential buildings. But, so far, it doesn't appear that the infusion of cash has trickled down to the rest of Miramar.

Miramar is home to Isla Grande Airport, San Juan's regional airport, which provides air service to the Caribbean.

Hato Rey, Río Piedras, and Bayamón

Outside San Juan's popular tourist areas are communities central to the lives of San Juan residents. Hato Rey is the city's business and financial district, chock-full of banks and restaurants that cater to businesspeople. It's connected by the 10-mile Tren Urbano metro system to Río Piedras, home of the Universidad de Puerto Rico, and the residential area of Bayamón.

Sights

OLD SAN JUAN

Historic Sites

★ CASTILLO SAN FELIPE DEL MORRO

It doesn't matter from which direction you approach **Castillo San Felipe del Morro** (501 Calle Norzagaray, Old San Juan, 787/729-6777, daily 9am-6pm, free, orientation talks every hour on the hour in English and Spanish), it's an impressive sight to behold. From San Juan Bay, which was constructed to protect from attack, it's an awesome feat of engineering and a daunting display of military defense featuring four levels of cannon-bearing batteries that rise 140 feet from the sea. From Old San Juan, the approach is more welcoming, thanks to an enormous expanse of grassy lawn and breathtaking views of the shore. It's easy to see why this is such a popular spot for kite-flyers.

Inside Castillo San Felipe del Morro is a maze of rooms, including gun rooms, soldiers' quarters, a chapel, turreted sentry posts, and a prison connected by tunnels, ramps, and a spiral stairway. The foundations for El Morro were laid in 1539, but it wasn't completed until 1787. It successfully endured many foreign attacks by the English in 1595, 1598, and 1797, and by the Dutch in 1625. During the Spanish-American War, the United States fired on El Morro and destroyed the lighthouse, which was later rebuilt.

On Saturdays and Sundays, guided tours are offered in Spanish and English.

★ CASTILLO DE SAN CRISTÓBAL

Castillo de San Cristóbal (Calle Norzagaray at the entrance to Old San Juan, 787/729-6777, daily 9am-6pm, $5) is the large fortress at the entrance to Old San Juan by Plaza de Colón. Before it was built, two significant attacks from land—first by the Earl of Cumberland in 1598, later by the Dutch in 1625—convinced the Spanish that protecting the walled city from attack by sea alone was not adequate.

The fort's construction began in 1634 and was completed in 1783. The fort eventually encompassed 27 acres of land, although some of it was destroyed to accommodate the expanding city. The fort's defense was tested in 1797 by another unsuccessful attack by the British. After the United States won the Spanish-American War, it took control of the fort and used it as a World War II observation post. Today, a section of the fort is open to the public, who can wander freely among its intriguing array of tunnels, ramps, stairways, batteries, magazines, soldiers' quarters, and turreted sentry posts.

CASA BLANCA

Casa Blanca (1 Calle San Sebastián, Old San Juan, 787/725-1454, Tues.-Sat. 9am-noon and 1pm-4pm, gardens open daily 8:30am-4:30pm, free) was originally built as a home for the island's first governor, Juan Ponce de León, although he died on his quest for the Fountain of Youth before he could ever take up residence. Construction began in 1523, and for more than 200 years it served as the residence of Ponce de León's descendants. Today it's a museum of 17th- and 18th-century domestic life featuring lots of impressive Spanish antiques. Don't miss the cool, lush gardens that surround the house and the views of both San Juan Bay and the Atlantic Ocean.

LA FORTALEZA

La Fortaleza (Calle Fortaleza, Old San Juan, 787/721-7000, ext. 2211, 2323, and 2358, Mon.-Fri. 9am-5pm, $3 donation) was the first fort built in Puerto Rico, completed in 1540 to provide refuge for the island's original Spanish settlers. Partially burned by the Dutch in 1625, it was rebuilt in the 1640s and received a new facade in 1846. It has been the official residence of the governor of Puerto Rico since the 16th century, which gives it the distinction of the longest continuous use of an executive

Old San Juan

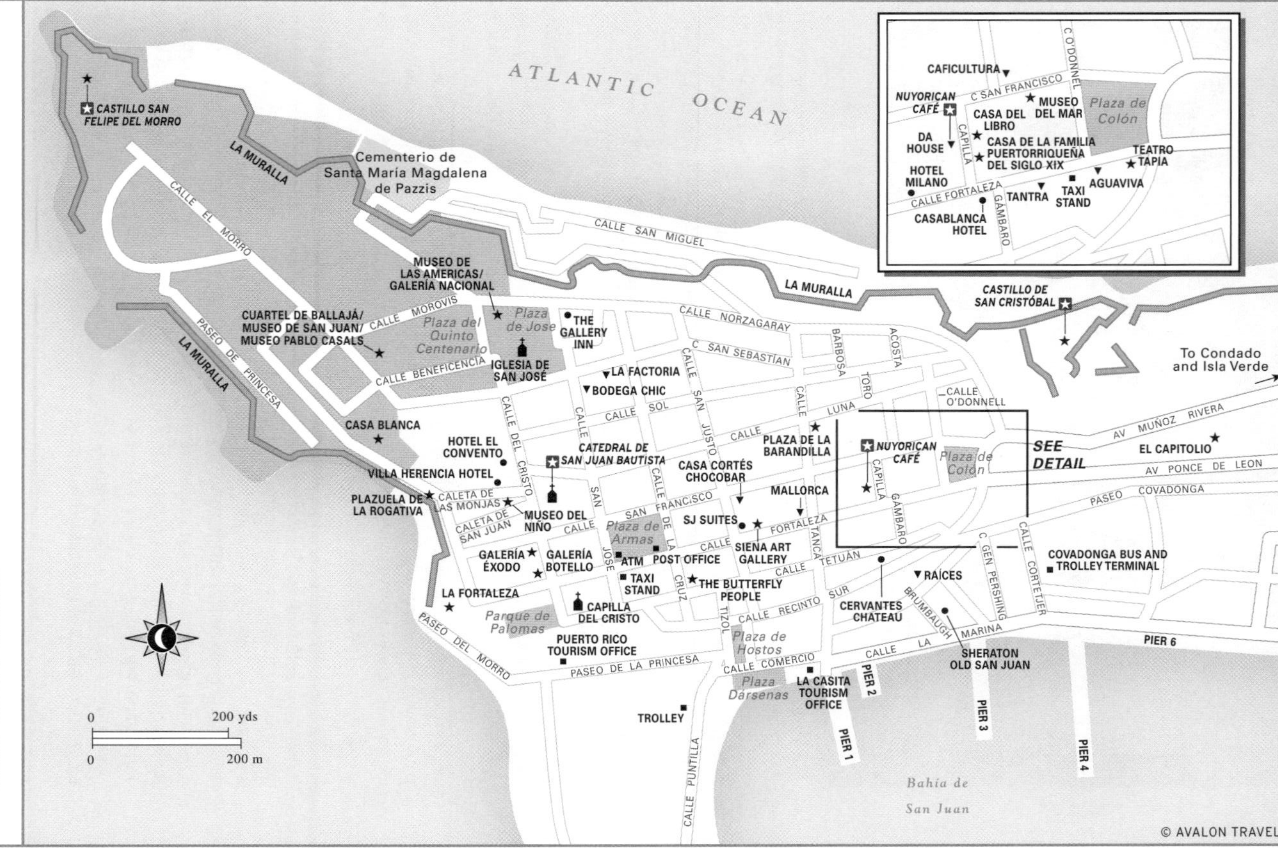
ATLANTIC OCEAN
CASTILLO SAN FELIPE DEL MORRO
LA MURALLA
Cementerio de Santa María Magdalena de Pazzis
CALLE EL MORRO
CALLE SAN MIGUEL
MUSEO DE LAS AMERICAS/ GALERÍA NACIONAL
LA MURALLA
CASTILLO DE SAN CRISTÓBAL
CUARTEL DE BALLAJÁ/ MUSEO DE SAN JUAN/ MUSEO PABLO CASALS
CALLE MOROVIS
Plaza del Quinto Centenario
Plaza de Jose
THE GALLERY INN
CALLE NORZAGARAY
C SAN SEBASTIÁN
BARBOSA
ACOSTA
To Condado and Isla Verde
PASEO DE PRINCESA
LA MURALLA
CALLE BENEFICENCIA
IGLESIA DE SAN JOSÉ
LA FACTORIA
BODEGA CHIC
CALLE SAN JUSTO
TORO
CALLE O'DONNELL
CALLE SOL
CALLE LUNA
CASA BLANCA
HOTEL EL CONVENTO
CALLE DEL CRISTO
CATEDRAL DE SAN JUAN BAUTISTA
CALLE
PLAZA DE LA BARANDILLA
NUYORICAN CAFÉ
Plaza de Colón
SEE DETAIL
AV MUÑOZ RIVERA
EL CAPITOLIO
AV PONCE DE LEON
VILLA HERENCIA HOTEL
CASA CORTÉS CHOCOBAR
CAPILLA
MALLORCA
PLAZUELA DE LA ROGATIVA
CALETA DE LAS MONJAS
CALETA DE SAN JUAN
MUSEO DEL NIÑO
CALLE SAN FRANCISCO
SJ SUITES
FORTALEZA
GAMBARO
PASEO COVADONGA
Plaza de Armas
CALLE DE LA
SIENA ART GALLERY
TANCA
CALLE TETUÁN
C GEN PERSHING
CALLE CORTETJER
COVADONGA BUS AND TROLLEY TERMINAL
GALERÍA ÉXODO
GALERÍA BOTELLO
JOSE
ATM
POST OFFICE
TAXI STAND
CRUZ
THE BUTTERFLY PEOPLE
CALLE SUR
RAICES
LA FORTALEZA
CAPILLA DEL CRISTO
TIZOL
CALLE RECINTO
CERVANTES CHATEAU
BRUMBAUGH
Parque de Palomas
Plaza de Hostos
CALLE LA MARINA
SHERATON OLD SAN JUAN
PIER 6
PASEO DEL MORRO
PUERTO RICO TOURISM OFFICE
PASEO DE LA PRINCESA
CALLE COMERCIO
Plaza Darsenas
LA CASITA TOURISM OFFICE
PIER 2
PIER 3
TROLLEY
PIER 1
PIER 4
CALLE PUNTILLA
Bahía de San Juan
0 200 yds
0 200 m
CAFICULTURA
C SAN FRANCISCO
C O'DONNEL
NUYORICAN CAFÉ
MUSEO DEL MAR
CASA DEL LIBRO
Plaza de Colón
DA HOUSE
CASA DE LA FAMILIA PUERTORRIQUEÑA DEL SIGLO XIX
TEATRO TAPIA
HOTEL MILANO
AGUAVIVA
CALLE FORTALEZA
TANTRA
TAXI STAND
CASABLANCA HOTEL
GAMBARO
© AVALON TRAVEL

mansion in the western hemisphere. Tours are limited mostly to the lovely gardens and first floor, with audio narration in Spanish and English.

LA MURALLA

La Muralla is the grand, dramatic, and impenetrable wall that once surrounded Old San Juan and still stands strong today along the coast and bay. Nearly 400 years old, the wall took 200 years to complete and stands 40 feet high and 45 feet thick in some places. The wall once had five gates that permitted access into the city, but only one remains today.

LA PUERTA DE SAN JUAN

The commanding red **La Puerta de San Juan** was built in the late 1700s and is on the western end of Old San Juan beside La Fortaleza. Sixteen feet tall and 20 feet thick, the door is best seen from the wide bayside promenade, Paseo de Princesa.

PASEO DE PRINCESA

Named after La Princesa, a 19th-century prison that now houses the Puerto Rico Tourism Company, the promenade **Paseo de Princesa** begins across from Plaza de Hostos at Calle Tizol near the cruise-ship piers in Old San Juan. Glorious royal palms, a view of the bay, the soaring city wall, the city gate, and an outlandish fountain comprising naked sea nymphs and goats are some of the sights along the way. The promenade continues along Castillo San Felipe del Morro, ending dramatically at the point containing the oldest part of the fort. Paseo de Princesa is the site of frequent festivals and events, and you can usually find a variety of vendors here selling *piraguas* (snow cones), popcorn, and *dulces* (sweets).

CUARTEL DE BALLAJÁ

Cuartel de Ballajá (Calle Norzagaray beside Plaza del Quinto Centenario near the entrance to Castillo San Felipe del Morro, Old San Juan) is a massive structure that once housed 1,000 Spanish soldiers. Built in 1854, the former barracks is three levels high with interior balconies and a dizzying series of arches that overlook an enormous courtyard. It was the last major building constructed by the Spanish in the New World. Today it houses several museums, including the Museo de las Americas, Museo Pablo Casals, and Cinema Bar 150 restaurant, which opened in 2014.

Castillo San Felipe del Morro

La Muralla

The most enduring symbol of Puerto Rico is La Muralla. Nearly 400 years old, the city wall is composed of rock, rubble, and mortar that wraps around Old San Juan from the cruise-ship piers on San Juan Harbor to the capitol on the Atlantic Ocean. Its iconic sentry boxes serve as a symbol of the island's Spanish heritage and resilience in an ever-changing world.

Begun by Spanish colonists in the 1600s, the wall took 200 years to complete and has withstood multiple attacks by the English, the Dutch, and the Americans. But what proved nearly impenetrable to foreign attack has been rendered defenseless by modern life. Automobile traffic, pollution, and misguided attempts to preserve it have endangered the wall.

La Muralla, a nearly 400-year-old wall that surrounds Old San Juan

Forty-five feet wide and 40 feet high in some spots, La Muralla is crumbling in places. In 2004 a 70-foot section below the heavily traveled Calle Norzagaray fell, underscoring the urgency of stepping up preservation efforts. It wasn't the first time the wall's fragility was made apparent. A larger section fell into San Juan Bay in 1938, and in 1999, a Soviet oil tanker ran aground, damaging the wall's northwest corner.

When the U.S. Army seized Puerto Rico in 1898, it took over maintenance of the wall and attempted its first preservation efforts. Concrete was used to patch La Muralla, but that only served to add weight to the wall and trap moisture inside it, which weakened the structure over time.

Now a National Historic Site, La Muralla is maintained by the National Park Service, which has been overseeing efforts to repair the wall. Experts have spent years studying the 16th-century methods used to build the structure in an attempt to recreate the magic mixture of sand, water, and limestone used to stucco the wall. Not only is the repair method they've developed more effective than concrete, it serves to preserve the wall's historical integrity. The process has been used to repair the wall's beloved sentry boxes. It's a painstaking and costly process.

But La Muralla endures. Along with the fortresses of El Morro and San Cristóbal that adjoin it, the wall attracts 1.2 million visitors a year. Chances are, with the help of preservation efforts, it will continue to assert its soaring beauty and cultural significance as the proud protector of Old San Juan for years to come.

CEMENTERIO DE SANTA MARÍA MAGDALENA DE PAZZIS

Cementerio de Santa María Magdalena de Pazzis is the city's historic cemetery, outside the city wall just east of Castillo San Felipe del Morro and accessible from Calle Norzagaray in Old San Juan. In addition to a neoclassical chapel, there are many significant burial sites of some of the city's early colonists, as well as the tomb of Pedro Albizu Campos, the revered revolutionary who sought independence for the island of Puerto Rico. Avoid going alone or at night. Next door is **La Perla,** an impoverished community notorious for its drug trade; its illicit activities are known to spill over into the cemetery. If you don't want to venture in, you can get a great view of it from Plaza del Quinto Centenario on Calle Norzagaray.

TEATRO TAPIA

Teatro Tapia (Calle Fortaleza at Plaza de Colón, Old San Juan, 787/721-0180 or 787/721-0169, www.teatropr.com) is one of the oldest theaters in the western hemisphere. The lovely

Romantic-style building was constructed in 1824 and renovated in 1987. Named after Puerto Rican playwright Alejandro Tapia y Rivera, the 642-seat theater still hosts a variety of performing arts events.

The only way to tour the interior is during an event, but this significant architectural landmark is worth viewing from the outside.

History Museums

MUSEO DE SAN JUAN

Museo de Arte y Historia de San Juan (150 Calle Norzagaray, Old San Juan, 787/724-1875, Tues.-Sun. 9am-noon and 1pm-4pm, free) is in the city's former marketplace, built in 1857. In 1979 it was converted into a city museum. It contains two exhibition spaces, one housing temporary exhibits illuminating various aspects of the city's history, the other a permanent exhibition that gives a comprehensive look at the city's history from its geographical roots to the 21st century. Superbly produced wall graphics and text include reproductions of old photographs, maps, prints, and paintings that tell the city's story. All the exhibits are in Spanish, but a photocopied handout in English encapsulates the exhibition highlights.

MUSEO DEL MAR

Museo del Mar (360 Calle San Francisco, Old San Juan, 787/977-4461, www.elmuseodelmar.com, Wed.-Sun. 10am-5pm, $5) boasts a small but impressive collection of nautical items, ranging from letters purportedly written by King Ferdinand V and Queen Isabella I to dozens of lifesavers from the world's largest collection (as proclaimed by Guinness World Records). The items are all from the private collection of José Octavio Busto, founder and president of Continental Shipping Inc.

CASA DE LA FAMILIA PUERTORRIQUEÑA DEL SIGLO XIX AND MUSEO DE LA FARMACIA

One house holds two museums: **Casa de la Familia Puertorriqueña del Siglo XIX** and **Museo de la Farmacia** (319 Calle Fortaleza, Old San Juan, 787/977-2700 or 787/977-2701, Wed.-Sun. 1pm-4:30pm, free). Upstairs is a re-creation of a typical (albeit wealthy) family's residence from the late 1800s filled with antiques, both locally made and imported from Germany, Belgium, and Italy. Downstairs is a re-created 19th-century pharmacy filled with authentic vessels, cabinets, and scales from a pharmacy in Cayey.

Cuartel de Ballajá used to house Spanish soldiers. Now it is home to several excellent museums.

MUSEO PABLO CASALS

Museo Pablo Casals (Cuartel de Ballaja, 1st Fl., on Calle Norzagaray beside Plaza del Quinto Centenario, Old San Juan, 787/723-9185, Tues.-Sat. 9:30am-4:30pm, $1 adults, $0.50 children age 12 and younger and seniors 60 and older) commemorates the career and accomplishments of Pablo Casals, the renowned cellist who performed for Queen Victoria and President Theodore Roosevelt, among other world movers and shakers. Born in Catalonia, Casals moved to Puerto Rico in 1956. A year later, the island established the annual Casals Festival of classical music, which continues today. The museum contains Casals's music manuscripts, cello, and piano, as well as recordings of his performances.

MUSEO DEL NIÑO

Museo del Niño (150 Calle del Cristo near Hotel El Convento, Old San Juan, 787/722-3791, www.museodelninopr.org, Tues.-Thurs. 10am-3:30pm, Fri. 10am-5pm, Sat.-Sun. noon-5:30pm, $5 adults, $7 children; ticket booth closed 1.5 hours before closing) is a children's museum containing exhibits in geography, nutrition, weather, astronomy, biology, and more.

Art Galleries and Museums

★ MUSEO DE LAS AMERICAS

Museo de las Americas (Cuartel de Ballajá, 2nd Fl., on Calle Norzagaray beside Plaza del Quinto Centenario, Old San Juan, 787/724-5052, www.museolasamericas.org, Tues.-Sat. 9am-noon and 1pm-4pm, Sun. noon-5pm, $3 adults, $2 children age 12 and younger, students, and seniors age 65 and older) is located inside an enormous structure that once housed 1,000 Spanish soldiers. The museum contains a fantastic collection of Latin American folk art, including masks, musical instruments, clothing, pottery, baskets, and tools. Highlights include altars representing Santería, voodoo, and Mexico's Day of the Dead celebration. Don't miss the collection of vintage santos, Puerto Rican wood carvings of saints. Wall text is in Spanish and English except in the second smaller exhibit dedicated to Puerto Rico's African heritage. The **Tienda de Artesanías** (787/722-6057, Tues.-Fri. 10am-4pm, Sat.-Sun. 11am-5pm), on the first floor, has a small but quality selection of locally made crafts for sale.

GALERÍA NACIONAL

Located in the 16th-century Convento de los Dominicos, **Galería Nacional** (Plaza de San Jose, Old San Juan, 787/725-2670, Tues.-Sat. 9am-noon and 1pm-5pm, $3 adults, $2 children) exhibits artwork by Puerto Rican masters, including Jose Campeche and Francisco Oller.

CASA DEL LIBRO

Tucked away on an alley between Calle San Francisco and Calle Fortaleza, the small, charming **Casa del Libro** (Calle Callejon de la Capilla, Old San Juan, 787/723-0354, Tues.-Sat. 11am-4:30pm, free) features an incredible collection of early manuscripts and books dating back to the 15th century.

GALERÍA BOTELLO

Galería Botello (208 Calle del Cristo, Old San Juan, 787/723-9987 or 787/723-2879, www.botello.com, Mon.-Sat. 10am-6pm, free) is a significant art museum dedicated to the work of Angel Botello. Born in Spain, the renowned artist spent most of his life in the Caribbean, eventually settling in Puerto Rico, where he opened this gallery. Although he died in 1986, the artist lives on through his paintings and sculptures on view at the gallery, which also exhibits solo shows by contemporary artists.

SIENA ART GALLERY

Siena Art Gallery (253 Calle San Francisco, Old San Juan, 787/724-7223, www.sienaart-gallery.com, Mon.-Sat. 11am-6pm, free) is a fine art gallery featuring Puerto Rican and Caribbean artists, including Mikicol and Rafael Colon Morales.

GALERÍA ÉXODO

Located in two galleries a few steps apart, **Galería Éxodo** (200-B Calle del Cristo and 152 Calle del Cristo, Old San Juan, 787/725-4252 or 787/671-4159, www.galeriaexodo.com, daily 11am-7pm, free) specializes in Caribbean art and represents 60 contemporary artists.

THE BUTTERFLY PEOPLE

The Butterfly People (257 Calle de la Cruz, Old San Juan, 787/723-2432 or 787/723-2201, www.butterflypeople.com, daily 11am-6pm, free) is a unique gallery that sells fantastic colorful pieces composed of real butterflies mounted in Lucite.

Religious Sites

★ CATEDRAL DE SAN JUAN BAUTISTA

Catedral de San Juan Bautista (151-153 Calle del Cristo, Old San Juan, 787/722-0861, www.catedralsanjuan.com, Mon.-Thurs. 9am-noon and 1:30pm-4pm, Fri. 9am-noon; Mass: Sat. 9am, 11am, and 7pm, Sun.-Fri. 12:15pm) holds the distinction of being the second-oldest church in the western hemisphere, the first being Catedral Basilica Menor de Santa in the Dominican Republic. The church was first built of wood and straw in 1521 but was destroyed by hurricanes and rebuilt multiple times. In 1917 the cathedral underwent major restoration and expansion. The large sanctuary features a marble altar and rows of arches with several side chapels appointed with elaborate statuary primarily depicting Mary and Jesus. In stark contrast is a chapel featuring an enormous contemporary oil painting of a man in a business suit. It was erected in honor of Carlos "Charlie" Rodríguez, a Puerto Rican layman who was beatified in 2001 by Pope John Paul II. Catedral de San Juan Bautista is the final resting place of Juan Ponce de León, whose remains are encased in a marble tomb. It also holds a relic of San Pio, a Roman martyr.

CAPILLA DEL CRISTO

Built in 1753, the tiny picturesque **Capilla del Cristo** (south end of Calle del Cristo, Old San Juan, 787/722-0861) is one of the most photographed sights in San Juan. Legend has it that horse races were held on Calle del Cristo, and one ill-fated rider was speeding down the hill so fast he couldn't stop in time and tumbled over the city wall to his death, and the chapel was built to prevent a similar occurrence. An alternative end to the legend is that the rider

Catedral de San Juan Bautista in Old San Juan

survived and the church was built to show thanks to God. Either way, the result was the construction of a beloved landmark.

Unfortunately, Capilla del Cristo is rarely open, but it's possible to peer through the windows and see the ornate gilded altarpiece. Beside it is **Parque de Palomas,** a gated park overlooking San Juan Harbor that is home to more pigeons than you might think imaginable. Birdseed is available for purchase if you want to get up close and personal with your fine feathered friends.

IGLESIA DE SAN JOSÉ

Iglesia de San José (Calle San Sebastián at Plaza de San José, Old San Juan, 787/725-7501) is one of the oldest structures in Old San Juan. Built in the 1530s, it was originally a chapel for the Dominican monastery, but it was taken over in 1865 by the Jesuits. The main chapel is an excellent example of 16th-century Spanish Gothic architecture. Originally Iglesia de San José was Juan Ponce de León's final resting place, but his body was later moved to Catedral de San Juan Bautista. Ponce de León himself is said to have donated the wooden 16th-century crucifix. Unfortunately, the church has been closed for many years.

Plazas and Parks

Most every town in Puerto Rico has a main plaza at its center that is flanked by a church and an *alcaldía* (town hall). Bigger towns like San Juan have several. There is no better way to spend the morning than strolling the perimeter of a plaza or spending time on a bench sipping coffee, fending off pigeons, and watching the parade of people pass by. The plazas are also popular sites for arts festivals and evening concerts. Not surprisingly, the largest concentration of historic plazas and parks is in Old San Juan.

PLAZA DE ARMAS

Plaza de Armas (Calle San Francisco, at Calle de la Cruz and Calle San José) is the main square in Old San Juan and a great place to people-watch. Once the site of military drills, it contains a large gazebo and a fountain surrounded by four 100-year-old statues that represent the four seasons. A couple of vendors sell coffee and snacks, and there's a bank of pay phones popular with cruise-ship visitors eager to check in with those back home. Across the street on Calle de la Cruz is a small grocery store. Across Calle Cordero is an ATM, and a taxi stand is just around the corner on Calle San José at Calle Fortaleza.

Plaza de Armas is Old San Juan's central square.

PLAZA DE COLÓN

Plaza de Colón (between Calle Fortaleza, Calle San Francisco, and Calle O'Donnell) is a large square at the entrance to Old San Juan by Castillo de San Cristóbal. In the center is a huge pedestal topped with a statue of Christopher Columbus, whom the plaza is named after. There's a small newsstand on one corner, and several restaurants and shops surround it on two sides. Unfortunately, there's little shade, so it's not that pleasant for lingering when the sun is high.

PLAZA DE LA BARANDILLA

Located by Carlos Albizu University, the large **Plaza de la Barandilla** (Calle Tanca between Calle San Francisco and Calle Luna) was buried beneath asphalt and concrete for 80 years until it was discovered in 2005. It was restored at a cost of more than $3 million. A popular spot for outdoor concerts, it is a welcome respite of open space and sky in the midst of Old San Juan's density, and it provides a welcoming access to Calle Luna via a sweeping set of steps.

PLAZA DEL QUINTO CENTENARIO

Plaza del Quinto Centenario (between Calle Norzagaray and Calle Beneficencia near the entrance to Castillo San Felipe del Morro, Old San Juan) is Old San Juan's newest park. Built in 1992 to commemorate the 500th anniversary of Christopher Columbus's "discovery" of the New World, the plaza features a striking 40-foot sculpture, Tótem Telúrico, created by local artist Jaime Suárez from black granite and ceramics. The plaza provides a great view of the historic cemetery, El Morro, and all the kite-flyers who gather on the fort's long green lawn.

PLAZUELA DE LA ROGATIVA

One of Puerto Rico's most beautiful pieces of public art is in **Plazuela de la Rogativa,** a tiny sliver of a park tucked between the city wall and Calle Clara Lair just west of El Convento in Old San Juan. At its center is a spectacular bronze sculpture called ***La Rogativa,*** designed by New Zealand artist Lindsay Daen in the 1950s. The piece depicts a procession of three women and a priest bearing crosses and torches. It commemorates one of San Juan's most beloved historic tales. In 1797 a British fleet led by Sir Ralph Abercrombie entered San Juan Bay and prepared to launch an attack in hopes of capturing the city. Because the city's men were away protecting the city's inland fronts, the only people remaining behind were women and clergy. In hopes of staving off an attack, the governor ordered a *rogativa,* a divine entreaty to ask the saints for help. As the story goes, the town's brave women formed a procession, carrying torches and ringing bells throughout the streets, which duped the British into thinking reinforcements had arrived, prompting them to sail away, leaving the city safe once again.

PLAZA DE JOSÉ

Plaza de José (Calle San Sebastián and Calle del Cristo, Old San Juan) is in front of the Iglesia de San José and features a statue of its most celebrated parishioner, Juan Ponce de León. After successfully thwarting another attack by the British in 1797, citizens of San Juan melted the enemy's cannons to make the statue. This is a popular gathering place for young locals, especially at night when the string of nearby bars gets crowded.

PLAZA DE EUGENIO MARÍA HOSTOS

Plaza de Eugenio María Hostos (between Calle San Justo and Calle Tizol, Old San Juan) is a bustling shady spot near the cruise-ship piers. On weekends it turns into a craft fair, and there are often food vendors selling fritters and snow cones. Just across the street, at **Plaza de la Dársena,** concerts are often held on the weekends on a covered stage overlooking the harbor.

PARQUE DE PALOMAS

Parque de Palomas (beside Capilla del Cristo on the south end of Calle del Cristo) is home to a gazillion pigeons. A vendor sells small bags of feed for those who take pleasure in being swarmed by the feathered urban dwellers. Kids love it!

BAHÍA URBANA AND AMPHITHEATRE

An exciting addition to San Juan's park system is **Bahía Urbana and Amphitheatre** (Pier 8, 98 Ave. Fernández Juncos, 787/977-2777), a great linear park on San Juan Bay (along Piers 6, 7, and 8). In addition to swaths of green space with gorgeous water views, wide walkways, and pleasant seating areas, there is a striking contemporary seahorse sculpture, a kids carousel, launch sites for boat and helicopter tours, the **Café 8** restaurant and bar, and an amphitheater that hosts more than 200 major concerts, festivals, and other events a year.

PUERTA DE TIERRA

PARQUE LUIS MUÑOZ RIVERA

Puerta de Tierra is a spot of land between Condado and Old San Juan that is home to **Parque Luis Muñoz Rivera** (between Ave. Ponce de León and Ave. Muñoz Rivera), a lovely, 27-acre green space established in 1929. Providing a welcome reprieve from the city's urban atmosphere, it features shady gardens, fountains, walking trails, a children's play area, and the Peace Pavilion.

FUERTE SAN JERÓNIMO

Fuerte San Jerónimo (behind the Caribe Hilton in Puerta de Tierra) is the only fort in San Juan that isn't part of the San Juan National Historic Site. Instead, it's overseen by the Institute of Puerto Rican Culture and managed by the Caribe Hilton, on whose property it now sits. Various sources date its origins to the 17th and 18th centuries, but little is known about it. Unfortunately, it's rarely open to the public, but it can be seen from Puente Dos Hermanos bridge in Condado and the grounds of Caribe Hilton in Puerta de Tierra.

EL CAPITOLIO

El Capitolio (Ave. Ponce de León at Ave. Muñoz Rivera, 787/724-2030, ext. 2472 or 2518, www.nps.gov, Mon.-Fri. 9am-5pm) is the seat of government for the island, and it is one of many government buildings located in Puerta de Tierra. The neoclassical revival-style building was completed in 1929, although the dome was added later in 1961. Inside are murals and mosaics that detail the island's history. Guided tours are available by appointment only.

CONDADO

PARQUE NACIONAL LAGUNA DEL CONDADO JAIME BENÍTEZ

Parque Nacional Laguna del Condado Jaime Benítez (Ave. Baldorioty de Castro on the eastern side of the Condado Lagoon between Condado and Miramar, daily 24 hours) features a wide boardwalk along the lagoon's edge, park benches, and a public ramp for launching kayaks and canoes. Several natural restoration projects are underway at the site, including a sea-grass restoration project in the lagoon and the cultivation of red mangrove trees, ceibas, and other native plants around its shore.

PARQUE LUCHETTI

A lovely oasis of quiet and lush green flora just two blocks away from the hubbub of Avenida Ashford, **Parque Luchetti** (between Calle Magdalena and Calle Luchetti at Calle Cervantes) is a hidden gem of a park. Shaded benches, flowering shrubs, palm trees, and bronze sculptures make this the perfect spot to relax or picnic. One of the highlights is a whimsical bronze sculpture called *Juan Bobo and the Basket.* Created in 1991 by New Zealand artist Lindsay Daen, who made the more famous *La Rogativa* statue in Old San Juan, it's inspired by a local fable.

VENTANA AL MAR

A welcome expanse of green space with a stunning view of the Atlantic along Condado's high-rise row, **Ventana al Mar** (1054 Ave. Ashford, beside La Concha Resort) provides easy access to the beach, as well as benches and lounges for relaxing. On one side is an

Puerta de Tierra, Condado, Ocean Park, and Isla Verde

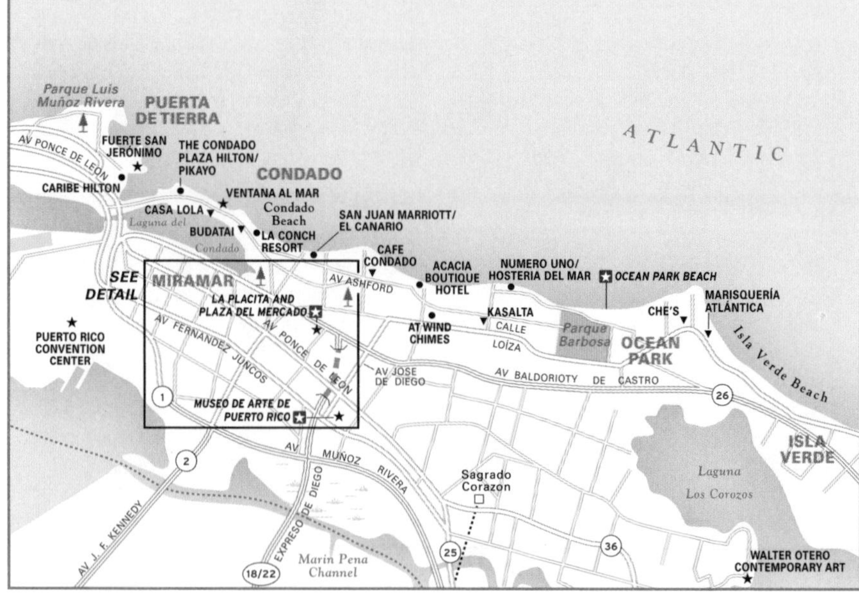

attractive strip of restaurants, ranging from casual to upscale, and an outdoor area filled with tables and chairs for dining alfresco. The first Sunday of every month, the park fills with white tents and the **Mercado Urbano** sets up shop, providing a place for food vendors and farmers to sell fruits and vegetables, baked and canned goods, smoothies and cocktails, and all variety of hot dishes prepared to order.

MIRAMAR

PUERTO RICO CONVENTION CENTER

Puerto Rico Convention Center (100 Convention Blvd., Miramar, 800/214-0420, www.prconvention.com) is a shiny new facility that opened in 2009, and it lays claim to being the largest, most technologically advanced convention center in the Caribbean, with 580,000 square feet of meeting space that can accommodate up to 10,000 people. Events include art fairs, Puerto Rico Comic Con, bridal shows, volleyball championships, and shopping expos. **Ficus Café** (Thurs.-Sat. 5pm-midnight) is an open-air restaurant serving tapas and cocktails.

CONSERVATORIO DE MUSICA DE PUERTO RICO

Renowned cellist Pablo Casals established the **Conservatorio de Musica de Puerto Rico** (951 Ave. Ponce de León, Miramar, 787/751-0160, www.cmpr.edu) in 1959, and it underwent extensive renovation in 2011. The music conservatory provides undergraduate, graduate, and community education programs in areas of musical performance, composition, jazz, and education. The conservatory hosts a family concert series featuring performances by students, faculty, and guest artists; tickets are $10. In addition, free student concerts are held most Tuesdays at 5pm in the Patio Luis Ferré, and free jazz concerts are held on Wednesdays at 6pm in the Anfiteatro Rafael Hernández, in the Plaza de la Laguna.

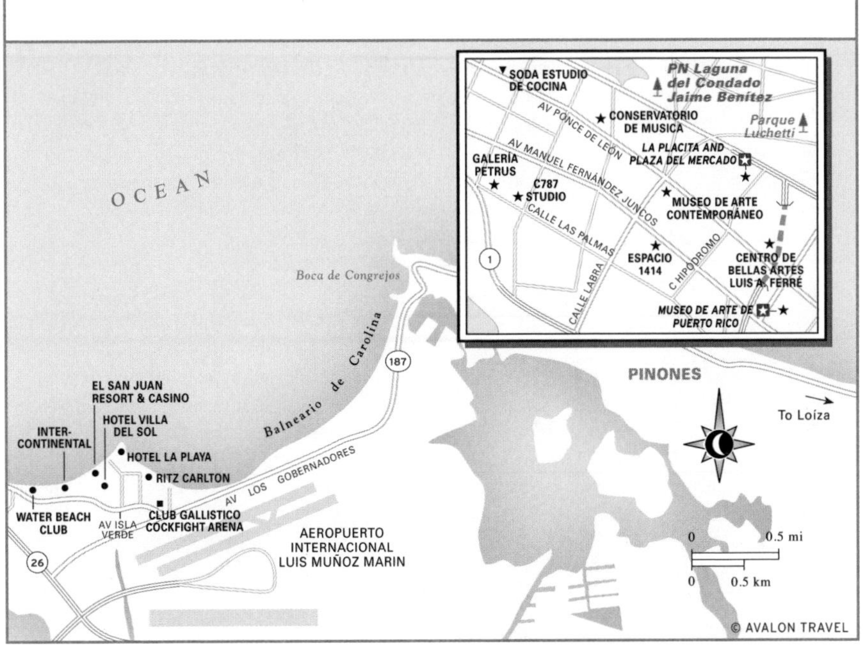

GALERÍA PETRUS

Galería Petrus (726 Calle Hoare, Miramar, 787/289-0505, www.petrusgallery.com, Mon.-Fri. 9am-6pm, Sat. noon-6pm) is a contemporary art gallery that hosts temporary shows featuring contemporary paintings, sculptures, and graphic arts from the 1960s to the present. The gallery specializes in Caribbean artists, including painters Carlos Dávila Rinaldi, Santiago Flores Charneco, painter Luis Hernández Cruz, and sculptor Carlos Guzmán.

SANTURCE

Art Galleries and Museums

★ MUSEO DE ARTE DE PUERTO RICO

Without a doubt, the crowning jewel of San Juan's cultural institutions is **Museo de Arte de Puerto Rico** (299 Ave. José de Diego, Santurce, 787/977-6277, www.mapr.org, Tues. and Thurs.-Sat. 10am-5pm, Wed. 10am-8pm, Sun. 11am-6pm, $6 adults, $3 children 5-12). Visitors with even a passing interest in art will be bowled over by the volume and quality of work produced by the many gifted artists who hail from this small island.

The 130,000-square-foot, neoclassical structure opened in 2000 and was renovated in 2011. It is devoted to Puerto Rican art from the 17th century to the present. The wall text is in Spanish and English. Exhibition highlights include works by the celebrated Francisco Manuel Oller, a European-trained, 17th-century realist-impressionist, as well as a striking selection of *cartels,* a midcentury poster-art form distinguished by bold graphics and socially conscious themes.

Contemporary art is on the second floor, and it is not to be missed. One room is devoted to Rafael Trelles's 1957 installation *Visits to the Wake,* inspired by Oller's famous 19th-century painting of a family attending a child's wake, called *El Veloria.* The piece combines video, sculpture, found objects, and life-size cutouts of the painting's characters to astounding effect. Another remarkable work is Pepón Osorio's installation titled *No Crying Allowed in the Barbershop.* The simulated barbershop explores issues of male vanity, rites of passage, and early lessons in masculinity.

There are also temporary exhibition spaces for rotating shows, a children's gallery, a five-acre modern sculpture garden, and the Raul Julia Theater, featuring an intriguing curtain made of *mundillo,* a traditional handmade lace. A museum shop is also on-site.

MUSEO DE ARTE CONTEMPORÁNEO DE PUERTO RICO

In a striking red-brick Georgian structure completed in 1918, **Museo de Arte Contemporáneo de Puerto Rico** (Escuela Rafael M. de Labra, corner of Roberto H. Todd and Ave. Ponce de León, Santurce, 787/977-4030, 787/977-4031, or 787/977-4032, www.museocontemporaneopr.org, Tues.-Fri. 10am-4pm, Sat. 11am-1pm, Sun. 1pm-5pm, $5 adults, $3 students with ID and seniors 60 and older) has two small exhibition spaces featuring rotating exhibitions from its permanent collection.

WALTER OTERO CONTEMPORARY ART

Located in a clean, modern space, **Walter Otero Contemporary Art** (402 Ave. Constitucion, Santurce, 787/998-9622 or 787/627-5797, www.walterotero.com, Tues.-Fri. 10am-6pm, Sat. 10am-2pm, free) represents more than 20 modern Caribbean artists and hosts rotating exhibits year-round.

ESPACIO 1414

Espacio 1414 (1414 Ave. Fernandez Juncos, Santurce, 787/725-3899, www.espacio1414.org, by appointment Mon.-Fri. 9am-1pm, free) was established by art collectors Diana and Moises Berezdivin to house their collection of contemporary conceptual art with an emphasis on emerging artists. The nonprofit gallery is also the site of occasional visiting exhibitions.

C787 STUDIO

C787 Studio (734 Calle Cerra, Santurce, www.c787studios.com, free) is a slightly off-the-grid space that presents 10 group exhibitions a year featuring emerging contemporary, conceptual, street, and experimental artists. A gift shop sells T-shirts, hats, and other objects designed by local artists.

Puerto Rico Convention Center in Miramar

Museo de Arte de Puerto Rico in Santurce

Performing Arts

CENTRO DE BELLAS ARTES LUIS A. FERRÉ

Centro de Bellas Artes Luis A. Ferré (Ave. Ponce de León, Santurce, 787/620-4444 or 787/725-7334, www.cba.gobierno.pr) is a fine arts performance space hosting classical, jazz, and folk concerts, as well as theater and dance productions. This is also the place to see *zarzuela*, a form of Spanish operetta, performed. Home to the Puerto Rico Symphony Orchestra and annual Festival Casals, it has four halls; the smallest seats up to 200 and the largest seats around 1,950. Ample parking is available on-site.

HATO REY AND RÍO PIEDRAS

EL JARDÍN BOTÁNICO

Maintained by the Universidad de Puerto Rico, **El Jardín Botánico** (Río Piedras, Hwy. 1 at Carr. 847 in Río Piedras, 787/250-0000, ext. 6578, or 787/767-1701, daily 6am-6pm, free, guides available by special arrangement 10am-1pm) is a 289-acre urban garden filled with tropical and subtropical vegetation, including orchids, heliconias, bromeliads, palms, and bamboo. There's also a native Taíno garden display of native plants.

PARQUE LUIS MUÑOZ MARÍN

Parque Luis Muñoz Marín (off Hwy. 18 between Ave. Jesús Piñero and Ave. F. D. Roosevelt, Wed.-Sun. and holidays 8:30am-5pm) in Hato Rey is a modern 140-acre park with walking and bike trails, a children's play area, golf practice grounds, an amphitheater, pavilions, and more.

CATAÑO

CASA BACARDI VISITOR CENTER

Casa Bacardi Visitor Center (Carr. 165, km 2.6, Bay View Industrial Park, Cataño, 787/788-8400, www.casabacardi.org, Mon.-Sat. 9am-6pm, last tour at 4:15pm; Sun. 10am-5pm, last tour at 3:45pm, free) is a tribute to the long, colorful role rum has played in the history and economic development of Puerto Rico and neighboring Cuba. Established in 1862 by Don Facundo Bacardi Masó, Bacardi is the top-selling rum in the United States and is still owned and operated by its founder's descendants. But don't be misled into thinking you will take a tour of Bacardi's rum distillery operations. No rum is made on-site. Instead, expect to see a film about the company's origins in Cuba, historic objects used to make rum in its early days, and displays of advertisements through the years. The tour ends in The Lounge, where a bartender demonstrates how to make a variety of rum drinks and tour-goers get to imbibe two free rum cocktails. Most visitors to the visitor center arrive by ferry from Old San Juan. When you exit AcuaExpreso Cataño, you'll be instructed to turn right and walk about a quarter mile to a parking garage; from there vans take visitors to Casa Bacardi. If you miss the vans, call a taxi. The walk is long and not pedestrian-friendly.

GREATER SAN JUAN

EL CAÑUELO

El Cañuelo (end of Carr. 870 on Isla de Cabras, Toa Alta, daily 8:30am-5:30pm, $2) is the ruins of a tiny fortress across the bay from Castillo San Felipe del Morro. Originally constructed of wood in the 1500s, it was destroyed in an attack by the Dutch in 1625. The current stone structure was built in the 1670s. Its purpose was to work in concert with El Morro to create cannon crossfire at the mouth of the bay. Unfortunately, the public is not allowed to enter the fort, but it provides a terrific view of El Morro. There's a small recreation area with picnic tables.

RUINAS DE CAPARRA

Ruinas de Caparra (Carr. 2, km 6.4, Guaynabo, 787/781-4795, Mon.-Fri. 8am-4:30pm) is the site of Juan Ponce de León's first settlement on the island, established in 1508. All that's left is a few crumbling walls and foundations, but there is a small museum containing some historical documents and Taíno artifacts pertaining to the site.

Sports and Recreation

Puerto Rico's west coast is better known for diving and surfing, but there is plenty of opportunity to do both in San Juan. The most popular water sport these days seems to be stand-up paddleboarding. Riding personal watercraft like Jet Skis is also popular. And good old-fashioned swimming, sailing, and fishing never go out of style.

BEACHES

Balneario El Escambrón

The closest beach to Old San Juan is **Balneario El Escambrón** (Ave. Muñoz Rivera, Puerta de Tierra, 8:30am-6pm daily Apr.-Aug. and Wed.-Sun. Sept.-Mar., $4 per vehicle). The publicly maintained site offers basic amenities, such as public restrooms, showers, snack bar, lifeguards, and an outfitter renting scuba gear, snorkel gear, and kayaks. The small crescent beach is on a cove protected by a coral reef, so the water is quite calm, and there is excellent snorkeling and diving to be had along a collapsed bridge. Steer clear at night. It attracts unsavory types after dark.

Condado Beach

Condado Beach (along Ave. Ashford) is a perfectly fine beach for swimming and sunning, although the terrain is hillier, the sand coarser, and the water less crystalline than San Juan's finest beaches in Isla Verde or Ocean Park. As in Isla Verde, the beach is lined with high-rise buildings, but it is easier for the public to access it thanks to several parks along the way, including **Ventana al Mar, Plaza Ancla,** and **Parque del Indio.**

★ Ocean Park Beach

Located along Park Boulevard, this gorgeous stretch of **Ocean Park Beach**—free from high-rise buildings—is called Ultimo Trolley by locals, because when the island's electric trolley system ceased to operate in 1946, the last trolley car was converted into a snack bar and placed in Parque Barbosa, a large recreation park located across the street with ample parking. The section of the beach directly across from the park is cleaned and raked daily, and a swimming area is protected with nets to keep out sea creatures. On weekends, lounge chairs are available for rent, and street vendors patrol the boardwalk selling snacks and beverages. Farther east the wind and surf are a little rougher, which makes it popular with sailboarders and kite-surfers.

Parque Barbosa (end of Calle McLeary) is right across the street from Ocean Park Beach and is the perfect place to park when visiting the beach. It isn't the prettiest or best-maintained park in San Juan, but it does have hiking, jogging, and bike paths. Its proximity to a large public-housing project may deter some visitors.

El Alambique Beach

El Alambique Beach (Calle Tartak, Isla Verde) is a stunning strip of beach that makes Isla Verde a popular destination for sun-worshippers. Roughly two miles long, its wide stretches of sand and rolling surf make for great swimming, surfing, and windsurfing. Like all beaches in Puerto Rico, Isla Verde Beach is open to the public, but because it's lined cheek by jowl with high-rise hotels and apartment buildings, access is limited. Thank goodness for El Alambique, located at the dead end of Calle Tartak by the San Juan Water Beach Club Hotel. Parking is limited, but there is a turnaround where you can unload your coolers and beach chairs. Once you find a spot to park the car, there is a pedestrian pathway from Avenida Isla Verde. On weekends you can find vendors along the beach renting beach chairs and selling *piraguas* (snow cones). This is a popular spot to windsurf, parasail, ride Jet Skis, and take out small sailboats.

Balneario de Carolina

Balneario de Carolina (Carr. 187, Ave. Boca de Congrejas, 787/778-8811, $2) is a huge public beach maintained by the municipality of Carolina not far from Boca de Congrejas. It's best suited for swimming and sunning. The facility features picnic shelters, bathroom facilities, and plenty of parking. Traffic can get congested here on weekends.

DIVING AND SNORKELING

San Juan may be home to some beautiful beaches, but its snorkel and dive spots are virtually nil. Local outfitters typically head east toward Fajardo for underwater exploration tours.

Ocean Sports (77 Ave. Isla Verde, 787/268-2329, Mon.-Fri. 9am-7pm, Sat. 9am-6pm, $115-175 pp) rents and sells snorkel and scuba equipment from its two stores and operates scuba and snorkel tours from Fajardo. Road transportation to and from San Juan is available.

Caribbean School of Aquatics (1 Calle Taft, 787/728-6606 or 787/383-5700, www.saildiveparty.com) offers full- and half-day sail, scuba, snorkel, and fishing trips from San Juan and Fajardo on a luxury catamaran with Captain Greg Korwek. Snorkel trips start at $69 per person; scuba trips start at $119 per person.

Scuba Dogs (Balneario El Escambrón, Ave. Muñoz Rivera, 787/783-6377 or 787/977-0000, www.scubadogs.net, Mon.-Thurs. 8am-4pm, Fri.-Sun. 8am-5pm) offers guided snorkel, scuba, and kayak tours, as well as rents all the scuba, snorkel, and kayak gear you need to do it yourself. At Playa Escambrón, a Discover Dive for first-timers is $95 and a single-tank dive for certified divers is $75. Kayak tours (2.5 hours) are $65 for adults and $55 for kids. Five-hour boat tours from Fajardo are $180 for first-time divers, $149 for certified divers, and $100 for snorkelers, including transportation from San Juan. Rental charges: full scuba gear for certified divers only, $55; regulator and tank, $40; full snorkel gear, $20; single kayak, $15 an hour; hybrid kayak or paddleboard, $20 an hour; double kayak, $25 an hour.

Caribe Aquatic Adventures (1062 Calle 19, 787/281-8858, www.scaribe-aquatic-adventures.com) offers snorkel and reef dives four times daily, as well as light-tackle and deep-sea fishing trips. A day-long dive and picnic costs $140. A reef dive is $60.

SURFING

Wow Surfing School & Water Sports (on the beach at The Ritz Carlton San Juan and El San Juan Resort & Casino, Isla Verde, 787/955-6059, www.wowsurfingschool.com, daily 9am-5pm) offers two-hour surf lessons for $85, including board. Group rates are available. Equipment rentals include surfboards ($25 an hour), paddleboards ($30),

Water Sports in San Juan

San Juan may be the most cosmopolitan city in the Caribbean, filled with sophisticated art museums, fine-dining restaurants, rooftop lounges, and designer shops, but it's the ocean that attracts most visitors, and there is no better way to enjoy it than mastering a new water sport. There are plenty of opportunities to take your first deep-sea dive, learn to ride the waves, or paddleboard, the hottest new water sport to hit the island.

- **Paddleboarding:** Having originated in Hawaii, the sport, which is sometimes called stand-up paddleboarding (SUP), involves standing on a board and using a long paddle to propel across the surface of the water. It can be done in the ocean, lagoons, and rivers, and it is a fun way to explore the island's waterways. In San Juan, **Velauno** offers private and group lessons at **Laguna del Condado,** as well as eco-tours throughout the island.

surfer crossing

- **Surfing:** Puerto Rico's primo surf spots are found on the west coast around Isabela, Aguadilla, and Rincón, but in San Juan, **Isla Verde**'s waves are just big enough to give novice surfers a challenge. Instructors with **Wow Surfing School & Water Sports** offer two-hour private lessons on land and in the water, as well as board rentals.
- **Diving:** Snorkeling can be fun, but if you really want to explore more exotic underwater sights, you need to strap on an air tank and take a deep-sea plunge. **Scuba Dogs** at **Playa Escambrón** in **Puerta de Tierra** offers first-timers what's called a Discover Dive, which includes instruction and an underwater escort right there at the beach. If that's too tame, Discover Dives are also offered on a boat tour out of Fajardo.

kayaks ($25), and snorkel equipment ($15 and up). Jet Ski rentals and tours are available from Condado, Isla Verde, and San Juan Bay. Call for prices. **Caribbean Surf School** (787/637-8363, www.caribbeansurfpr.com) also offers lessons, tours, and equipment rental. Surfboard rentals are $30 per day and a one-hour surfing class is $65 (price includes day-long surfboard rental).

Tres Palmas Surf Shop (1911 Calle McLeary, Ocean Park, 787/728-3377, trespalmaspuertorico@yahoo.com, Mon.-Sat. 9am-7pm, Sun. 10am-6pm) is the source for all your surfing needs, including boards, board shorts, flip-flops, sunglasses, T-shirts, bathing suits, and more. Rentals are $30 for surfboards, $35 for fun boards, $40 for long boards, and $25 for body boards.

PADDLEBOARDING

Velauno (2430 Calle Loíza, Punta Las Marias, Isla Verde, 787/728-8716, www.velauno.com, Mon.-Fri. 10am-7pm, Sat. 11am-7pm) operates a retail space selling paddleboarding, kayaking, and windsurfing equipment. Equipment rental is available at Laguna del Condado. Options include paddleboard equipment for $25 an hour, $35 for two hours, or $50 for two paddleboards for two hours. Private windsurfing lessons are available for $59-199 for 1-4 hours. Single kayak rentals are $20 an hour; double kayaks are $25 an hour.

BOATING

There are three marinas in San Juan. All three have fuel and water. The largest is **San Juan**

Bay Marina (Calle Lindburgh, 787/721-8062), with a capacity of 191 boats, including 125 wet slips, 60 dry-stack spaces, and six spaces for yachts more than 100 feet long. There's also a restaurant on-site.

Club Náutico de San Juan (482 Ave. Fernández Juncos, Miramar, 787/722-0177, www.nauticodesanjuan.com) is a secure port in San Juan Harbor featuring 117 wet slips that can accommodate vessels 30-250 feet long. Amenities include a clubhouse, a fueling port, and 24-hour guard service. Club Náutico de San Juan also offers sailing lessons (787/667-9936) for children age 6 and older, and it hosts the annual International Regatta (Feb.) and the International Billfish Tournament (Sept.).

Cangrejos Yacht Club in Piñones (Carr. 187, km 3.8, Boca de Cangrejos, Piñones, 787/791-1015) has 180 wet slips, a boat ramp, and a restaurant.

FISHING

Caribbean Outfitters (Cangrejos Yacht Club, 787/396-8346, www.fishinginpuertorico.com) offers fishing and fly-fishing charters throughout Puerto Rico, Vieques, Culebra, the Dominican Republic, and St. Thomas with Captain Omar. Three-quarter-day kayak fishing trips are $600 for one person, $750 for two, including gear and bait. Light tackle fishing ventures start at $350 per person for half-day and $450 for three-quarters of a day. Deep-sea fishing starts at $575 for half-day, $825 for three-quarters of a day, and $1,150 for a full day. Stay two nights at **Tarpon Nest Lodge** (Carr. 187, km 5.6, Loíza, 787/640-6848, 787/783-7227, www.tarponnest.com) and enjoy a light tackle fishing venture ($775 half-day, $875 three-quarter-day) or deep-sea fishing ($687 half-day, $787 three-quarter-day). Prices include accommodations.

Magic Tarpon (Cangrejos Yacht Club, 787/644-1444, www.puertoricomagictarpon.com) offers half-day tarpon and fly-fishing charters for $330-460 for 1-4 people.

CLIMBING, CAVING, AND ZIPLINES

Hacienda Campo Rico (Carr. 3, km 2, Carolina, 787/523-2001, www.haciendacamporico.com) is a 2,300-acre estate featuring ziplining (starting at $119), horseback riding (starting at $55 for two hours, $20 children), ATV riding (starting at $75 for two hours), and a golf academy (private instruction starting at $100).

The go-to outfitter in San Juan for

Tres Palmas Surf Shop in Ocean Park

rappelling in the rainforest, cave tubing, zipline rides, and hiking is **EcoQuest** (New San Juan Building 6471, Ste. 5A, Isla Verde, 787/616-7543 or 787/529-2496, www.ecoquestpr.com). A hiking, kayaking, and zipline tour featuring five zipline courses is $119-169, including transportation.

TENNIS

There is no shortage of tennis courts in San Juan. Many of the large hotels have courts. In addition, there are several public courts, including: **Caribbean Mountain Villas Tennis Court** (Carr. 857, km 857, Canovanillas Sector, Carolina, 787/769-0860), **Central Park** (Calle Cerra off Carr. 2, Santurce, 787/722-1646), and **Isla Verde Tennis Club** (Villamar, Isla Verde, 787/727-6490). The general court rental rates are $4-10 per person, per hour.

GOLF

Río Bayamón Golf Course (Carr. 171 at Ave. Laurel, Bayamón, 787/740-1419, www.municipiodebayamon.com, Mon.-Sat. 7am-6pm, Sun. 6am-8pm, $30 greens fees) is the only golf course in the metropolitan San Juan area. The public course is 6,870 yards and par 72.

Caribbean Golf Academy (Hacienda Campo Rico, Carr. 3, km 2, Carolina, 787/523-2001, www.haciendacamporico.com) provides individualized instruction for beginning and advanced duffers. One-on-one instruction here is $100 per hour and a three-hour group session for a minimum of three people is $175 per person.

HORSEBACK RIDING

Tropical Trail Rides (Hacienda Campo Rico, Carr. 3, km 2, Carolina, 787/523-2001, www.haciendacamporico.com) provides horseback riding for $55 per person for two hours.

BICYCLING

Rent the Bicycle (100 Calle del Muelle, Pier 6, Old San Juan, 787/602-9696 or 787/692-3200, www.rentthebicycle.net) will deliver bikes to your hotel. Rental rates are $17 for three hours, $27 a day. Bike tours of Old San Juan, Condado parks and beaches, and Piñones are $27 for three hours, with a two-person minimum.

YOGA AND SPAS

Ashtanga Yoga (1950 Calle McLeary, Ocean Park, 787/677-7585, www.ashtangayogapuertorico.com, Ashtanga $17 for drop-ins, Mysore $20 for drop-ins, $3 towel rental, $1 mat rental) offers all levels of yoga, workshops, and teacher training.

Eden Spa (331 Recinto Sur, Bldg. Acosta, Old San Juan, 787/721-6400, Mon.-Sat. 10am-7pm) offers pure luxury pampering, including caviar facials, four-hands massage, honey-butter body wrap, chakra-balancing treatments, Reiki—you name it, Eden Spa has got it. Packages run $148-198.

Zen Spa (1054 Ave. Ashford, Condado, 787/722-8433, www.zen-spa.com, Mon.-Fri. 9am-7pm, Sat. 9am-6pm) offers massage, body wraps, facials, manicures, and hair care. Day-spa packages run $145-450. There's also a health club on the premises.

Entertainment and Events

NIGHTLIFE

If club- and bar-hopping is your thing, you've come to the right place. San Juan definitely knows how to party. Electronic music is prevalent, as is hip-hop and reggaetón, Puerto Rico's homegrown brand of hip-hop, combined with Jamaican dancehall and Caribbean musical styles. And there's always plenty of salsa to go around. The legal drinking age is 18, and there's no official bar-closing time, so many establishments stay open until 6am. Things often don't get started until after midnight, so take a disco nap and put on your dancing shoes. It's sure to be a long, fun-filled night.

Old San Juan

There are two sides to Old San Juan's nightlife. On the southern end near the cruise ship docks are the more commercial and chain establishments like Señor Frog's. But the farther north you go toward Calle San Sebastián, the more authentic the offerings get. And there's only one true nightclub with live music and dancing, but it's a good one.

★ NUYORICAN CAFÉ

By far the best nightclub in San Juan for live contemporary Latin music—from rock and jazz to salsa and merengue—is **Nuyorican Café** (312 Calle San Francisco, 787/977-1276, www.nuyoricancafepr.com, Tues.-Wed. 7pm-3am, Thurs.-Sun. 7pm-5am, Sat.-Thurs. free, Fri. $5, full bar). Don't bother looking for a sign; there isn't one. Just look for a gaggle of club-goers clustered around a side door down Capilla alley, which connects Calle San Francisco and Calle Fortaleza. Locals and tourists alike pack in, especially on weekends when the tiny dance floor gets jammed. The kitchen serves a limited menu of Puerto Rican cuisine until midnight. The music usually starts around 11pm. There's no direct link between this café and New York City's Nuyorican Poets Café, which was and still is the epicenter of the Nuyorican movement, although the name is a nod to the club in NYC.

BARS

If you need a place to rest your feet and just chill with a cool beverage, there are a wide variety of bars, both casual and upscale, where you can actually have a conversation, at least in the early part of the evening. The later it gets, though, the more crowded and louder it gets.

Located in the space formerly occupied by Los Hijos de Borinquen bar, **La Factoria** (148 Calle San Sebastián, no phone, daily 6:30pm-4am, $6-16) is a popular new bar with a vintage vibe, thanks to the distressed walls, strings of filament light bulbs draped across the room, and two enormous mirrors behind the bar, lined with old liquor bottles. Check the chalkboard for drink specials, like the spiced old fashioned made with rum and housemade bitters, and drinks made with lavender-infused vodka. Pass through the plywood door behind the bar and you enter the semi-secret wine bar, **Vino @ Factoria,** where DJs spin until the wee hours. Both venues serve from the same eclectic menu of tapas, including skirt steak steamed buns, burger sliders, pork-stuffed burritos, and *bánh mì*. The kitchen is open until 2am.

Beer aficionados flock to **La Taberna Lúpulo** (151 Calle San Sebastián, 787/721-3772, Mon.-Thurs. 6pm-2am, Sat. 1pm-2am, Sun. noon-2am, $11-30). The corner bar with dramatic archways and shelves lined with beer bottles sets the stage for sampling more than 30 craft beers on tap, as well as a pub menu of quesadillas, empanadas, and the like. There's also a full bar.

At **El Farolito** (277 Calle Sol, Old San Juan, no phone, daily noon-midnight or later) artwork by local artists hangs on the walls and a chess set sits on the tiny bar of this narrow

The History of Puerto Rican Rum

Sugar production was integral to Puerto Rico's modern history. It was the bounty of sugarcane that first brought an influx of Europeans to the island in the 1800s. Eventually the island was dotted with sugarcane plantations, sugar refineries, rum distilleries, and shipping operations. Around the turn-of-the-19th century, the sugar industry declined, but that didn't stop the rum-making operations. Today, most of the world's supply of rum is produced in Puerto Rico. **Bacardi** is the top-selling brand, but it's not the only game in town. Serralles Distillery in Ponce produces the well-regarded brand **Don Q.** Most locals recommend **Ron del Barrilito,** made in Bayamón, as the island's most prized brand. In recent years, several small-batch craft rums have come to market, including **Rum Caray** made in Juncos and **Trigo** from Bayamón.

Here are some ways to explore the flavors and history of the island's favorite elixir.

Casa Bacardi Visitor Center is a popular tourist attraction in Cataño devoted to the history of the top-selling rum in the United States, which is still owned and operated by descendants of founder Don Facundo Bacardi Masó. But don't be misled into thinking you will take a tour of Bacardi's rum distillery operations. No rum is made on-site. Instead, expect to see a film about the company's origins in Cuba, historic objects used to make rum in its early days, and displays of advertisements through the years. The tour ends with two free rum cocktails.

Castillo Serrallés is proof of how lucrative rum production was for its makers. Built atop a mountain overlooking Ponce in 1934 for Eugenio Serrallés, founder of Serrallés Rum Distillery, this stunning four-story Spanish Moroccan-style mansion contains many of the Serrallés family's original furnishings. One room in the house has been converted into an exhibition space that explains and illustrates how sugar cane is processed and turned into rum.

Casa Melaza is a petite shop in Old San Juan that bills itself as a "rum boutique." Owner Antonio Lizardi is a wealth of information about local rums. In addition to all the major brands, he carries an excellent selection of small-batch and aged rums ideal for sipping. You'll also find locally produced sangrias and coffees.

The **Piña Colada,** a frozen concoction of rum, coconut cream, and pineapple juice, originated in San Juan. There's no disputing that. But, the question remains: Who invented it? Ramon "Monchito" Marrero, a bartender at **Caribe Hilton** hotel, claimed to have made the first one in 1954 after three months of experimentation. Rumor has it that Joan Crawford said the drink was "better than slapping Bette Davis in the face." But Spanish-born bartender Ramon Portas Mingot also claims to have made the first one at **Barrachina** restaurant in 1963. The difference between the two versions is Caribe Hilton makes it with ice and Barrachina makes it with water and freezes it before blending it. You can try one at both establishments and decide for yourself which one is best.

Chichaito is a clear, thimble-sized drink often served after a traditional Puerto Rican meal, as well as in most bars. (Its name is slang for "little fornicator.") It is made from equal parts rum and anise-flavored liqueur and is downed in a single gulp that packs a powerful punch. **La Casita Blanca** in Santurce sends out a complimentary round after dinner, and **Tres Cuernos** in Old San Juan serves 31 flavored versions.

Taste of Rum (www.tasteofrums.com, Mar.) offers the opportunity to sample an array of Puerto Rican rums at this annual festival held at Paseo La Princesa in Old San Juan. The one-day event also features educational seminars, competitions, live music, dancing, and food vendors.

---

drinking spot favored by locals. This is not the place for fruity, frozen drinks. Your best option is to stick with beer and shots, such as the *chichaito,* a rum and anise-flavored blast of booze.

Tres Cuernos (359 Calle San Francisco, 787/724-3840 or 787/723-2733, Tues.-Sun. 10am-2am, Mon. 10am-6pm) is a large, bare-bones dive bar specializing in 31 flavors of $1 *chichaitos*, a traditional anise-flavored shot, and $1.50 Medalla beers. A changing menu of Puerto Rican dishes such as *arroz con pollo* and *carne guisada* is served for lunch (daily 10:30am-3pm, $6 a plate).

A favorite late-night spot for pub crawlers is **Blessed Café** (353-1 Calle San Francisco, 787/604-5432, Tues.-Sun. 11am-midnight or later, depending on the crowd), a divey reggae bar offering live music on Saturdays, starting at 10pm. This is a no-frills place, featuring TV screens playing Bob Marley videos, serving $2 cans of Medalla beer and $9 rum punches. There is a surprisingly pricey menu ($15-22) of Jamaican dishes, including oxtail stew and jerk chicken.

Although primarily an Indo-Latino fusion restaurant, **Tantra** (356 Calle Fortaleza, 787/977-8141, www.tantrapr.com, Sun.-Thurs. noon-11pm, Fri.-Sat. noon-midnight) turns into a late-night party spot with the after-dinner crowd who flock here for the sophisticated ambiance, the creative martinis, and a toke or two on one of the many hookahs that line the bar. The kitchen serves a limited late-night menu.

Looking for all the world like an old jail cell, **El Batey** (101 Calle del Cristo, 787/725-1787, daily noon-4am, cash only) is a barren dive bar covered top to bottom with scrawled graffiti and illuminated by bare bulbs suspended from the ceiling. There's one pool table and an interesting jukebox with lots of jazz mixed in with classic discs by the likes of Tom Waits, Jimi Hendrix, and Sly Stone. If you order a martini, they'll laugh at you. This is a beer and shots kind of place.

Isla Verde

One of San Juan's most glamorous bars is **Mist** (2 Calle Tartak, 787/728-3666, www.waterbeachhotel.com), atop the San Juan Water Beach Club Hotel. This posh rooftop bar features white leather sofas and beds arranged around tiny tables under a white awning. The minimal lighting is limited to elaborate Indonesian lanterns and candles, which complement the panoramic view of the city lights.

On the first floor of the San Juan Water Beach Club Hotel is **Zest** (2 Calle Tartak, 787/728-3666 or 888/265-6699, www.waterbeachhotel.com), a more intimate restaurant and bar. The attraction here is the interesting wall behind the bar—it's made from corrugated tin over which water pours all night long.

Another popular hotel hot spot is **Brava** (El San Juan Resort, 6063 Ave. Isla Verde, 787/791-2761 or 787/791-2781, www.bravapr.com). This popular dance club, which underwent renovation in 2014, packs in the upscale, trendy set, who dance to an eclectic mix of dance-club tunes, salsa, and '80s rock. Reservations are required for table service.

Condado

From the street level, **Di Zucchero Lavazza Restaurant & Lounge** (1210 Ave. Ashford, 787/946-0835, http://dizuccheropr.com, lounge Fri.-Sat. 11pm-4am) is a hip Italian coffee bar and restaurant specializing in pasta, pizza, and panini in a dramatic red-and-black setting appointed with ornate white chandeliers. Venture upstairs and discover a massive two-level nightclub that continues the baroque theme from downstairs but sets it against an industrial-chic backdrop. Five extensively stocked bars serve up to 500 club-goers who come to dance to techno music, check out experimental film projections on the walls, and canoodle on overstuffed couches in dark corners.

The large open-air pavilion bar **La Terraza Condado** (intersection of Ave. Ashford and Calle McLeary, 787/723-2770, Sun.-Thurs. 5pm-midnight, Fri.-Sat. 5pm-2am) is popular with a young crowd that flocks here on the weekends for the cheap drinks, and it's an ideal perch for people-watching. There's a full bar, and it serves Puerto Rican cuisine ($9-18).

Ocean Park and Santurce

At the nexus of all that is hip in Santurce, which is experiencing an arts renaissance, is **La Respuesta** (1600 Ave. Fernandez Juncos, Santurce, no phone, www.larespuestapr.com), a graffiti-covered industrial space that hosts DJs, live bands, and art exhibitions that celebrate both emerging young artists and oldsters with an edge. Musical acts run the gamut from hip-hop and R&B to metal and Latin jazz. Wednesday night is *Noche de Cine,* featuring film screenings. By day this place looks like an abandoned warehouse, but it smokes at night.

Loíza 2050 Whiskey Bar (2050 Calle Loíza, Santurce, 787/726-7141, Wed.-Sat. 6pm-midnight, Sun. 6pm-4am) got its start 25 years ago as a pizza joint, but it has become a popular hot spot for the young, hip crowd, attracted by the large selection of craft beers and whiskeys. And you can still get a pizza to soak up the booze.

It's a bookstore, but **Libraría Libros AC Barra & Bistro** (1510 Ave. Ponce de Leon, Santurce, 787/998-5132, www.librosac.com, Mon.-Wed. 10am-10pm, Thurs.-Sat. 10am-midnight, Sun. 10am-6pm) is also a major music venue for local rock, jazz, and Latin bands.

Mango's (1954 Calle McLeary, Ocean Park, 787/998-8111, www.mangosocean-park.com, Tues.-Fri. 11:30am-2am, Sat.-Sun. 9:30am-2am, $10-30) is marketed as a restaurant, and the brunch is very popular, but this casual spot with a small interior restaurant and a large covered patio turns into a loud, rowdy bar where recorded pop music throbs until the wee hours. The bar offers a large selection of craft beers and an economical menu of Puerto Rican cuisine. The kitchen serves food until midnight. Be prepared to be patted down and have your purse searched before you enter.

GAY BARS

San Juan's gay bars are located in Santurce, and they don't get started until at least 10pm at the earliest. The later it gets, the livelier they become.

Shoot pool, play video games, sing karaoke, check out the drag show, and hit the dance floor at **Circo Café** (650 Calle Condado, Santurce, 787/725-9676, daily until the wee hours, no cover). **La Jirafe Verde** (365 Ave. de Diego, Santurce, 787/723-6643 or 787/429-1402, www.lajirafeverde.com, Thurs. 10pm-2am, Fri.-Sat. 10pm-4am) is a dark, sexy, multi-level dance club with a rooftop bar and private, curtained nooks.

Formerly Junior's Bar, **Scandalo** (613 Calle Condado, Santurce, no phone, $5 cover) is a small dance club with DJs, go-go boys, and drag shows. For a bevy of male strippers, visit **MetroSex Club** (1204 Ave. de Diego, Santurce, no phone, Wed.-Sat. 10pm-3am, $5 cover). For an older crowd, stop by **Tia Maria's Liquor Store** (326 Ave. de Diego, Santurce, 787/724-4011), a small, low-key bar with two pool tables and a reputation for stiff drinks.

Hato Rey

Located in San Juan's business district, Hato Rey, **Downtown Bar & Restaurant** (Ave. Arterial B, in front of Choliseo, 787/523-6666, Wed.-Sun. 11am-2am) is a large, chic music venue that hosts live performances by big name, contemporary Latino bands. In addition to a full bar, there is a large selection of craft beers and a full menu.

PARTY DISTRICTS

There's no doubt about it: Puerto Ricans love a good party, and it seems as if there's always one going on somewhere. San Juan has a couple of unofficial party districts where the concentration of bars and restaurants creates a street-party atmosphere that attracts young locals and tourists alike to bar-hop and people-watch. Although generally safe and contained, these areas can experience a certain level of rowdiness and petty crime, particularly the later it gets and the more alcohol is consumed. Visitors are encouraged to have a good time, but they should take care to keep their wits about them.

★ La Placita and Plaza del Mercado

Santurce's historic marketplace, **La Placita and Plaza del Mercado** (Calle Roberts), is at the heart of this street party that spills into the surrounding narrow roads. La Placita attracts a mostly local, middle-class crowd, which gives it an authentic feel. Instead of partying down with tourists, beachcombers, and novice drinkers, you can share a drink with folks who are blowing off steam after a hard day's work.

A high concentration of small bars and restaurants serve cheap drinks and local cuisine, and a bandstand hosts live music. The streets get especially crowded Thursday, Friday, and Saturday nights.

Boca de Cangrejos

Boca de Cangrejos (end of Ave. Isla Verde, just past the airport) is a sandy patch of beachfront bars, restaurants, clubs, and food kiosks. Since this is also a popular weekend beach spot, the party tends to start early here, but the fun still lasts late into the night. The best way to get to Boca de Cangrejos is to drive or take a taxi, although you'll have to call one to pick you up when you're ready to leave. If you drive, be sure not to leave anything of value visible in the car; break-ins are not uncommon.

Although most establishments are open-air concrete structures, there are a few more-upscale places, such as **Soleil Beach Club** (Carr. 187, km 4.8, Piñones, 787/253-1033, www.soleilbeachclub.com, Sun.-Thurs. 11:30am-10pm, Fri.-Sat. 11:30am-midnight, $10-25), near Boca de Cangrejos in Piñones. The beachside establishment with the palm-frond entrance serves Puerto Rican cuisine and offers live Latin music.

Calle San Sebastián

In Old San Juan, party central is along Calle San Sebastián. Restaurants, bars, clubs, and pool halls of every stripe line the street, making it a great place to bar-hop door-to-door. Standard stops include **Nono's** and **Balcones de Nono's** (109 Calle San Sebastián, 787/725-7819, daily noon-3am), **La Taberna Lúpulo** (151 Calle San Sebastián, 787/721-3772, Mon.-Thurs. 6pm-2am, Sat. 1pm-2am, Sun. noon-2am), and **La Factoria** (148 Calle San Sebastián, no phone, daily 6:30pm-4am).

CASINOS

Puerto Rico's greatest concentration of casinos can be found in San Juan. Its gambling palaces are all in hotels. Although jacket and tie are not required, attire tends to be dressy. All the casinos have banks of slot machines, blackjack tables, and roulette wheels. Most have craps tables, Caribbean stud poker, and three-card poker. Some have mini-baccarat, let it ride, progressive blackjack, and Texas hold 'em.

La Placita is a popular nighttime party district around Plaza del Mercado in Santurce.

Old San Juan

Old San Juan has only one casino, **Sheraton Old San Juan Hotel & Casino** (100 Calle Brumbaugh, Old San Juan, 787/721-5100, www.sheratonoldsanjuan.com, daily 8am-2am).

Condado

For a concentration of casino action, Condado is the place to go. **Condado Plaza Hotel** (999 Ave. Ashford, 787/721-1000, daily 24 hours) boasts 402 slots, as well as 13 blackjack tables, six mini-baccarat games, and Texas hold 'em. Other 24-7 casinos in the area include **San Juan Marriott Resort & Stellaris Casino** (1309 Ave. Ashford, 787/722-7000, www.marriott.com, daily 24 hours) and the small **Diamond Palace Hotel and Casino** (55 Ave. Condado, 787/721-0810, daily 24 hours). Condado is also home to **Radisson Ambassador Plaza Hotel & Casino** (1369 Ave. Ashford, 787/721-7300, www.radisson.com, daily 10am-4am), with a whopping 489 slots.

Isla Verde

The largest casino is at the **Ritz-Carlton San Juan Hotel** (6961 Ave. of the Governors, Isla Verde, 787/253-1700, www.ritzcarlton.com, daily 24 hours, table games noon-6am). Within its 17,000 square feet are 335 slots, 11 blackjack tables, four mini-baccarat games, and Texas hold 'em.

Another 24-hour casino in Isla Verde is **Casino del Sol** (7012 Boca de Cangrejos Ave., Carolina, 787/791-0404, daily 24 hours) in the Courtyard by Marriott Isla Verde Beach Resort. **El San Juan Resort & Casino** (6063 Ave. Isla Verde, Isla Verde, 787/791-1000, www.elsanjuanresort.com, daily 10am-4am) has the largest number of blackjack tables—14—and the added bonus of proximity to one of the most glamorous old-school hotel lobbies on the island, filled with gorgeous ornate woodwork and a massive antique chandelier. Other casinos in the area include **InterContinental San Juan** (5961 Ave. Isla Verde, Isla Verde, 787/791-6100, daily 10am-4am) and **Embassy Suites Hotel** (8000 Calle Tartak, Isla Verde, 787/791-0505, daily 10am-4am).

Miramar

San Juan's newest casino is **Casino Metro** (Sheraton Convention Center Hotel & Casino, 200 Convention Blvd., Miramar, 787/993-3500, www.casinometro.com, daily 24 hours). It features more than 400 slot machines and 16 table games, including blackjack, roulette, baccarat, pai gow poker, and three-card poker. The Mezzanine Stage features live entertainment most nights of the week, and players receive complimentary snacks and beverages. Take a break from the action in the Metro Lounge, where you can enjoy a specialty cocktail and watch the game on one of 12 high-definition TVs.

MOVIE THEATERS

Puerto Rico gets all the major Hollywood releases, as well as a steady offering of Spanish-language films that don't make it to the States. Offering a modern megaplex experience is **Caribbean Cinemas Fine Arts Miramar** (654 Ave. Ponce de León, 787/721-4288, www.caribbeancinemas.com), showing a variety of English and Spanish films, most of which are subtitled. A second location is at **Popular Center** (Torre Norte, 208 Ave. Juan Ponce de León, Hato Rey, 787/765-2339).

HORSE RACING

Just 20 minutes east of San Juan, **Hipódromo Camarero** (Carr. 3, km 15.3, Canóvanas, 787/641-6060, http://camarero-racepark.com, races Wed.-Sun. 3pm-6pm, free) is a modern upscale racetrack with a restaurant, sports bar, and clubhouse with a panoramic view of the track.

COCKFIGHTS

Granted, cockfighting isn't for everyone, but it is a part of Puerto Rican culture. Most cockfight arenas are in rural areas, but San Juan has a large, modern, tourist-friendly facility in **Club Gallistico de Puerto Rico** (Ave. Isla

Verde at Ave. Los Gobernadores, 787/791-1557, 787/791-6005, Wed.-Thurs. 4:30pm-10pm, Sat. 2:30pm-10pm, $10 entry fee). Most of the betting action takes place in the seats closest to the ring. Odds are haggled over and then bets are placed on the honor system by shouting wagers until a taker is secured. Bets are made not only on which bird will win, but on how long the fight will last. Regulars tend to be high rollers who take their bets seriously, so novices may have difficulty placing bets. Food and beer are available for purchase. This is a highly charged, testosterone-rich environment. Women are welcome, but they are advised not to dress provocatively or go alone.

FESTIVALS AND EVENTS

San Juan loves a festival. It seems as though there's one going on every weekend. Some have traditional origins, and others are products of the local tourism department, but they all promise insight into the island's culture and are loads of fun.

Noches de Galerías is held the first Tuesday of the month in February-May and September-December. Roughly 20 museums and galleries throughout Old San Juan open 6pm-9pm for this festive gallery crawl. Though its intentions may be high-minded, as the night progresses the event becomes more of a raucous pub crawl as young adults and teenagers fill the streets in revelry. Arts and crafts booths also line Plaza de San José.

Held in June, **Noche de San Juan Bautista** is the celebration of the island's patron saint. Festivities last several days and include religious processions, concerts, and dance performances. But the highlight of the event is on June 24, when celebrants from all over the island flock to the beach for the day for picnics and recreation. Then at midnight, everyone walks backward into the ocean three times to ward off evil spirits.

Street festivals don't get any more lively than **Festival de la Calle de San Sebastián** (787/724-0910), held in January on Calle San Sebastián in Old San Juan. For three days the street is filled with parades, folkloric dances, music, food, and crafts. As many as 100,000 people flood the streets of Old San Juan, and the later it gets, the younger the crowd becomes.

In 2008, the Puerto Rico Hotel & Tourism Association launched the annual **Saborea Puerto Rico** (http://saboreapuertorico.com), a four-day culinary festival held in April, featuring dinners, cooking demonstrations, tastings, entertainment, and more with local and visiting celebrity chefs.

Taste of Rum (www.tasteofrums.com) is an annual festival held in March at Paseo La Princesa in Old San Juan. The one-day event features tastings of Puerto Rican rums, educational seminars, competitions, live music, dancing, and food vendors.

Founded in honor of the renowned cellist and composer Pablo Casals, the **Casals Festival** (787/918-1106, www.festcasalspr.gobierno.pr) is held in early spring and features a slate of classical music concerts with world-renown guest artists at the Pablo Casals Symphony Hall at the University of Puerto Rico and the Puerto Rico Music Conservatory.

Santurce es Ley (www.santurceesley.com) is an annual independent artists street festival held in August. Area galleries and design studios throughout Santurce stay open until late, hosting art exhibitions and musical performances featuring the work of more than 100 emerging local artists. The event also features the creation of elaborate murals on sides of buildings.

Each spring, the **Heineken Jazz Festival** (Anfiteatro Tito Puente, Hato Rey, 866/994-0001) selects a single jazz master to celebrate with three nights of concerts (8pm-midnight).

The Puerto Rico Tourism Company presents an annual three-day arts festival in early June called **Feria de Artesanías** (787/723-0692, www.gotopuertorico.com). More than 200 artisans fill the walkways along Paseo La Princesa and Plaza de la Dársena, and the days are filled with music and dance performances as well as a folk-singer competition.

Less an actual festival and more a cultural

series, **La Casita Festival** takes place every Saturday 5:30pm-7:30pm year-round in Plaza de la Dársena by Pier 1 in Old San Juan. Musicians and dance groups perform, and artisans sell their wares.

Similarly, **LeLoLai Festival** (787/723-3135, 787/791-1014, or 800/223-6530) presents traditional concerts and dance performances year-round at various sites throughout the island, including InterContinental San Juan Resort in Isla Verde and Castillo de San Cristóbal in Old San Juan.

Shopping

In the current era of globalization, shopping is fast becoming similarly homogenized the world over, and Puerto Rico is no different. The island is rife with large shopping malls and outlet stores selling the same designer names you could buy at Anywhere, USA. But there is also a strong culture of artisanship in Puerto Rico, and many stores sell locally made traditional crafts and contemporary artwork in varying degrees of quality. Haitian, Indonesian, and Indian import shops are plentiful too, as are high-end fine-jewelry stores. And thanks to Condado, San Juan is the place to go for high-end fashion, including Louis Vuitton and Cartier.

OLD SAN JUAN

Visitors love to shop in Old San Juan because it offers the widest variety of unique shopping options in one pedestrian-friendly place. This is the place to go for fine jewelry, imported clothing and furnishings, cigars, folk art, tourist trinkets, and American chain stores, such as Marshalls, Walgreens, and Radio Shack.

Antiques and Collectibles

Thrift-store shoppers and collectors of vinyl will love **Frank's Thrift Store** (363 Calle San Francisco, 787/722-0691, daily 10am-6pm). Come here to peruse the enormous used-record collection, from 1980s kitsch to fresh electronica. There's even a turntable available, so you can listen to the stock before you buy. This cluttered labyrinth of rooms is also packed with the widest assortment of junk and collectibles you could ever imagine: decorative items, old photographs, dishes, toys, clothes—you name it.

Galería Don Pedro (254 Calle San Justo, 787/721-3126 or 787/429-7936, Mon.-Thurs. and Sat. 10:30am-7pm, Fri. 10:30am-5:30pm, closed Sun.) has three floors of antiques, vintage collectibles, and original artwork by local artists.

Arts and Crafts

For visitors seeking high-quality crafts by local artisans, **Puerto Rican Arts and Crafts** (204 Calle Fortaleza, 787/725-5596, daily 9:30am-6pm) is your one-stop shopping spot. This large two-level store has everything from original paintings and prints to ceramics, sculpture, jewelry, and more.

Another good option is **Age Art Gallery** (150 Calle del Cristo, 787/724-8282, www.agepr.net, daily 10am-7pm), which specializes in pottery, ceramics, jewelry, and glasswork by local artisans.

For a small selection of authentic Caribbean crafts, stop by **Tienda de Artesanías** (Museo de las Americas in Ballajá Barracks, on Calle Norzagaray beside Quincentennial Plaza, 787/722-6057, www.museolasamericas.org, Tues.-Sat. 9am-noon and 1pm-4pm, Sun. noon-5pm). It has a nice but small mix of quality baskets, shawls, pottery, jewelry, santos, art posters, and CDs.

Máscaras de Puerto Rico (La Calle, 105 Calle Fortaleza, 787/725-1306, http://home.coqui.net/chilean, Mon.-Sat. 10am-6:30pm, Sun. 10:30am-5:30pm) is a funky, narrow shop in a covered alleyway selling quality contemporary crafts, including masks and small reproductions of vintage *cartel* posters. In the back is Café El Punto restaurant, serving traditional Puerto Rican cuisine.

There are two nearly identical shops on the same street called **Haitian Gallery** (367 Calle Fortaleza, 787/721-4362, and 206 Calle Fortaleza, 787/725-0986, www.haitiangallerypr.com, daily 10am-6pm). They both sell a great selection of Haitian folk art, including brightly colored primitive-style paintings and tons of woodwork, from sublime bowls to ornately sculpted furniture. There's a small selection of Indonesian imports, such as leaf-covered picture frames and photo albums, and tourist trinkets.

The Poets Passage (203 Calle Cruz, 787/567-9275, daily 10am-6pm) offers a funky collection of local arts, crafts, and books. The store is owned by local poet and publisher Lady Lee Andrews. Poetry nights are held every Tuesday at 7pm.

Cigars and Rum

Like Cuba, Puerto Rico has a long history of hand-rolled cigar-making, and you can often find street vendors rolling and selling their own in Plaza de Hostos's Mercado de Artesanías, a plaza near the cruise-ship piers at Calle Recinto Sur. There are also several good cigar shops selling anything you could want—except Cubans, of course. The biggest selection is at newly renovated **The Cigar House** (257 Calle Fortaleza, 787/725-0652, www.thecigarhousepr.com, Sun.-Thurs. 10am-9pm, Fri.-Sat. 10am-11pm) with an inviting smoking lounge. Trinidad, Monte Cristo, Padron 1926 and 1964, Cohiba, Perdomo, Macanudo, Partagas, Romeo and Julieta, and Puerto Rican cigars aged in rum are among those sold.

For a more intimate setting, visit **El Galpón** (154 Calle del Cristo, 787/725-3945 or 888/842-5766, www.elgalpon.net, Mon.-Sat. 10am-6pm, Sun. 10am-5pm). This small, selective shop sells a variety of quality cigars, Panama hats, masks, art prints, and superb vintage and contemporary santos.

Billing itself as a "rum boutique," **Casa Melaza** (74 Caleta de San Juan, 787/462-4782, www.casamelaza.com, daily 11am-7pm) is a small store, but it sells a big selection of Puerto Rican rums, including locally made craft varieties Rum Caray made in Juncos and Trigo from Bayamón, and limited reserve varieties from major distilleries Don Q and Bacardi. You'll also find locally produced sangrias and coffees. Owner Antonio Lizardi is a fountain of information about local rums.

Clothing and Accessories

For a large inventory of Panama hats, visit **Vaughn's Gifts & Crafts** (262 Calle Fortaleza, 787/721-8221, vaughns@operamail.com, Mon.-Sat. 10am-6pm, Sun. 11am-5pm). Other hat styles, as well as handbags and souvenirs, can be found here.

Costazul (264 Calle San Francisco, 787/722-0991 or 787/724-8085, Mon.-Sat. 9am-7pm, Sun. 11am-5pm) sells a great selection of surf and skate wear for men and women, including Oakley sunglasses and clothes by Billabong and Quiksilver. During surf season, it also stocks boards and related gear.

Concalma (207 Calle San Francisco, 787/342-9757, www.shopconcalma.com or www.concalmalinea.com, Mon.-Sat. 9:30am-7pm, Sun. 10am-6pm) is a chic shop specializing in locally made tote bags, purses, and pouches. The variety of fabrics and patterns range from playful to sophisticated.

All along Calle del Cristo are a dozen or so designer outlets and stores including **Tommy Hilfiger, Coach, Guess, Crocs, Ralph Lauren, Dooney & Bourke, Polo Chopard, Harry Winston,** and **H. Stern.**

Fine Jewelry

There are dozens of high-end fine-jewelry stores in Old San Juan, especially along Calle Fortaleza, including **N. Barquet Joyers** (201 Calle Fortaleza, 787/721-3366 or 787/721-4051, nbarquet@spiderlink.net, daily 10:30am-5pm); **Casa Diamante** (252 Calle Fortaleza, 787/977-5555, daily 10am-6pm); and **Emerald**

Isles (105 Calle Fortaleza, 787/977-3769, Mon.-Sat. 11am-6pm).

Vogue Bazaar (364 Calle San Francisco, 787/722-1100, Mon.-Wed. and Fri.-Sat. 10am-6:30pm) specializes in pre-Columbian reproductions, gemstones from South America, and purses from Thailand.

Imports

San Juan has several Indonesian import shops. **Eclectika** (204 Calle O'Donnell, Plaza de Colón, and 205 Calle de la Cruz, 787/721-7236 or 787/725-3163, www.eclectikasanjuan.com, daily 10am-7pm) has Indonesian imports specializing in home decor, purses, and jewelry.

Hecho a Mano (260 Calle San Francisco, 787/722-0203, and 250 Calle San José, 787/725-3992, www.hechoamanopr.com) sells Indonesian decorative imports, locally designed women's wear, funky purses, and jewelry. There's another location in Condado (1126 Ave. Ashford).

Markets

A small market, **Mercado Agricola Natural** (150 Calle Norzagaray, Old San Juan, Sat. 8am-1pm, www.mercadoagricolanatural.com, free), with an emphasis on natural products, occurs at Museo de San Juan, selling organic fruit and vegetables, baked goods, coffee, cheese, and bread.

Established in 1910, **La Placita and Plaza del Mercado** (between Calle Dos Hermanos and Calle Canals, http://placitasanturce.com, Mon.-Sat. 6am-6pm, Sun. 6am-noon, free) is the main farmers market in the San Juan area offering a huge selection of fresh produce, meats, seafood, botanicals, and fresh fruit smoothies. If you're hungry and can't wait to go home to cook up your purchases, stop by one of the many surrounding restaurants for a meal of local cuisine, ranging from super cheap to high-end.

Artisans markets, selling locally crafted jewelry, leather goods, gourd art, musical instruments, paintings, and cigars, are often held at two plazas in Old San Juan—**Plaza Dársenas** (Calle Comercio by La Casita) and **Plaza Eugenio María de Hostos** (between Calle San Justo and Calle Tizol). Don't be surprised if there's also live entertainment and a food truck or two.

Spicy Caribbee (154 Calle del Cristo, 888/725-7529, www.spicycaribbee.com, Mon.-Sat. 10am-6pm, Sun. 11am-5pm) sells Caribbean sauces, spice mixes, coffees, soaps, fragrances, candles, cookbooks, and more.

CONDADO

Condado has several high-end stores like Cartier, Louis Vuitton, Gucci, and Salvatore Ferragamo, but in recent years more reasonably priced clothing stores have opened up. Don't be surprised if you try to enter a storefront along Condado and find the door locked during regular business hours. Many of the smaller shops are managed by a single person; the doors are kept locked for their safety. Just ring the doorbell and the proprietor will buzz you in.

Clothing and Accessories

For one-of-a-kind designs, visit the eponymous store of one of the island's most renowned designers of casual wear and haute couture for both men and women, **Nono Maldonado** (1112 Ave. Ashford, 2nd Fl., 787/721-0456, www.nonomaldonado.com, Mon.-Fri. 10am-6:30pm, Sun. 2pm-7pm). The former fashion editor of *Esquire* magazine, Maldonado also designs interiors for many of the island's high-end hotels.

If you don't mind dropping $400 for a tank top, **Olivia Boutique** (1400 Ave. Magdalena, 787/722-6317, Mon.-Sat. 10:30am-6pm) sells high-end designer leisurewear and beachwear for women. Labels include Missoni and Helmut Lang. Don't miss the shoes—they're works of art from Italy and Spain.

Monsieur (1126 Ave. Ashford, 787/722-0918, Mon.-Sat. 10am-6:30pm, Sun. 2pm-7pm) sells casual designer menswear for the young and clubby. Labels include Thomas Dean, Stone Rose, Ballin, Alberto, and Robert Graham. There's also a second location (1373 Garden Hills Plaza, Guaynabo).

Also for men, **Root** (1129 Ave. Ashford, 787/946-7668, www.rootformen.com, Mon.-Thurs. 11am-7pm, Fri.-Sat. 11am-10pm, Sun. noon-6pm) is a tiny, black-and-white store that sells two things: limited edition T-shirts designed by graphic artists ($25) and limited edition handmade dress shirts ($49). Only 18 of each T-shirt is made, and only six of each dress shirt design, so it's a safe bet you'll be the only one on your block to have one when you go back home. The high style of the shop's unique designs can be traced to the Argentinean owners.

Across the street from La Concha Resort, **Piña Colada Club** (1102 Ave. Magdalena, 787/998-1980, Mon.-Sat. 11am-7pm, Sun. noon-5pm) specializes in stylish resort- and beachwear. Labels include Trina Turk, Vitamin A Swim, Maaji, Echo, Bianca Coletti, Hale Bob, and the Piña Colada Club line of terrycloth and jersey beachwear. Note: Don't confuse this clothing shop with the restaurant and bar of the same name located in the Caribe Hilton.

Charmé (1374 Ave. Ashford, 787/723-9065, Mon.-Sat. 10am-6:30pm) is a tiny shop packed to the rafters with flowing resort-wear for mature women, including the Flax Designs linen clothing line.

Nativa Boutique (55 Calle Cervantes, 787/724-1496, 350 Ave. Roosevelt, 787/783-0099, www.nativaboutique.net, Mon.-Sat. 10am-6pm) is a clothing boutique selling micro mini club wear, crochet maxi dresses, and sky-high heels. It carries Maaji swimwear and designs by Maritza Camareno and Luis Antonio. Along the same vein, **Glam Boutique** (1357 Ave. Ashford, 787/722-9197, Mon.-Sat. 10am-7pm, Sun. noon-5pm) sells club wear and beachwear for the young and trendy.

Imports

Mozaik (1214 Ave. Ashford, Condado Village, 787/724-3769, www.mozaikbazaar.com, Mon. 10am-2pm, Tues.-Sun. 10am-10pm) bills itself as a world village bazaar, but its goods are primarily from Turkey and Puerto Rico. But that's okay because it offers a well-curated selection of exceptionally well-made and unique fair trade products including shoes, purses, clothing, lamps, jewelry, toys, candles, incense, wall art, and food items.

Indonesian imports and locally designed women's wear are available at **Hecho a Mano** (1126 Ave. Ashford, 787/722-5322, www.hechoamanopr.com, Mon.-Wed. 10am-7pm, Thurs.-Sat. 10:30am-8pm, Sun. 11am-6pm). It also has two locations in Old San Juan (260 Calle San Francisco and 250 Calle San José).

Markets

The first Sunday of every month, oceanfront Plaza Ventana al Mar fills with white tents as the **Mercado Urbano** (1054 Ave. Ashford, Condado, first Sun. 9am-5pm, free) sets up shop, providing a place for food vendors, farmers, and artisanal cheese makers to sell theirs fruits and vegetables, baked and canned goods, smoothies and cocktails, and all varieties of hot dishes prepared to order. The market has grown so popular that it pops up in other locations such as the Yacht Club Marina in Palmas del Mar.

ISLA VERDE

Owned by local designer Chrisnelia Guzman, **Dressed** (5980 Ave. Isla Verde, 787/726-3327, Mon.-Sat. 10:30am-7pm, Sun. noon-4pm) specializes in one-of-a-kind ball gowns, prom dresses, and club wear at surprisingly affordable prices. Most gowns are in the $100-200 range. **Creaciones Phylipa** (Ave. Isla Verde, 787/791-5051, daily 10am-7pm) is a tiny shop packed full of inexpensive cotton gauze dresses for girls and women, jewelry made from beads and wood, purses, and tourist souvenirs.

Located at the end of La Plazoleta de Isla Verde shopping center, **Surf Face** (6150 Ave. Isla Verde, 787/640-9830 or 787/640-9638, Mon.-Sat. 9am-7pm, Sun. 9am-5pm) sells surfboards and skateboards, bathing suits, T-shirts, sunglasses, and flip-flops.

SANTURCE AND MIRAMAR

Clothing and Accessories

For a carefully curated collection of vintage men and women's clothing and accessories, visit **Len. T. Juela Vintage Boutique** (1852 Calle Loíza, Santurce, 787/408-7111, Mon.-Sat. 11am-7pm). There's also a small selection of garments made by local designers.

Check out the flirty, feminine haute couture and ready-to-wear dresses, skirts, and blouses by local designer **Noe Amador** (1804-A Calle Loíza, Santurce, 787/428-8140, Mon.-Fri. 9am-2pm, Sat. 9am-4pm).

Gifts and Music

Gemileo (1808 Calle Loíza, Santurce, 787/727-4110, Mon.-Fri. 9am-6pm, Sat. 9am-7pm) is the place to go for floaty, colorful Indonesian dresses and blouses, and other imported items including jewelry, Hindu statuary, yard art, incense, and candles.

It's a restaurant, but **Kamoli Café** (1706 Calle Loíza, Santurce, 787/721-4326, Mon.-Fri. 7:30am-9pm, Sat.-Sun. 8:30am-9pm, Amex not accepted) sells a nice, small selection of jewelry, T-shirts, and purses by local artisans, as well as tins of loose-leaf teas.

Located in a former church, **Viera Discos** (909 Ave. Fernández Juncos, Miramar, 787/725-1105, www.vieradiscos.com, Mon.-Fri. 9am-6pm) has an enormous selection of new and collectible Latin music CDs and DVDs. Be sure to check out the collection of instruments and autographed photographs of celebrated musicians in the foyer.

HATO REY

For all your American chain store needs, **Plaza Las Americas** (525 Ave. Franklin Delano Roosevelt, Hato Rey, www.plazalasamericas.com, Mon.-Sat. 9am-9pm, Sun. 11am-7pm) is a two-level mall with more than 300 stores, including Macy's, JCPenney, Victoria's Secret, Ann Taylor, Foot Locker, Gap Kids, and Sears.

Accommodations

In addition to an enormous array of hotels, inns, and guesthouses offering every kind of accommodation imaginable, San Juan has a variety of daily, weekly, and monthly apartment rentals available to those seeking a homier or long-term place to stay. **The Caleta Realty** (151 Calle Clara Lair, 787/725-3436, www.thecaleta.com) has many properties in Old San Juan and Condado.

OLD SAN JUAN

Aside from a Sheraton located near the cruise-ship docks, accommodations in Old San Juan are small boutique hotels and inns. In recent years a small hotel group has changed the landscape by developing several unique properties that are modestly priced but big on design, including Da House, Casablanca Hotel, and Villa Herencia. No matter where you stay in Old San Juan, you're within easy walking distance to some of the city's finest restaurants, shops, and cultural sights.

$50-100

Centrally located right on Plaza Colon, **Posada San Francisco** (405 Calle San Francisco, 787/996-0324, www.posada-colonial-puertorico.com, $49-50 s/d, $20 dorm) is a guesthouse and hostel offering very basic but comfortable accommodations for visitors who just need a clean, safe place to crash at night. Rooms range from private single and double rooms (one with a 26-inch flat screen TV) with refrigerators to bare-bone dormitories designated for men, women, or both genders. All rooms are air-conditioned, and there are coin laundry machines and two kitchens available for use. There are no private bathrooms, and a $5 surcharge is tacked on for late-night arrivals. Whether you stay here or not, be sure to check out the stunning ceiling murals by Henry Antoni Pospieszalski in the lobby that depict the mythological origins of the Antilles islands at the hands of Neptune and Vulcan and the clash between the island's Taíno Indians with Spanish conquistadors.

Catering to a young clientele, **Da House** (312 Calle San Francisco, 787/366-5074 or 787/977-1180, www.dahousehotelpr.com, $80-120 s/d) is owned and operated by the folks behind one of the city's hottest music clubs, Nuyorican Café. It's also located directly above the nightclub, making it a great spot for the late-night party crowd. Those inclined to go to bed early will likely be kept awake by the club downstairs, which doesn't close until 3 or 4 in the morning. But night owls looking to stay in elegant but casual surroundings on a student's budget would be hard-pressed to find a better hotel. The 27 units are small and sparsely furnished with just the basics—bed, lamp, mini-fridge, ceiling fan, and remote-control air-conditioning. There is no TV; fresh linens, irons, and hair dryers are available only upon request. There's also no elevator, so be prepared to walk up as many as four flights to your room—carrying your own luggage. Service is minimal—the pierced and tattooed employees that run the reception desk often do double duty in the bar downstairs. So what makes Da House so great? Besides the inexpensive rates and location in the heart of Old San Juan, it is a gorgeous building filled with fantastic contemporary art exhibitions that change every month. There's also a very good shop in the lobby that sells artisan-made crafts.

$100-150

For modern, generic accommodations in an excellent, central location, **Hotel Milano** (307 Calle Fortaleza, 787/729-9050, www.hotelmilanopr.com, $148-175 s/d plus tax) provides 30 clean, corporate-style rooms appointed with queen-size beds, air-conditioning, satellite TV, hair dryers, and mini-refrigerators. Breakfast is served on a lovely rooftop terrace.

$150-250

A dramatic lobby and bar drenched in red velvet, crystal chandeliers, Moroccan lanterns, and Pop Art paintings create a hip vibe at the 35-room ★ **Casablanca Hotel** (316 Calle Fortaleza, 787/725-3436, http://hotelcasablancapr.com, $179-322 plus tax), managed by the folks at Da House. Accommodations range from very small standard rooms to more spacious superior rooms complete with sitting area and balcony. There's no elevator, so be prepared to carry your luggage up a flight or two of stairs. All rooms have air-conditioning, pillow-top mattresses, private baths, and iPod docks. Some rooms have satellite TV. Other amenities include a rooftop sun deck, complimentary high-speed Internet access, next-day laundry service, a business center, concierge service, and free shoeshine.

A classic colonial home built in the 1700s has been converted into ★ **Villa Herencia Hotel** (23 Caleta Las Monjas, 787/722-0989, www.villaherencia.com, $199-349 s/d, plus tax), a stunning eight-room, limited service hotel featuring antique furnishings and huge, original Pop Art paintings by Puerto Rican artist Roberto Parrilla. A manager is on-site during the day only, and amenities are limited to an honor bar, a rooftop terrace, and some gorgeously appointed common areas. It's hard to find such high style in Old San Juan at this price.

On the edge of Old San Juan overlooking the Atlantic Ocean is ★ **The Gallery Inn** (204-206 Calle Norzagaray, 787/722-1808, www.thegalleryinn.com, $170-350 s/d, plus tax, includes breakfast buffet), one of the unique hotels in San Juan. This 18th-century home is packed with 22 small rooms tucked into a multilevel labyrinth of patios, courtyards, balconies, archways, fountains, and interior gardens. As if that weren't enough, the hotel is chock-full of portrait sculptures and plaster reliefs by artist-owner Jan D'Esopo, as well as potted plants, hanging baskets, and an assortment of tropical birds, which have the run of the place. If the chockablock decor begins to feel a bit claustrophobic, there's an elegant, airy music room with a grand piano and a rooftop deck for a change of scenery. Small rooms are well appointed with quality antiques and reproductions. A restaurant serves dinner daily beginning at 5pm.

Nearby is the equally modern, corporate-style **SJ Suites** (253 Calle Fortaleza, 787/977-4873, 787/977-4873, or 787/725-1351, www.sjsuites.com, $150-190 s/d, plus 9 percent tax). Fifteen spanking-new, self-serve suites come with air-conditioning, satellite TV, and mini-refrigerators. There's no reception desk or on-site management. Check-in is inside Kury Jewelry Store next door.

Over $250

To get a true sense of history, spend the night in a Carmelite convent completed in 1651 by order of King Phillip IV of Spain. ★ **Hotel El Convento** (100 Calle del Cristo, 787/723-9020, 787/721-2877, or 800/468-2779, www.elconvento.com, $250-370 s/d, $630-1,440 suite, plus tax and resort fees) is a recipient of many awards and accolades. The 58-room hotel encompasses a four-floor colonial structure with an enormous well-landscaped courtyard in the center. Common areas are filled with gorgeous Spanish antiques and reproductions. Rooms come with air-conditioning, cable TV, VCR, stereo, telephone, and refrigerator. Amenities include a fitness center, plunge pool, and whirlpool bath on the fourth floor, which overlooks Old San Juan and the bay. The hotel has four restaurants.

Elegant simplicity defines ★ **Cervantes Chateau** (329 Recinto Sur, 787/724-7722, www.cervantespr.com, $238 s/d, $300 junior suite, $451 signature suites, $1,073 penthouse suite, plus tax and resort fees), a luxury boutique hotel near the piers in Old San Juan. Tastefully but playfully decorated by clothing designer Nono Maldonado, each room is different but features original artwork and a subdued modernist aesthetic in shades of gray, gold, and russet. The stunning penthouse suite takes up the whole top floor and features an outdoor terrace and a dining room table that seats up to 10. Each room has air-conditioning, flat panel TVs with cable access, free wireless Internet, and complimentary continental breakfast. Downstairs is a tiny lobby and Panza restaurant, serving international and local cuisine.

Hotel El Convento, formerly a Carmelite convent built in 1651

If you want to know exactly what to expect, stay at the **Sheraton Old San Juan Hotel & Casino** (100 Calle Brumbaugh, 787/721-5100, www.sheratonoldsanjuan.com, $249 s/d, $279-329 suite, plus tax and hotel service charges). The high-rise hotel by the cruise-ship docks features all the comforts one expects from the chain. Amenities include 42-inch LCD cable TVs, high-speed Internet, a rooftop pool, a health club, and a 7,000-square-foot casino. There are two restaurants: a seafood spot called Palio and Chicago Burger Company.

PUERTA DE TIERRA

Over $250

Puerta de Tierra is a small bit of land between Condado and Old San Juan, just west of the bridge that connects those two communities.

It includes a small beach, a large park, a stadium, several government buildings, and one classy hotel.

★ **Caribe Hilton** (1 Calle San Geronimo, 787/721-0303, www.hiltoncaribbean.com, $249-269 s/d, $369 suite, plus tax and resort fees) is proof that all Hilton hotels are not alike. This stunning display of modernist architecture and design is a beloved blast from the past, a reminder of a time when the Condado was an epicenter of glamour. Built in the late 1940s, the sprawling hotel features an enormous lobby awash in curved lines and modular shapes that merge elegantly with blond woods, polished steel, and thick glass. Be sure to gaze up at the ceiling, a stunning wooden structure that mimics the swooping shape of ocean waves. Rooms in the main building were renovated in 2013; rooms in the tower building were renovated in 2015. There are seemingly countless bars, including a swim-up bar at the pool. The Caribe Hilton is one of two places in Puerto Rico (the other being Barrachina in Old San Juan) that claims to have invented the piña colada, so tourists often stop by to have one, whether they're staying at the hotel or not. And don't miss the hard-to-find Tropical Garden. Tucked away in a quiet corner is an oasis of lushly landscaped grounds built around a pond and gazebo where peacocks, geese, and black swans roam freely. There are 916 units, including villas, and nine restaurants, including Morton's The Steakhouse. There is also a spa and boutiques for shopping.

CONDADO

$100-150

Located in the heart of Condado and two blocks from the beach, **Coral Princess Hotel** (1159 Ave. Magdalena, 787/977-5959 or 787/977-7700, www.coralpr.com, $135-225 s/d, plus tax and fees) is a compact, 25-room hotel with a small pool, complimentary continental breakfast, free Internet, flat screen TVs with cable, and a rooftop whirlpool tub.

For clean, modern, no-frills accommodations at a budget rate, **El Canario** (1317 Ave. Ashford, 787/722-3861, www.canaryboutiquehotel.com, $105-134 s, $134-149 d, plus tax) offers a pleasant lobby and 25 small units.

$150-250

★ **The Condado Plaza Hilton** (999 Ave. Ashford, 787/721-1000 or 866/316-8934, www.condadoplaza.com, $239-269 s/d, $449-549 suites, plus tax and resort fees) is an interesting bookend to the 1940s-era modernism

Built in the late 1940s, Caribe Hilton in Puerta de Tierra features many mid-century architectural details.

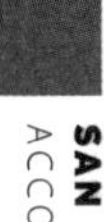

of the Caribe Hilton. The Condado Plaza is a 21st-century modernist's dream with a minimalist aesthetic and a tastefully rendered nod to Pop Art sensibilities. The lobby is blindingly white with occasional touches of brilliant orange that draw the eye around the room, from the low-backed couches to the textured wooden wall treatments to the private nooks and crannies tucked behind beaded curtains. Modernist touches continue in the guest rooms, where billboard-size black-and-white photographs hang over the beds and the shower is a clear glass cube situated in the center of the spacious bathroom. The casino is open 24 hours a day, and there are multiple restaurants, including Pikayo, local celebrity chef Wilo Benet's popular restaurant serving contemporary interpretations of Puerto Rican cuisine. Other amenities include a fitness center, a business center, and two pools, one of which is filled with saltwater.

Opened in 2012, **Olive Boutique Hotel** (55 Calle Aguadilla, 787/705-9994, www.oliveboutiquehotel.com, $175 s, $200-240 d) is a small boutique hotel with small, beautifully appointed rooms designed in Mediterranean themes. Ideal for couples, the hotel features a rooftop bar with a view of Laguna del Condado, see-through showers right in the rooms, and the fine dining restaurant Olivda, serving creative Italian cuisine.

Over $250

For your standard corporate stay, **San Juan Marriott Resort @ Stellaris Casino** (1309 Ave. Ashford, 787/722-7000, www.marriott.com, $269-349 s/d, $395 suite, plus tax and resort fees) is a high-rise hotel on the ocean offering spectacular views. Amenities include two restaurants, two bars, a coffee shop, swimming pool, fitness room, and a casino.

La Concha Resort (1077 Ave. Ashford, 787/721-7500, www.laconcharesort.com, $249 s/d, $279-399 suite, plus tax and fees) was built in 1958 and is another huge, shimmering modernist hotel on the Condado. It closed and lay dormant for years, but a recent renovation has returned it to its former glory and beyond. Amenities include multilevel swimming pools with waterfalls and a sandy beach with food and beverage service, two lounges, and four restaurants, including Perla, an upscale restaurant serving contemporary American cuisine heavy on seafood in a stunning clamshell-shaped space right on the beach.

OCEAN PARK

Ocean Park boasts one of the better beaches in the metro area and some small, charming, gay-friendly guesthouses that pay a lot of attention to the kinds of details that can make an overnight stay memorable. Because this is primarily a residential neighborhood, there aren't a lot of restaurants, bars, or shops within walking distance. Also note that if you have a rental car, street parking can be scarce, especially on the weekends when locals flock to the beaches.

$100-150

It's at the far eastern end of Condado, several blocks from the nearest restaurant or shop, but **At Wind Chimes Inn** (1750 Ave. McLeary, 787/727-4153, www.atwindchimesboutiquehotel.com, $80 s, $109-159 d, plus tax) is just a block from the beach. Two Spanish-style haciendas have been combined to create a quaint, artful, 22-room boutique hotel. Each room has air-conditioning, cable TV, telephone, and wireless Internet; some rooms have kitchenettes. Rooms are tastefully decorated with high-quality furnishings and bright cheery bedspreads. Amenities include a small pool with jets and a waterfall, and a shady courtyard bar and grill.

Tucked inside the gated residential neighborhood of Ocean Park is **Dreamcatcher Guest House** (2009 Calle España, 787/455-8259, www.dreamcatcherguesthouse.com, s/d $79-159, t/q $129-189, plus tax), a nine-room guesthouse with a hippie, Zen vibe. Decorated with India print wall hangings, candles, ornate mirrors, wind chimes, and dream catchers, each room is different. Some have en-suite bathrooms, others have shared bathrooms,

At Wind Chimes Inn is a small guesthouse in Ocean Park.

and there's a strictly vegetarian shared kitchen. A three-course breakfast ($15) featuring healthy fare such as pumpkin oatmeal and chia seed pudding is served. Nighttime yoga sessions are offered three times a week under the stars in the courtyard. There is no TV or phones, but there's free high-speed Internet, and each bedroom has air-conditioning.

Andalucia (2011 Calle McLeary, 787/309-3373, www.andalucia-puertorico.com, s/d $89-135, plus tax) is a small, modest spot if you don't need a lot of amenities and just need a comfortable, economical place to sleep. Each of the 11 rooms has an en-suite bathroom, cable TV, air-conditioning, and a mini-refrigerator. Some rooms have kitchenettes. There is one room that is designated handicapped accessible, and there is a computer for guest use in the lobby.

Two side-by-side houses, connected by a courtyard, create **Tres Palmas Guest House** (2212 Park Blvd., 787/727-4617, 888/290-2076, or 866/372-5627, www.trespalmasinn.com, $131-155 s, $148-167 d, plus tax), containing 18 modest guest rooms, offering possibly the most economical stay you can find this close to the beach in greater San Juan. Amenities include a tiny pool and two small hot tubs on the rooftop sundeck overlooking the ocean, which is about 15 steps away, right across the street. Rooms come with air-conditioning, cable TV, free wireless Internet, refrigerator, and complimentary continental breakfast. This is a great place to stay if you want to escape the city's congested tourist areas. All the action is just a short taxi ride away.

$150-250

Located in the heart of Ocean Park's commercial district, **Oceana Hostal Playero** (1853 Calle McLeary, 787/728-8119, www.oceanopuertorico.com, $198-218 s, $238 d, $180 q, $258-458 suite, plus tax; two-night minimum required) is a modest, compact building with 27 rooms. Rooms come with air-conditioning, cable television, wireless Internet, complimentary parking, and continental breakfast. Amenities include a tiny pool.

Acacia Boutique Hotel (8 Calle Taft, 787/268-2803, www.acaciaboutiquehotel.com, $105 s, $175-210 d) is a small, newish beachfront property from the folks at nearby At Wind Chimes. Modern, modest rooms have air-conditioning and basic cable TV; some have balconies. Wireless Internet is available in the common areas. Guests can use the bar and pool of At Wind Chimes Inn (1750 Ave. McLeary, 787/727-4153, www.atwindchimesboutiquehotel.com).

Numero Uno Guest House (1 Santa Ana, 787/726-5010 or 866/726-5010, www.numero1guesthouse.com, $199-259 s/d, $679 two-bedroom apartment, plus tax) is a small, well-maintained guesthouse with attentive service. There's no lobby to speak of, just a tiny reception office beside a petite black-bottomed pool. But the 11 rooms are newly furnished, tastefully decorated, and comfortable, if you don't mind the compactness. Amenities include air-conditioning, a minibar, and wireless Internet. The guesthouse also boasts the popular fine-dining restaurant Pamela's

Caribbean Cuisine, serving internationally inspired cuisine.

You know you're in for something unique as soon as you pass the tall contemporary waterfall and koi pond at the entrance to **Hostería del Mar** (1 Calle Tapia, 787/727-3302, www.hosteriadelmarpr.com, $89-199 s/d, $179-239 ocean view, $244-264 suites and one-bedroom apartment, plus 9 percent tax). This compact oceanfront hotel has a lot of pizzazz in its common areas. The small lobby features an artful mix of antiques and tropical-style decor that gives way to a tastefully designed Polynesian-style bar and restaurant filled with warm woods and rattan furnishings. The wooden, top-hinged windows open out from the bottom, revealing the sand and sea just a few steps away. The restaurant, Uvva, specializes in what it calls Nuevo Mediterranean cuisine and serves three meals a day. The small, basic guest rooms have air-conditioning, cable TV, and telephones. A second-floor room is recommended for those sensitive to noise, which sometimes emanates from the bar at night.

ISLA VERDE

When it comes to accommodations, Isla Verde is mostly home to luxury chain hotels such as the Ritz-Carlton and the InterContinental. But it has a handful of small independent hotels and one swanky hotel for the glamour set.

$100-150

In a cheerful yellow faux hacienda-style building two blocks from the beach, **Hotel Villa del Sol** (4 Calle Rosa, 787/791-2600 or 787/791-1600, www.villadelsolpr.com, $100 s, $130 d, $180 mini-suite) has 24 units with air-conditioning, cable TV, and mini-refrigerators. Some rooms are starkly furnished; others are a little nicer. Amenities include a tiny pool, restaurant, bar, free parking, and free wireless Internet in the common areas. Vias Car Rental service is on-site.

$150-250

★ **San Juan Water Beach Club Hotel** (2 Calle Tartak, 787/728-3666 or 888/265-6699, www.waterbeachhotel.com, $195-319 s, $234-259 d, $351-389 suite) is a modern, high-design boutique hotel offering super-luxurious accommodations for the young, trendy, and well-heeled crowd. The hotel's 75 rooms come with air-conditioning, satellite TV, CD players, two-line telephones, data ports, high-speed Internet, minibars, in-room safes, and superior beds topped with down comforters. Water is the theme of this stark white and aqua property: Bubbles float in Lucite countertops at the reception desk, and water features abound. Liquid, the lobby bar, has a corrugated tin wall with a constant flow of water trickling over it. Wet, the rooftop bar, features stunning views of the city and huge leather couches and beds—yes, beds—that spill out around the pool. The restaurant, Tangerine, serves American Asian cuisine.

Tucked away from the fray, **Hotel La Playa** (6 Calle Amapola, 787/791-1115 or 787/791-7298, www.hotellaplaya.com, $175-200 s/d, plus tax) is a very casual, modest, motel-style property right on the water. The quality and comfort of the rooms vary; some are windowless and stark while others have more stylish furnishings and terraces. The open-air lobby doubles as a bar and restaurant serving creative Caribbean cuisine. A tall vacant building next door mars the view. Beach access is across the street.

Catering to business travelers, **Verdanza Hotel** (820 Calle Tartak, 855/222-5956, www.verdanzahotel.com, $168-188 s/d) is not located on the beach, but it's not a far walk. The 220-room hotel offers all the amenities visitors could want, including a swimming pool with food and beverage service, a children's play area, a business center, a fitness center, and four restaurants serving Asian, Caribbean, Puerto Rican, and Spanish cuisine.

Over $250

The classic elegance of ★ **El San Juan Resort & Casino** (6063 Ave. Isla Verde, 787/791-1000 or 888/579-2632, www.elsanjuanresort.com, $299-679 s, $359 d, $889

Hotel InterContinental San Juan Resort & Casino in Isla Verde

suite, $889-1,189 two-room suite, plus tax and resort fees) is apparent as soon as you step into the expansive lobby featuring a massive crystal chandelier, carved mahogany wood panels and columns, rose-colored marble floors, and antique French tapestries. Built in the late 1950s by Pan Am Airlines, the sprawling, 385-room resort is steeped in old-school luxury and consummate service. There are eight restaurants, including Meat Market steakhouse, Yamato (complete with sushi bar), and La Piccola Fontana. On the rooftop is Brother Jimmy's BBQ, a fun play on a Carolina-style barbecue joint and sports bar. There's also a discrete mini-mall of shops selling clothing, shoes, sunglasses, jewelry, and sundries. Other amenities include a nightclub, spa, beauty salon, fitness center, casino, three pools, tennis courts, and a gorgeous stretch of beach with food and beverage service.

Equally elegant is **Hotel InterContinental San Juan Resort & Casino** (5961 Ave. Isla Verde, 787/791-6100, www.ichotelsgroup.com, $229-399 s/d, $609-809 suites), a classic, ocean-side hotel built in 1963. The lobby features long, low archways, burnished wood accents, marble tile floors, and subdued lighting that casts a flattering warm glow. There are 398 rooms, including junior and executive suites, and each one features a curved balcony that creates an undulating effect reminiscent of a waterfall on the building exterior. The grounds are lushly landscaped around a freeform, lagoon-style pool featuring waterfalls and a swim-up bar. Hotel amenities include a spa, fitness center, business center, and casino. The property has five restaurants, including Ruth's Chris Steak House and Alfredo's, where the namesake dish—fettuccine Alfredo—is the house specialty.

The Ritz-Carlton, San Juan (6961 Ave. of the Governors, 787/253-7100, www.ritzcarlton.com, $489-809 s/d, $1,139 suites) features more than 400 luxury guest rooms on eight acres of beachfront property. It has a 24-hour casino and five restaurants, including BLT Steak and Il Mulino New York. Other amenities include a spa, fitness center, oceanfront pool, and concierge service.

MIRAMAR

$150-250

Hotel Miramar (606 Ave. Ponce de León, 787/977-1000, www.miramarhotelpr.com, $149-154 s/d plus tax, including complimentary continental breakfast) is a modest high-rise hotel featuring cable television, air-conditioning, microwaves, mini-refrigerators, and free wireless Internet in the rooms. Other amenities include a fitness center, laundry facilities, and a sundeck terrace. Bistro 606 serves breakfast and dinner daily and has a small bar. Check the board for dinner specials.

Over $250

Rooms at the **Sheraton Convention Center Hotel & Casino** (200 Convention Blvd., 787/993-3500, www.starwoodhotels.com, $273-473 s/d, including tax and fees) run the gamut from standard guest rooms to a variety of multi-room suites, each one featuring a 40-inch flat screen TV with cable, high-speed

Internet, and iPod docking station radio. Microwaves and mini refrigerators are available upon request. Amenities include a fitness center, full-service spa, two restaurants, a lounge, name-brand boutiques, a fourth-floor infinity pool with whirlpool tub, wading pool and sun deck, and Casino Metro. A business center provides copy shop services.

Food

San Juan's dining scene continues to evolve, becoming as sophisticated and unexpected as the city itself. Inventive reinterpretations of traditional *criolla* cuisine—called nueva criolla—are in vogue these days, but traditional Puerto Rican dishes, as well as New American and global cuisines, are reaching new heights at the hands of trained chefs and home-style cooks throughout the metro area. Fast on the heels of homegrown celebrity chefs Roberto Treviño and Wilo Benet are young up-and-comers like Jose Enrique and Christophe Gourdain, who are transforming the culinary landscape.

OLD SAN JUAN

Puerto Rican

The hokey theme setting of ★ **Restaurante Raíces** (315 Calle Recinto Sur, 787/289-2121, www.restauranteraices.com, Mon.-Sat. 11am-11pm, Sun. 11am-10pm, $12-39) threatens to undermine just how good the traditionally prepared *criolla* cuisine is here. Based on a Disneyfied interpretation of the *jíbaro* (hillbilly) lifestyle, the enormous restaurant comprises multiple rooms tricked out like palm-thatched huts from the mountain region. Female servers wear long white dresses and turbans; male servers wear guayabera shirts and Panama hats. Drinks are served in tin cups. If you can look past the artifice, you can expect to dine on generous servings of expertly prepared rice and beans, *mofongo, churrasco, escabeche, alcapurrias,* and *chuleta can can,* an enormous fried pork chop with ribs. Stop by the little shop in the center of the restaurant to pick up some traditional candies made from coconut and dried fruits. The original location is in Caguas (Urb. Villa Turabo, 787/258-1570).

It began as a catering business, but now chef Mari Blanca has a brick-and-mortar store at **Restaurante Airenumo** (102 Calle Tanca, 787/723-0984, www.airenumo.com, daily 11am-11pm, $16-25). Nosh on a wide assortment of Puerto Rican and Spanish inspired appetizers ($8-14), ranging from scallops with pumpkin and rosemary to fried Brie cheese with guava sauce. Entrées include *mofongo*, rabbit with mushrooms, and seafood casserole. There's also an extensive vegetarian menu and a children's menu.

Opened in late 2014, **Cinema Bar San Juan 150** (Cuartel de Ballajá, Calle Norzagaray at Calle Morovis, 1st Fl., 787/708-6113, www.cinemabar150.com, Sun. and Wed.-Thurs. noon-9pm, Fri.-Sat. noon-11pm, $10-24) serves standard Puerto Rican fare and an array of fruit-flavored mojitos in a newly decked-out restaurant made to look like a turn-of-the-century parlor. Plans are to open a movie theater next door with dinner service. One of the best reasons to go here is to enjoy a cocktail on the patio overlooking the grounds of El Morro.

For a more authentic experience, **La Fonda El Jibarito** (280 Calle Sol, 787/725-8375, daily 11am-9pm, $6-18) is one of the best bets for authentic Puerto Rican cuisine, including codfish stew, fried pork, fried snapper, great rice and beans, and *mofongo* (cooked and mashed plantain seasoned with garlic). It's a major staple. Sometimes it's stuffed with meat or seafood. Patrons share tables in this casual restaurant designed to look like a traditional country house. Between the blaring TV and many families with small children, the noise level can be overwhelming. Thank goodness there's a full bar.

Café Puerto Rico (208 Calle O'Donnell, 787/724-2281, www.cafepuertorico.com, Mon.-Sat. 11:30am-3:30pm and 5:30pm-11pm, Sun. noon-9pm, $9-24) has a whole new lease on life. The plain little café beside Plaza Colón that has been there forever and never changed a bit is no more: The place has been outfitted in rich, dark wood paneling and a new tile bar with tastefully lit contemporary artwork hanging on the walls. It's quite a transformation, but the coffee is still outstanding, and the Puerto Rican cuisine is still good solid fare. You can get everything from *asopao* and *mofongo* to paella and steak.

Nueva Criolla

Enter the dimly lit bar of ★ **Bodega Chic** (5 Calle del Cristo, 787/722-0124, Tues.-Sat. 6:30pm-midnight or later, Sun. 11:30am-midnight or later, $15-26) and it feels as though you've time traveled back in time to the 1950s. Ceiling fans slowly turn over a few four-top tables on a red cement floor surrounded by green walls hung with vintage black-and-white pages from old magazines. The ambiance is so authentic you might think you walked onto a movie set. But the more contemporary dining room next door gives it away with its bright yellow walls and the restaurant's name emblazoned on the wall in huge letters. Atmosphere aside, the reason to come is the food. The chef-owner is Christophe Gourdain, who trained with the world-renowned French chef Jean-George Vongerichten, and the menu reflects his French-Algerian-meets-Puerto Rican roots. Dishes include roasted chicken breast with curry banana sauce, braised lamb shank, and a ceviche of mussels and calamari. For dessert, take a break from the ubiquitous offering of flan and indulge in the delicate profiteroles.

The locally owned OOF! Restaurants group was a pioneer in bringing San Juan into the 21st century of the culinary world. The first of its four restaurants is **The Parrot Club** (363 Calle Fortaleza, 787/725-7370, www.oofrestaurants.com, lunch Mon.-Fri. 11:30am-3pm and Sat.-Sun. 11:30am-4pm, dinner daily 5pm-10pm, bar Sun.-Wed. until midnight, Thurs.-Sat. until 1am, $17-32), which opened in 1996. At first glance, this wildly popular restaurant might look like a prefab tourist attraction. It boasts an over-the-top tropical-island theme, complete with faux palm trees and wooden parrots, and the din around the crowded bar can make conversation a challenge. But the reality is that Parrot Club serves some of the island's finest interpretations of nueva criolla cuisine. If you prefer a nice, quiet, leisurely served meal, bypass the bar and ask to be seated in the calm, low-lit courtyard out back. The restaurant specializes in a smorgasbord of crisp, refreshing ceviches, featuring a wide selection of seafood marinated in fresh citrus juices and served chilled. The shrimp, *chillo* (snapper), and dorado (mahimahi) are the best of the bunch. If you want something a little heartier, try the thick slab of blackened tuna steak served in a dark, slightly sweet sauce of rum and orange essence. It's an addictive dish that will have you coming back for more.

Located in the space formerly occupied by Amadeus, **Aureola Café Restaurant** (106 Calle San Sebastián, 787/977-0100, Tues.-Sun. noon-midnight, $10-25) serves creative Caribbean cuisine specializing in seafood, including *chillo* fillet stuffed with shrimp, salmon pizza, mixed seafood ceviche, and *tostones* (fried plantains) topped with caviar in a colorful atmosphere. In addition to the dining room, there is seating in an enclosed patio or outside on Plaza San Jose, located across the street.

Breakfast and Cafés

Thank goodness for ★ **Cafeteria Mallorca** (300 Calle San Francisco, 787/724-4607, daily 7am-6pm, $6-18). Now that the venerable diner La Bombonera has closed, this is the most authentic option for enjoying the traditional breakfast item for which this no-frills diner is named: the *mallorca* ($3-7), a light, flaky swirl of delicately sweetened pastry split open; stuffed with your choice of ham, cheese, egg, or bacon; heated on a grill press; and dusted with powdered sugar. The menu also features standard Puerto Rican dishes, including rice and beans, roast pork, *chicharrones de pollo* (fried chunks of chicken on the bone), and an array of baked goods.

Although it serves three meals a day, breakfast is the best reason to visit ★ **Caficultura** (401 Calle San Francisco, 787/723-7731, info@caficulturapr.com, Mon.-Thurs. 8am-5pm, Fri. 8am-10pm, Sat.-Sun. 8am-8pm, breakfast $6-13, lunch $8-13, dinner $15-20). Pancakes banana flambé and coconut milk French toast are a few of the specialties that keep fans coming back.

Catering to the literary minded, **Poetic Café** (203 Calle Cruz, 787/721-5020, daily 8am-9pm, $2-6) is a clever coffeehouse associated with the Poets Passage next door. Drink names sport literary references, such as the haiku espresso and couplet double espresso, and paper and pencil are provided on each table in case the writing muse strikes while you sip your metaphor café latte. A limited menu offers sandwiches and pastries, and there is a small bar.

Located beside Capilla del Cristo, **Waffle-era Tea Room** (Calle Tetuá, 787/721-1512, http://waffle-era.com, Mon.-Fri. 10am-3pm, Sat.-Sun. 8am-6pm, $3-12) serves Belgian waffles, flambé dishes, coffees, and tea infusions.

Lunch and Brunch

Bright, cheery **Hecho en Casa** (249 Calle San Francisco, 787/289-9898, daily 9:30am-7:30pm, $4-17) serves excellent fare, ranging from burgers, sandwiches, and *mallorcas* to grilled charrusco, pork chops, and mahimahi. There's also a bakery and a full bar. The house specialties are the passion fruit sangria and carrot cake. The staff is very friendly and the place is filled with colorful folk art.

If you need a quick snack and a drink, and you don't mind taking it with you, stop by tiny **Mate** (366 Calle San Francisco, 787/725-0271, Mon.-Thurs. 8am-8pm, Fri.-Sun. 10am-6pm, $5) and pick up a baked empanada (beef, cheese, spinach) and a rum smoothie. Or get two Medalla beers for $5.

Providing a welcome departure from more filling fare is **St. Germain Bistro & Café** (156 Calle Sol, 787/725-5830, Tues.-Sat. 11:30am-3pm and 6pm-10pm, Sun. 10am-3pm and 6pm-10pm, $5-12, $17 Sun. brunch), serving a variety of soups, salads, sandwiches, quiches, pita pizzas, and cakes. A prix fixe brunch menu is served on Sundays.

American

Owned by the folks behind Restaurante Airenumo, **Taberna La Rubia** (107 Calle Tanca, 787/725-6951, daily 11am-11pm, $6-16) serves upscale burgers, empanadas, craft beers, and house-made pastries. There's a full bar, too.

Asian

Dragonfly (364 Calle Fortaleza, 787/977-3886, www.oofrestaurants.com, daily 6pm-11pm, $19-28), another OOF! Restaurant establishment frequented by the young and beautiful party set, has recently been expanded from a tiny intimate space to encompass a lounge and second bar. Nevertheless, be prepared for the wait to get in, unless you go early in the night. The menu encompasses a wide selection of Asian inspired foods, including sushi and noodle dishes, as well as Latin-Asian fusion dishes, such as Korean kimchee fajitas and sweet and sour pulled pork lettuce wraps.

J-Taste (307 Calle Recinto Sur, 787/724-2003, www.j-taste.com, daily noon-11pm or later, $17-25) serves Japanese cuisine, including sushi, teriyaki, tempura, rice, noodles, teppanyaki, and more. It has a full bar.

French

For traditional French cuisine in a classic elegant setting featuring an enormous crystal chandelier and walls surrounded by long white flowing drapes, there's **Trois Cent Onze / 311** (311 Calle Fortaleza, 787/725-7959, www.311restaurantpr.com, Wed.-Fri.

noon-3pm, Tues.-Thurs. 6pm-10:30pm, Fri.-Sat. 6pm-11:30pm, $24-35). This is the place to go for snails and foie gras. Check out their highly lauded wine-pairing dinners.

Mediterranean

Located in the lobby of Cervantes Chateau, **Panza** (329 Calle Recinto Sur, 787/724-7722, www.cervantespr.com, Wed.-Sun. noon-3pm and 6pm-11pm, $21-32) is a fine dining restaurant offering a quiet, elegant respite from the crowds and chaos that sometimes reign on the streets of Old San Juan. Marble tile floors, white linen tablecloths, and gold banquettes provide a serene atmosphere for a menu that combines Italian-influenced cuisine with flavors from the island. First-course offerings include dishes such as ceviche *taquitos* and sweet potato gnocchi; main courses include pan-seared cod loin and pan-roasted Peking duck breast. Four- and eight-course tasting menus are offered ($50 and $95 per person, respectively); the entire table is required to participate.

A whimsical atmosphere sets the scene for **Al Dente** (309 Calle Recinto Sur, 787/723-7303, Mon.-Thurs. 11:30am-10pm, Fri.-Sat. 11:30am-11pm, closed Sun., $17-32). Three intimate dining rooms are separated by huge red arches; the ceiling is hung with stained-glass stars. A wooden, U-shaped bar is just inside the entrance, and large, colorful contemporary paintings brighten the walls. The menu features pastas, risottos, fresh catch of the day, and heavier traditional dishes such as *braciola* and *bistecca alla Fiorentina*, a one-pound steak served in a reduction of Barolo wine and fresh rosemary.

You'll think you've been transported to Turkey when you step into **Istanbul Turkish Restaurant** (325 Calle Recinto Sur, 787/722-5057, www.istanbulturkishrestaurant.com, Sun.-Thurs. 11am-9:30pm, Fri.-Sat. 11am-10:30pm, $13-18). The high red and white walls are hung with a jumble of tapestries, flags, vintage pictures of Turkey, and large, severe portraits of Mustafa Ataturk, founder of the Turkish Republic. Waiters in fezzes wind their way around the tight-knit jumble of tables and chairs, carrying heaping platters of dolma (stuffed grape leaves), kebabs, lamb chops, and baklava. In addition to a full bar, beverage offerings include traditional Turkish coffee.

Mexican

Located in the space formerly occupied by Baru, **La Mala Vida** (150 Calle San Sebastián, 787/723-7575, www.lamalavidapr.com, Wed.-Sat. 6pm-11pm, Sat.-Sun. 10am-3pm, dinner $7-18, brunch $4-13) serves Mexican influenced American cuisine, ranging from tacos and burritos to burgers and baby back ribs. Tacos, burgers, and burrito bowls appear on the brunch menu, too, along with stuffed croissants, bagels, and egg dishes. There's a second location (211 Calle Canals) at La Placita in Santurce.

Italian

Black-and-white tile floor and strings of lights across the ceiling make small, cozy **Pirilo Pizza Rustica** (201-2 Calle Fortaleza, 787/721-3322, Sun.-Mon. and Wed. 11:30am-midnight, Thurs.-Sat. 11:30am-2am, $12-28) a festive place to dine on Puerto Rican and Argentinean style pizzas, fried calamari, and rice-and-bean fritters. The pizzas are very thick and overloaded with meaty toppings, so come with an appetite. There are 30 craft beers on tap to wash it all down.

Barrachina (104 Calle Fortaleza, 787/721-5852 or 787/725-7912, www.barrachina.com, Sun.-Tues. and Thurs. 10am-10pm, Wed. 10am-5pm, Fri.-Sat. 10am-11pm, $14-49) is one of two places in Puerto Rico (the Caribe Hilton being the other) that claims to have invented the piña colada, which is disappointingly served here from a slushy-style machine, but is surprisingly tasty.

Café La Princesa (Paseo La Princesa, 787/724-2930 or 787/635-4173, www.cafelaprincesa.com, Mon. 11am-3pm, Tues.-Thurs. 11 am-3pm and 5pm-10pm, Fri. 11am-3pm, Sat. 6pm-midnight, Sun. 2pm-10pm, $10-19) is a shady sidewalk café located just outside the city wall that is particularly inviting at night, thanks to the dramatic lighting and sounds of live salsa music emanating from within. The menu features hearty fare, including paella, crab-stuffed *chillo* and *churrasco,* served three ways: in *chimichurri* sauce, in a red wine sauce, or stuffed with chorizo and mushrooms and topped with marinara and Swiss cheese.

Those in the know head to **Café El Punto** (105 Calle Fortaleza, 787/646-4943, www.cafeelpunto.com, Tues.-Sun. 10am-8pm, $8-15), tucked in the back of a gift shop, to dine on authentic *criolla* cuisine accompanied by fresh salads and tropical fruit shakes. *Tostones* (fried plantains) stuffed with shrimp or chicken are popular, as is the avocado stuffed with shrimp salad. And if you've had your fill of fried foods, try the baked empanadas. The flan comes highly recommended, too.

It's hard to tell that **The House of Mofongo Los Yeyos** (353-2 Calle San Francisco, 787/725-9362, daily 10am-6pm, $8) is a restaurant. It looks more like a dim, blue hallway with newspaper clippings, outdated calendars, and family graduation pictures tacked up on the wall. There is a small sign outside, a couple of small tables inside, and seemingly just one employee, a friendly but slightly harried woman who takes the orders and serves up delicious *mofongo,* crab stew, and *carne guisado* on sectioned, school cafeteria-style plates, with plastic utensils and sodas in a can.

Spanish

In the historic Hotel El Convento, **El Picoteo** (100 Calle del Cristo, 787/723-9020 or 800/468-2779, www.elconvento.com, daily noon-11pm, $7-29) overlooks the central courtyard and serves a menu of traditional Spanish tapas, ranging from simple slices of Manchego cheese and Serrano ham to grilled lamb chops and berry chutney. For larger appetites, try one of the paellas, including one prepared with nutty, earthy black rice chock-full of shrimp, calamari, and chunks of dorado.

Steak and Seafood

For a hip, hot restaurant where the gorgeous wait staff is attitude-free, the seafood is amazing, and the decor is evocative of dining in an aquarium, get thee to ★ **Aguaviva** (364 Calle Fortaleza, 787/722-0665, www.oofrestaurants.com, daily 11:30am-4pm, Mon.-Thurs. and Sun. 6pm-11pm, Fri.-Sat. 6pm-midnight, $17-30), another of the OOF! Restaurants, purveyors of contemporary cuisine. The space is drenched in bright white, chrome, and aqua, with glass jellyfish lights hanging from the ceiling. In addition to an oyster and ceviche bar, dishes on a recent visit included grilled dorado with smoked shrimp salsa, grilled marlin with chorizo, and *nueva paella* with seared scallops. At the blue-lit bar, where seashells float in Lucite, sublime cocktails are prepared with fresh juices. Be sure to try the watermelon sangria.

The atmospheric **El Asador Grill** (350 Calle San Francisco, 787/289-9966, www.elasadorpr.com, daily 8am-1am, $16-26), located in a contemporary faux hacienda-style setting, specializes in grilled fish, ceviche, *mofongo,* linguine, and risottos. At night, it turns into a club, with techno music, dancing, and hookahs ($20). The breakfast menu ($3-10) includes omelets, pancakes, and *mangu,* a traditional Dominican dish of cooked, pureed green plantains topped with onions. Cream-colored stucco walls, dark wood beams, terracotta tile floors, and dramatic archways create an inviting environment.

It has relocated up the hill near Plaza del Quinto Centenario, expanded its outdoor performance space, and altered its name, but **Ostra Cosa @ Totem** (corner of Calle del Cristo and Calle San Sebastián, 787/722-2672, Mon.-Fri. 10am-11pm, Sat.-Sun. 10am-2am, $12-26) is still a romantic, alfresco restaurant. The menu has been updated to include *tostones* (fried plantains) with caviar and sardines in roasted red pepper vinaigrette; its specialty is crepes stuffed with lobster or beef tenderloin. More emphasis has been placed on entertainment on Friday-Sunday, featuring DJs and salsa bands.

Bringing a bit of a New England vibe to the island, **Old Harbor Brewery Steak & Lobster House** (202 Calle Tizol, 787/721-2100, www.oldharborbrewery.com, daily 11:30am-1am, $10-44) is a microbrewery producing handcrafted beers made on-site, including Coqui, a golden lager; Old Harbor Beer, a copper-colored pale ale; Kofresi, a dark stout; and Santo Viejo, a golden pilsner. As the name implies, the menu is heavy on local lobster and all varieties of beef, including Angus, Kobe, and dry aged. Lighter fare includes pizza and penne pasta served in a choice of sauce. Expect live entertainment on the weekends. Reservations are accepted.

La Cueva del Mar (305 Recinto Sur, Old San Juan, 787/725-8700, http://cueva.r-leon.info, Sun.-Thurs. 11am-9:30pm, Fri.-Sat. 11am-11pm, $10-20; additional locations at 1904 Calle Loíza, Santurce, 787/726-8700, and Carr. 19, km 0.7, Guaynabo, 787/793-8700) serves a huge variety of Puerto Rican-style seafood dishes from conch salad to *mofongo relleno de camarones* (mashed, garlicky plaintain stuffed with shrimp). Seafood stuffed tacos, *empanadillas,* and salads, as well as salmon, mahimahi, and grouper dishes, round out the menu. The house specialties are *Arroz con Mariscos La Cueva*, featuring seasoned rice and a variety of seafood, and flan de Nutella. There's a full bar, a kids' menu, weekly specials, and a full bar.

Eclectic

Late night hot-spot ★ **La Factoria** (148 Calle San Sebastián, no phone, daily 6:30pm-4am, $6-16) is a popular bar, with a semi-secret wine bar, **Vino @ Factoria,** behind an unmarked door. But it also serves an eclectic menu of tapas, including skirt-steak steamed buns, burger sliders, pork-stuffed burritos, and *bánh mìs.* The kitchen is open until 2am.

Carli's Fine Bistro & Piano (Banco Popular building, corner of Recinto Sur and Calle San Justo, 787/725-4927, www.carlisworld.com, Mon.-Sat. 3:30pm-11:30pm, music starts at 8:30pm, $16-34) is a romantic, sophisticated lounge and restaurant serving a variety of dishes, including risottos, raviolis, quesadillas, and Caribbean-inspired tapas. The owner, jazz pianist Carli Muñoz, performs nightly with a changing array of guest musicians. It's also a great place to just sit at the bar and enjoy one of a large selection of specialty cocktails. There's alfresco dining on the sidewalk too.

★ **Marmalade** (317 Calle Fortaleza, 787/724-3969, www.marmaladepr.com, Mon.-Thurs. 6pm-11pm, Fri.-Sat. 6pm-midnight, Sun. 6pm-10pm, bar daily 5pm-close, $13-44, tasting menus $65-85, wine pairings extra) beckons likes a fanciful oasis with its romantic bar, dramatically lit and draped with swaths of organza. In the back is an elegant, sophisticated restaurant. But that's all just packaging. It's the impressive wine list; the creative cocktails made from fresh juices, herbs, and flowers; and the changing seasonal menu of small plates and entrées that attract return visits. Recent offerings included Heritage Berkshire pork cheeks with peach-poblano marmalade and wild sea bass with pineapple-ginger relish. Order à la carte or enjoy a tasting menu of four, five, or six courses, with or without wine pairings.

Dark red tiles, upholstered banquettes, and a large, arched window overlooking Plaza Colon give **Café Berlin** (407 Calle San Francisco, 787/722-5205, www.cafeberlinpr.com, daily 9am-10pm, breakfast $8-12, lunch $7-14, dinner $16-25) a moody, romantic atmosphere. The diverse menu features Puerto Rican, European, vegetarian, and gluten-free dishes. It's a great stop for a hearty breakfast of banana raisin walnut pancakes or spinach quiche. Lunch features a variety of soups, salads, and sandwiches. Dinner ranges from pasta to *mofongo,* but the house specialty is dorado (mahi) in coconut sauce. There's a full bar, a small wine list, a children's menu, and outdoor dining.

Dessert

★ **Casa Cortés ChocoBar** (210 Calle San Francisco, 787/722-0499, www.casacortespr.com, Tues.-Sun. 8am-6pm, $3-15) is a hot new addition to Old San Juan's dining scene that combines contemporary high design and wildly inventive cuisine with a deep history of chocolate making. Casa Cortés has been making chocolate since 1929; now they're serving it up in croissants, panini, cocktails, beverages, and unusual appetizers such as *mofonguitos de amarillos con chocolate*—small, sweet plantain *mofongos* filled with chocolate and bacon. For a bracing, complex cocktail, try the Don Pedro, featuring rum, ginger, lemon, and dark chocolate. Before you leave, check out the bakery case and small selection of chocolate bars and drink mixes.

Groceries

Supermax (201 Calle Cruz, 787/725-4839, www.supermaxpr.com, Mon.-Sat. 6am-midnight, Sun. 10am-8pm) is a modern, full-service grocery store with a bakery, deli, fresh meat counter, and produce section. It carries a large selection of spirits and a wide variety of local coffees, but you'll have to get a clerk to unlock the case for you.

CONDADO

Puerto Rican

It's rare to find a true locals' place in touristy Condado, and that's what makes ★ **Cafe Condado** (Ashford Medical Center, Ave. Ashford, 787/722-5963, Mon.-Thurs. 5am-5pm, Fri. 5am-4pm, Sat. 5am-2pm, $3-9) so appealing. More no-frills diner than café, it features a long pink Formica bar with 16 aqua vinyl bar stools and a dozen or so four-top tables in an otherwise drab room. The food is crazy cheap and authentic. The *pollo* empanada (fried chicken breast), *cubano* sandwich, and red beans and rice are outstanding. They deliver, too.

The late-night party crowd likes **Latin Star Restaurant** (1128 Ave. Ashford, 787/724-8141, daily 24 hours, $11-40) less for the food and more for the fact that it's open 24-7. It serves a huge menu, including authentic local dishes such as goat or rabbit stew, tripe soup, and brandied guinea. There's indoor and sidewalk dining, and if you want to keep the party going, Dom Perignon is on the wine list. Breakfast and daily specials are also served.

Orozco's Restaurant (1126 Ave. Ashford, 787/721-7669, Wed.-Mon. 8am-11pm, Tues. 4pm-11pm, breakfast daily except Tues. 8am-3pm, live music Fri.-Sat., $11-25) serves traditional Puerto Rican cuisine featuring *mofongo*, grilled steak, pork, and chicken, plus daily specials. There is a full bar; try the house-made sangria.

Café Berlin in Old San Juan

Nueva Criolla

Celebrated local chef Roberto Treviño's signature venture, ★ **Casa Lola Criolla Kitchen** (1006 Ave. Ashford, 787/998-2918, www.casalolarestaurant.com, Sun.-Thurs. 11:30am-11pm, Fri.-Sat. 11:30am-midnight, $21-38), has moved into the space that once housed Ajili-Mójili. Not only has Treviño updated the space, giving it a playful pop of purple, but he's infused the *criolla* cuisine with his creative touch. Traditional corn sticks become *sorullitos* of blue cheese, empanadas are stuffed with a Cuban stew of *ropa vieja,* and the traditional mashed plantain dish of *mofongo* goes upscale with scallops, fish, shrimp, and calamari.

Previously located at Museo de Arte de Puerto Rico, the critically acclaimed ★ **Pikayo** (999 Ave. Ashford, 787/721-6194, www.condadoplaza.com, www.wilobenet.com, daily 6:30pm-11pm, small plates $12-19, entrées $37-50) is now located at Conrad Condado Plaza Hotel, where celebrity chef Wilo Benet continues to push culinary boundaries with dishes like duck *magret* in chocolate sherry sauce, Gouda cheese lollipops, octopus *escabeche,* and Serrano ham.

Breakfast

Fruit bowls and smoothies that promote energy and healthy skin are served up fresh and fast at **Crush Juice Bar** (1703 Ave. Ashford, 939/644-8672, daily 8am-10pm, $6-8). Yogurt and granola are also available.

Waffler Avenue (Ave. Ashford, Ventana al Mar, 787/705-9365, www.waffleravenue.com, Sun.-Thurs. 7am-11pm, Fri.-Sat. 7am-midnight, $8-10, no American Express) serves sweet and savory Belgian waffles stuffed with everything from Tuna Niçoise to ham and Swiss cheese, or waffles topped with an assortment of goodies from ice cream to fresh fruit. There's also an extensive coffee menu. The food is carry out only, but there are tables and chairs right outside in Ventana al Mar park.

American

For an American style sports bar with a big beer selection, **The Place at Condado** (1378 Ave. Ashford, 787/998-4209 or 787/998-4213, Sun. and Wed.-Thurs. 11:30am-10pm, Fri.-Sat. 11:30am-midnight, $3-16) is the place to feel like you never left the United States. Dine on burgers, pizza, and chicken wings surrounded by TVs, loud rock music, and a staff with attitude. There's a full bar.

Angus burgers, grilled beef hot dogs, hand-cut French fries, and milkshakes are on the menu at **Buns Burger Shop** (1515 Ave. Ashford, 787/725-7800, www.bunsburgershop.com, Mon.-Thurs. 11:30am-10pm, Fri.-Sat. 11:30am-1am, Sun. 11:30am-10:30pm, $3-7). There's another location (283 Calle A-E) in Guaynabo.

Tiny, divey **Punk Burger & Bistro** (1129 Ave. Ashford, 787/723-4750, Mon.-Fri. 7am-4am, Sat.-Sun. 8am-midnight, $2-9) lives up to its name with its weird rustic decor. The people-watching is great as you nosh on eggs and bacon at breakfast or burgers made from beef, salmon, or turkey for lunch. Plus, there's a full bar. (Avoid the latrine-like bathroom if at all possible.)

Asian

To step into ★ **Budatai** (1056 Ave. Ashford, 787/725-6919, www.ootwrestaurants.com, Mon.-Wed. 11:30am-11pm, Thurs.-Sat. 11:30am-midnight, Sun. 11:30am-10pm, $26-48) is to forget where you are. Nothing could seem farther away from the bustling tropical street outside than this luxurious, two-story restaurant and lounge. Deep red walls and drapes, iridescent stone tile columns, and massive gold light fixtures that resemble sea anemones create an exotic setting for premier chef Roberto Treviño, a competitor on the Food Network show *Iron Chef,* to serve his melding of Latin and Asian cuisines. Dishes include slow-roasted duck with Peking glaze, veal pot stickers, duck fried rice, and a variety of ceviches and sushi. The mixologist behind the bar surprises with creative twists on favorite cocktails, making margaritas with cilantro and caipirinhas with fresh watermelon juice.

Overlooking the Caribe Hilton's Tropical Garden, complete with pond, gazebo, and black swans, **Lemongrass Pan Asian Latino** (Caribe Hilton, 1 Calle San Germano, daily 5:30pm-10:30pm, $27-33) creates some lively dishes, including smoked eel over Chilean sea bass in a foie gras reduction and sea scallops and lamb cakes in mustard sesame sauce with fennel.

The elegant minimalist space at **Nori Sushi and Grill Bar** (1051 Ave. Ashford, 787/977-8263, Mon.-Thurs. 11am-3pm and 6pm-1:30am, Fri.-Sun. 11:30am-1:30am, $6-26) creates a fine dining atmosphere for sushi, tempura, teriyaki, and hibachi dishes. House special rolls include the Mango Dragon Roll, featuring eel, crab, avocado, and sliced mango, and sushi pizza made with a choice of spicy salmon, tuna, eel, shrimp, or scallops. Chef specials include pineapple seafood fried rice. Bento box lunch specials are served noon-3pm.

Cuban

A trendy take on Cuban cuisine can be found at **Ropa Vieja Grill** (1025 Ave. Ashford, 787/725-2665, Sun.-Wed. 11am-10:30pm, Thurs. 11:30am-11pm, Fri. 11:30am-midnight, Sat. 6pm-midnight, $15-25). A modern space with a large cherrywood bar, tile floors, and a wall of windows that provides great people-watching, the restaurant serves risotto with pork rinds, filet medallions in Roquefort sauce, and grilled sea bass in pesto sauce.

Italian

In the spot previously occupied for decades by Paris Bistro is ★ **Bistro Hijole** (1504 Ave. Ashford, 787/993-5710, www.blondacondadopr.com, daily 7am-10pm, brunch $9-24, entrées $11-29), a chic, European-style eatery that serves an unusual combination of Italian and Mexican cuisines. Thin crust pizza, gnocchi, fettuccine, filet mignon fajitas, and *churrasco* quesadillas are menu highlights. Served daily, the outstanding brunch features huevos rancheros, croque monsieur, and French toast. Servings are massive, so consider sharing or be prepared to take home leftovers. There's a full bar, and the staff is very attentive.

Via Appia's Deli (1350 Ave. Ashford, 787/725-8711 or 787/722-4325, daily 11:30am-11pm or midnight, $11-20) serves standard red-sauce Italian dishes, including pasta, sandwiches, and pizzas. It has indoor and sidewalk dining.

Dine on prosciutto di Parma, fettuccine with basil tomato sauce, pizza, and panini at **Di Zucchero Lavazza Restaurant & Lounge** (1210 Ave. Ashford, 787/946-0835, http://dizuccheropr.com, Sun.-Thurs. 11am-11pm, Fri.-Sat. 11am-midnight, $14-17) while a DJ spins techno in this hip, black-and-red coffee bar and restaurant. After 11pm, the upstairs turns into a nightclub.

Mike's Pizzeria (1024 Ave. Ashford, 787/723-0242, 787/723-0118, 787/722-2480, or 787/722-2484, www.mikespizzeriapr.com, Sun.-Thurs. 11am-midnight, Fri.-Sat. 11am-2am, $6-18) serves New York-style pizza, salads, subs, calzones, pasta dishes, and burgers, plus it has a full bar. Delivery is free, but a $12 minimum purchase is required.

Mediterranean

Turkish and Middle Eastern cuisine is on the menu at **Ali Baba** (1214 Ave. Ashford, Condado Village, 787/722-1176, www.alibabarestaurantpr.com, Tues.-Sat. 4pm-11pm, Sun. noon-10pm, $11-30). Service can be slow, but the grape leaf dolmas, chops, kebabs, and gyros are pretty good. There's a full bar.

Mexican

If you're looking for nachos, slushy margaritas, and mariachi music, keep on looking. **Agave Cocina Mexicana Creativa** (1451 Ave. Ashford, 787/963-1793, daily noon-midnight, $10-30) is one of the first truly sophisticated Mexican restaurants on the island. The setting is sleek and understated, and the dishes are unexpected, ranging from beef ribs cooked in tequila and cola to Napoleon *chilaquiles* topped with a fried egg to fresh tuna seasoned with chilies, cinnamon, and achiote, served with clementines, plantains, and habanera foam. Valet parking is available.

Serving basic Tex-Mex cuisine, **Tijuana's Bar & Grill** (1350 Ave. Ashford, 787/723-3939, www.tijuanaspr.com, Sun.-Thurs. 11:30am-11pm, Fri.-Sat. 11:30am-midnight, $8-25) serves nachos, tacos, quesadillas, enchiladas, burritos, and fajitas indoors or on an outside terrace. Specialties include shrimp diablo and Mexican lasagna. It has a full bar. Another location is in Old San Juan (Pier No. 2, Fernández Juncos, 787/724-7070).

Spanish

Another Roberto Treviño eatery, the sidewalk patio at **Bar Gitano** (1302 Ave. Ashford, 787/294-5513, www.ootwrestaurants.com, Mon.-Wed. 11:30am-11pm, Thurs.-Sat. 11:30am-midnight, Sun. 11:30am-10pm, $6-28) is a great place to people-watch, sip craft cocktails ($8-10), and enjoy a small menu of tapas ($6), including jerk chicken *pinchos*, fish tacos, and a manchego cheese and Serrano ham board. For bigger appetites, share paella, featuring meat, seafood, or veggies. The dark, moody interior features rough-hewn dark woods, a tile floor, and a wall of framed mirrors. There is live flamenco on Thursday and Sunday at 8:30pm.

Next door to Bar Gitano is its sister bar and restaurant, **Barril** (1302 Ave. Ashford, 787/725-6919, www.ootwrestaurants.com, Wed.-Thurs. 8pm-3am, Fri.-Sat. 8pm-4am, $6-28), serving the same menu, but featuring entertainment in the form of live salsa bands, DJs, and sporting events broadcast on big-screen TVs. The space is also available for private rental.

Steak and Seafood

Central Steakhouse (1104 Ave. Magdalena, 787/908-6960, Wed.-Thurs. and Sun. 5pm-11pm, Fri.-Sat. 5pm-midnight, $25-40) is a dark, stylish spot of contemporary design in shades of red, black, and gray, serving up cuts of beef served in your choice of sauces and flourishes, including bacon jam, *chimichurri*, chorizo, and fried egg. There are plenty of seafood dishes, too. This is a great spot for craft cocktails (mole bitters anyone?) and creative appetizers, including roast pork poutine with yucca fries and blue cheese fondue. The **Moonbar** lounge pumps techno music upstairs.

Sit at the bar and watch the grill-master cook your dinner over an open flame at **Ummo Argetinian Grill** (1351 Ave. Ashford, 787/722-1700, www.ummoargentiniangrill.com, Mon.-Sat. noon-midnight, Sun. noon-10pm, $17-39). Sausages, sweetbreads, short ribs, steak, and *churrasco* dominate the menu, but there are a few seafood and pasta options for non-meat eaters.

A stunning example of midcentury modern architecture at its best, **Perla** (La Concha Resort, 1077 Ave. Ashford, 787/977-3285, www.perlarestaurant.com, Sun.-Thurs. 6pm-10pm, Fri.-Sat. 6pm-11pm, $18-36) creates the sensation of dining inside a giant clam shell—albeit a devastatingly posh one—with views of an infinity pool and the Atlantic Ocean. Dinner selections include delicacies such as pan-roasted sea bass with lobster and truffle risotto and braised lamb shank with flaming raisin jam. Three- and five-course tasting menus ($40 and $55, respectively) are available; wine pairings are extra.

Its search for a chef was turned into a competition and televised on the Food Network with chef Anne Burrell. The winner didn't stick around long, but **Oceano** (2 Calle Vendig, 787/724-6300, www.oceanopr.com, Tues.-Wed. noon-10pm, Thurs.-Sat. noon-11pm, Sun. 11am-10pm, $18-36) is still ready for its close-up. The glamorous, multi-level, beachfront restaurant serves creative seafood fare, including snapper ceviche with passion fruit dressing and diver scallops with sweet potato puree and baked prosciutto di parma with romantic views of the ocean.

Waikiki Caribbean Food & Oyster Bar (1025 Ave. Ashford, 787/977-2267, daily 11am-late, $12-35), a casual oceanfront restaurant, features a long pinewood bar, sidewalk dining, a stone-grotto-style dining room inside, and a wood deck on the beach for alfresco dining. Dishes include mahimahi nuggets, crab-stuffed mushrooms, lobster tail, osso buco, and seafood *criolla*.

Dessert

Moyo (1452 Ave. Ashford, 787/294-6025, Mon.-Sat. 10am-11pm, Sun. 11am-11pm, $4-12) bills itself as a "frozen yogurt lounge." Decked out in eye-popping shades of bright pink and green, a graffiti mural covers one wall. In addition to self-serve frozen yogurt, complemented by an array of toppings, coffee drinks, smoothies, crepes, and sandwiches round out the menu.

The artisan bakery trend has happily arrived in Puerto Rico with the **Vanilla Bean Cupcakery** (1400 Ave. Magdalena, 787/289-8383 or 787/289-6868, Tues.-Sat. 9am-8pm, Sun. 11am-8pm, $1.25-3). This petite, pink confection serves creative cupcake flavors including s'mores, chocolate hazelnut, snickers, and mango. Mango pops, frosting shots, and coffee drinks are also available, as are special orders.

Groceries

Freshmart (1310 Ave. Ashford, 787/999-7800, www.freshmartpr.com, daily 7am-11pm) is a bright, clean, modern grocery and deli specializing in organic produce, grass-fed beef, free-range chicken, and chemical-free vitamins and supplements. There's also a large selection of freshly prepared foods, including gourmet pizzas, pastas, and salads. Additional locations can be found at Carolina Commerical Park in Carolina and Garden Hills Plaza in Guaynabo.

Located in Miramar, **Supermax** (113 Ave. de Diego, 787/723-1611, www.supermaxpr.com, daily 24 hours) is a modern, full-service grocery store with a bakery, a deli, a fresh meat counter, and a produce section. It carries a large selection of spirits and a wide variety of local coffees, but you'll have to get a clerk to unlock the case for you.

Eros Food Market (1357 Ave. Ashford, 787/722-3631, Mon.-Sat. 7:30am-10pm, Sun. 8am-9pm) is a convenient place to stock up on provisions, including the essentials: coffee and rum. It includes a good supply of canned goods, health and beauty items, snacks, beverages, cigarettes, and more.

For 24-hour needs, **Convenience Store** (Ashford Gallery shopping center, 1482 Ave. Ashford, 787/946-7776) sells cold drinks, snacks, cigarettes, and liquor, and it has a small grill serving hot food.

OCEAN PARK

The restaurant scene has picked up momentum here in recent years. There are several new options and the quality overall tends to be good to excellent.

Puerto Rican

Despite its name, ★ **Kasalta Bakery** (1966 Ave. McLeary, 787/727-7340 or 787/727-6593, www.kasalta.com, daily 6am-10pm, lunch $9, dinner $12-25) is much more than a bakery. This large, professionally run operation sells piping hot *empanadillas, pastelillos,* and *alcapurrias,* and super-thick toasted sandwiches, including exceptional *cubanos, medias noches,* and a variety of breakfast sandwiches. In addition to a variety of soups and salads, lunch features hot daily specials (Mon.-Fri. 11:30am-3pm), featuring dishes such as asparagus risotto and pork tenderloin. At night, table service is offered for dinner entrées, including grilled skirt steak and seared ahi tuna. But Kasalta is still a bakery, so be sure to check out case after glass case of freshly made cookies, pastries, and slices of cheesecake. It also sells whole cakes and has an excellent wine and liquor selection. Order at the counter and grab a seat at shared tables to feast. If you drive, there's a free parking lot next door, but be prepared to wait for a parking space and stand in line to order on the weekends.

Bagua Restaurant (51 Maria Moczo, 787/200-9616, Mon. and Wed. 11am-10pm, Thurs.-Sat. 11am-1am, Sun. 10:30am-10pm, $10-30) is a colorful new addition to the neighborhood. The two-story, blue and green restaurant serves Puerto Rican fare heavy on seafood, as well as pizza and sandwiches, in a rustic setting. Recommended dishes include the *tacoviche*—a taco made from fried plantain stuffed with fish or shrimp ceviche. Vegetarian fare and a kids' menu are also available.

More like a bar that serves food than a true restaurant, **Mango's** (1954 Calle McLeary, 787/998-8111, www.mangosoceanpark.com, Tues.-Fri. 11:30am-2am, Sat.-Sun. 9:30am-2am, $10-30) offers a large selection of craft beers and an economical menu of Puerto Rican cuisine, including *mofongo*, rice and beans, and *tostones* (fried plantains), as well as burgers and wings. The kitchen serves food until midnight, and the weekend brunch is popular. There is a small indoor dining room and a huge covered patio; all of it has a worn, beer hall feel to it. At night the music gets loud and the scene turns into a rowdy, crowded bar scene that caters to a Puerto Rican clientele.

Nueva Criolla

In Numero Uno guesthouse, **Pamela's Caribbean Cuisine** (1 Calle Santa Ana, 787/726-5010, www.numero1guesthouse.com/tropical-cuisine, lunch daily noon-3pm, tapas daily 3pm-6pm, dinner daily 6pm-10:30pm, $25-44) is the most popular restaurant in Ocean Park. This elegant fine-dining restaurant with excellent service features white linen tablecloths and mission-style furnishings inside, with casual seating inside and out, right on the sandy beach. Specialties include paella, pan-seared mahi in coconut fennel curry broth, coconut shrimp in a piña colada balsamic glaze, and veal chop with chorizo sauce.

American

Uvva (Hostería del Mar, 1 Calle Tapia, 787/727-3302, www.hosteriadelmarpr.com, daily 8am-10pm, $21-38) is another popular, upscale (in price) restaurant located in a beachside guesthouse. More casual than Pamela's, it features a small, two-level dining room decked out in warm woods and rattan furnishings overlooking the ocean. Dinner entrées include pan-seared duck breast in fig sauce and salmon in coconut ginger broth. Lighter fare, including burgers and beer-batter fried fish, is available for lunch.

Italian

You've never had pizza like this. **Pizza Cono** (1059 Calle McLeary, 787/317-3725, daily 11am-10pm, $2.50) is a closet-sized spot

a classic *cubano* sandwich from Kasalta Bakery

serving pizza cones to go. The sauce, cheese, and toppings are stuffed into a cone-shaped crust. Appropriate to the concept, it's served carryout only.

Located one block from the beach, **Relax @ Ocean Park** (Calle Saldado, between Calle Cacique and Calle McLeary, 787/728-0954, daily 10am-8pm, $6-15) is the kind of place you can patronize in your bathing suit with no problem. This laid-back, casual spot with indoor and outdoor seating serves an all gluten-free menu, specializing in *pizzetas* made with a cornmeal crust; try the Manhattan, featuring blue cheese and prosciutto. The menu changes every six months. Fresh fruit smoothies, coffee drinks, house-baked breads, sandwiches, salads, and wraps are also on the menu.

Mexican

San Juan is experiencing a newfound boom in Mexican restaurants. Everywhere you look, a new one has popped up. **La B de Burro** (2000 Calle McLeary, 787/242-0295, Mon.-Wed. 11am-10pm, Thurs.-Sat. 11am-midnight, Sun. noon-10pm, $4-11) is a funky little joint serving all varieties of tacos, tostados, burritos, quesadillas, and chimichangas. But they also serve lettuce tacos and an assortment of *aguas frescas* and fresh-made fruit juices, which the staff is happy to whip up into margaritas. Try a tamarind margarita and the spicy house salsa served with crispy corn tortilla halves while you peruse the menu and check out all the Mexican Day of the Dead decor. The waitstaff is very young, hip, and friendly.

Dessert

Clean, modern **Yogen Fruz** (51 Calle McLeary, 787/200-4450, www.yogenfruz.com, Mon.-Wed. 11am-10pm, Thurs.-Sun. 11am-11pm, $3.50-5.70) serves refreshing frozen nonfat yogurt in cups or cones with your choice of fresh fruits and other toppings, including shaved chocolate or nuts. Additional locations are throughout Puerto Rico, including Condado, Isla Verde, and Old San Juan.

Groceries

McLeary Mini Mart (1951 Calle McLeary at Calle Santa Ana, 787/236-5057, Mon.-Tues. 8am-8pm, Wed.-Fri. 8am-9pm, Sat.-Sun. 9am-7:30pm) is a convenient spot to pick up drinks and snacks for a day at the beach, or other last-minute essentials.

SANTURCE

The dining scene has exploded in Santurce, especially along Calle Loiza. Once a crowded, busy strip of discount stores that catered to a working class clientele, Calle Loiza has become one of the hippest places in San Juan, thick with tattoo shops, vintage clothing stores, artisanal bakeries, and lots of great new restaurants.

Puerto Rican

La Placita and Plaza del Mercado (Calle Dos Hermanos and Calle Capital, http://placitasanturce.com, Mon.-Sat. 6am-6pm, Sun. noon-6pm) is a terrific open-air farmers market by day, but at night the market closes up, sidewalk bars open for business, and adjacent restaurants and bars fill up with patrons, turning the surrounding neighborhood into a lively street party. Check out **Boronia** (Calle Capital at La Placita, 787/724-0636, www.boroniarestaurante.com, daily noon-10pm, $9-20) a modest, casual spot serving traditional *criolla* cuisine with a few surprises, such as mashed celery root with codfish for an appetizer and rabbit fricassee. There's live music on weekends. Other popular options in the neighborhood include **Taberna los Vázquez** (1348 Calle Orbeta, 787/723-1903) and **El Coco de Luis** (corner of Plaza del Mercado, 787/721-7595).

Located on the first floor of a four-story apartment building, **Bebo's Café** (1600 Calle Loíza, 787/726-1008, daily 7:30am-12:30am, $6-21) is a casual restaurant serving an exhaustive menu of traditional *criolla* cuisine. Literally, just about anything you can think of is served here: Cuts of chicken, pork, and beef are prepared fried, breaded, grilled, stuffed, or stewed. Shrimp, crab, octopus, and conch are

La Casita Blanca in Santurce serves classic Puerto Rican cuisine.

served in salads or stuffed in *mofongo.* All varieties of fritters, sandwiches, soups, fish, and flan are also represented, as are fruit shakes and frappes. Check the daily specials for delicacies such as stewed oxtail, goat fricassee, and *pastelón,* a dish similar to lasagna that uses plantain or breadfruit in place of pasta. This place is the real deal.

★ **La Casita Blanca** (351 Calle Tapía, Santurce, 787/726-5501, Mon.-Thurs. 11:30am-4pm, Fri.-Sat. 11:30am-9pm, Sun. noon-4pm, $7-15) is a warm and endearingly rustic restaurant tricked out like a 1950s-era living room serving some of the best traditional Puerto Rican cuisine found in San Juan. The menu changes daily but typically includes classics such as *arroz con pollo, carne guisado, pastélon con carne, amarillos, tostones,* and *picadillo.* All meals end with a tasty complimentary shot of *chichaito,* made from rum and anisette.

Nueva Criolla

Hands down one of the best meals you can have—not only in the area of La Placita but in all of Puerto Rico—is at the eponymous, chef-owned ★ **Jose Enrique** (176 Calle Duffaut near La Placita, 787/725-3518, Tues.-Fri. 11:30am-10:30pm, Sat. 6:30pm-10pm, $10-26). There's no sign, but it's easy to spot this foodie mecca by the size of the crowd congregated outside. The menu changes every night, depending on what's fresh, but always features creative interpretations of traditional Puerto Rican cuisine. A recent night's offerings included house-smoked *longaniza* (pork sausage), *carne guisada* (beef stew), *churrasco* (Argentinean skirt steak), *dorado ajillo* (mahimahi in garlic sauce), and *tembleque* (a congealed coconut dessert). Reservations are not accepted, so be prepared to wait up to two hours; but not to worry—you can head someplace nearby for pre-dinner drinks, and the hostess will call your cell phone when your table is ready. Ask to sit outside if there's space; the candlelit setting is more serene and atmospheric than the crowded, brightly lit dining room.

Also in La Placita area is the upscale **Santaella** (219 Calle Canals, 787/ 725-1611, www.santaellapr.com, Tues.-Fri. 11:30am-11pm, Sat. 6:30pm-11pm, $26-36) serving up a creative menu of baby octopus casserole with chorizo and chickpeas in sherry and steamed halibut in leek sauce. Chef-owner José Santaella, who trained with Ferran Adrià at elBulli and Eric Ripert, started out as a caterer before opening this sleek, low-lit, special occasion restaurant. Save room for one of the unusual desserts, like the Nutella sandwich with Frangelico whipped cream or cherry tomatoes in syrup with fresh cheese and basil ice cream. And although they're pricey ($13-14), consider starting your meal with craft cocktails such as the ginger margarita or rum mango julep. If you like Santaella's cuisine, check out his 2014 cookbook, *Cocina Tropical: The Classic and Contemporary Flavors of Puerto Rico* (Rizzoli).

For a more casual nueva criolla experience, look for the bright yellow storage container-turned-restaurant ★ **Tresbé** (1765 Calle Loíza, 787/294-9604, www.cafetresbe.com, daily 11am-midnight, $4-12). Order at the window, take a seat at one of the metal picnic tables on the patio, and dine on marlin *pinchos* (kabobs), breadfruit *tostones,* tamarind chicken wings, burgers, tacos, and ceviche. For something light, try a fresh fruit smoothie or a cupcake. It's a popular spot for lunch and late-night snacks.

Breakfast

In the funky, two-story blue building at the corner of Calle Taft, **Kamoli Café & Boutique** (1706 Calle Loíza, 787/721-4326, Mon.-Sat. 11am-4pm, $5.50-13) serves breakfast all day, with an emphasis on healthy options including fresh fruit smoothies, multi-grain pancakes, organic juices, and fruit bowls with yogurt and granola. Service tends to be very casual and slow for no apparent reason, so don't go here if you're in a hurry or hope to chat up your barista. The boutique part sells bohemian clothing and jewelry by local artisans.

French

Located across from the Museo de Arte de Puerto Rico, **Bistro de Paris** (310 Ave. de Diego, 787/998-8929 or 787/721-8925, www.bistrodeparispr.com, Mon.-Wed. 11:30am-10pm, Thurs. 11:30am-11pm, Fri.-Sat. 11:30am-midnight, Sun. 11am-10pm, $25-37) specializes in authentic French nouvelle cuisine, including shrimp flambé and filet mignon topped with sautéed duck liver. Globe light fixtures and art posters create a cozy ambiance in the dining room, while more casual dining is available on the patio. Brunch is served Saturday and Sunday 11am-4pm.

Italian

What started as a family-owned pizza joint has turned into one of the hippest hot spots along Loiza's burgeoning nightlife corridor. **Loíza 2050 Whiskey Bar** (2050 Calle Loíza, 787/726-7141, Wed.-Sat. 6pm-midnight, Sun. 6pm-4am, $9-18) serves thin, crispy pizzas topped with smoked salmon and goat cheese or bourbon pork. A large selection of craft beers and whiskeys rounds out the bar.

Mexican

A hip Mexican restaurant and self-described dive bar, **Panuchas** (1762 Calle Loíza, 787/545-2845, Mon.-Thurs. 3pm-midnight, Fri.-Sun. 11am-2am, $5-15, no American Express or Discovery) serves everything from tacos to tuna steak. Specialties include *ropa vieja* enchiladas with sweet plantains and a

Tresbé serves meals from a former storage container in Santurce.

variety of tortas. Spice it up with the housemade hot sauces and wash it down with a margarita while you check out the pink and black-stenciled wall featuring repeated images of Frida Kahlo, mustachioed skulls, and banditos.

La Mala Vida (211 Calle Canals, at La Placita, 787/717-4979, www.lamalavidapr.com, Wed.-Sat. 6pm-11pm, Sat.-Sun. 10am-3pm, dinner $7-18, brunch $4-13) serves Mexican influenced American cuisine, ranging from tacos and burritos to burgers and baby back ribs. Tacos, burgers, and burrito bowls appear on the brunch menu, too, along with stuffed croissants, bagels, and egg dishes. There's a second location (150 Calle San Sebastián) in Old San Juan.

Peruvian

Peruvian food is on the menu at **La Chola** (1859 Calle Loíza, 787/200-5877, Tues.-Thurs. 5pm-10pm, Fri.-Sat. 5pm-11pm, Sun. noon-10pm, $9-14). Dine on *chaufa* (a traditional Peruvian rice dish) with seafood, chicken, or beef, as well as a variety of ceviches and grilled or fried meats.

Seafood

Get your seafood fix at **La Cueva del Mar** (1904 Calle Loíza, 787/726-8700, http://cueva.r-leon.info, Sun.-Thurs. 11am-9:30pm, Fri.-Sat. 11am-11pm, $10-20; additional locations at 305 Recinto Sur, Old San Juan, 787/725-8700, and Carr. 19, km 0.7, Guaynabo, 787/793-8700). Tricked out in a 1980s-era nautical theme complete with fishing nets and wooden ship wheels, this popular spot with locals serves a huge variety of Puerto Rican-style seafood dishes from conch salad to *mofongo relleno de camarones* (mashed, garlicky plantains stuffed with shrimp). Seafood stuffed tacos, *empanadillas,* and salads, as well as salmon, mahimahi, and grouper dishes round out the menu. But the house specialties are *Arroz con Mariscos La Cueva*, featuring seasoned rice and a variety of seafood, and flan de Nutella. There's a full bar, a kids' menu, and weekly specials.

Spanish

Set in a colonial mansion appointed with stained-glass windows, archways, patios, intricate tile work, and lush landscaping, **La Casona** (609 Calle San Jorge, corner of Ave. Fernández Juncos, 787/727-2717 or 787/727-3229, http://restaurantelacasonapr.com, Mon.-Fri. noon-3pm, Mon.-Sat. 6pm-11:30pm, $25-35) serves a menu of classic Spanish dishes. An extensive wine list complements the paella, rack of lamb, and pâté. It's a particularly popular spot for business lunches, banquets, receptions, and other private parties.

Fine Dining

Opened in 2013, **Gallo Negro** (1107 Ave. Ponce de León, 787/554-5445, Tues.-Sat. 6pm-midnight, Sun. 11am-4pm, $22-35) is a welcome addition to the Santurce fine-dining scene. Small and sophisticated, the chef-run restaurant features outstanding craft cocktails and an ever-changing menu of creative global dishes, ranging from lettuce wraps with Korean barbecue style duck confit with Gochujang sauce to coq au vin.

Groceries

Plaza del Mercado (Calle Dos Hermanos and Calle Capital, www.placitasanturce.com, Mon.-Sat. 6am-6pm, Sun. noon-6pm) is a picturesque, colonial-style, open-air farmers market built in 1910 where shoppers can pick up a wide variety of fruits, vegetables, fresh meats, frozen fruit frappes, and herbal remedies. At night the markets close up, sidewalk bars open for business, a live band strikes a tune, adjacent restaurants and bars fill up with patrons, and the surrounding neighborhood turns into a lively street party.

MIRAMAR

Puerto Rican

From the same folks who run the popular Casita Blanca in Santurce, equally popular **Casita Miramar** (605 Ave. Miramar, 787/200-8227, Mon.-Fri. 6pm-10pm, Sat. 11:30am-10pm, Sun. 11:30am-9pm, $18-32) serves traditional Puerto Rican cuisine in a

two-story colonial building with a second-floor patio. The menu changes daily based on what's fresh and in season. Be prepared to wait up to two hours if you go at prime time.

Nueva Criolla

One of the most exciting new additions to the San Juan dining scene is ★ **Soda Estudio de Cocina** (562 Calle Cuevillas, 787/998-9920, http://restaurantesoda.com, Tues.-Thurs. noon-10pm, Fri.-Sat. noon-11pm, $7.50-17, no Discovery or American Express). Judging from the rustic beer bar vibe, the crudely rendered pop culture murals, and the hipster waitstaff, it would be easy to assume this place is a college bar serving pizza and pitchers of suds. But the opposite is true. This is some of the most expertly prepared creative cuisine in the city. Duck breast stuffed with sweet plantains served with mango salsa is the perfect combination of salty savory fruity char. It's hard not to lick the plate when this dish is gone. Other menu options include coconut arepas stuffed with *ropa vieja* made from antelope, and fried dumplings filled with duck and pork belly. For a refreshing beverage, try the blackberry mojito made from plump fresh fruit and a fistful of fresh mint. As for the hipster waitstaff? They couldn't be more friendly and helpful.

Breakfast

At **Abracadabra Counter Café** (1661 Ave. Ponce de León, 787/200-0447, Tues.-Thurs. 8:30am-7pm, Fri. 8:30am-9pm, Sat.-Sun. 10am-3pm, $5-15), bright yellow-and-white striped wallpaper and vintage photographs cover the walls of this whimsical bistro frequented by a hip, young clientele, as well as families attracted by the local coffee and the fresh, organic menu. Breakfast and brunch dishes are its specialties, including the caprese omelet, Nutella-filled croissants, and bacon maple cupcakes. Live entertainment runs the gamut from magic shows to film nights to live musical performances. A full bar and free wireless Internet are available.

Al Gusto Deli (950 Ave. Ponce de León, 787/723-4321, Mon.-Fri. 7:30am-3:30pm, $6-9) serves breakfast sandwiches and burritos, as well as deli sandwiches, wraps, salads, soups, and quesadillas. Neon green walls and bright orange chairs create a cheery place to start the day.

French

Although **Augusto's Cuisine** (801 Ave. Ponce de León, 787/725-7700, www.marriott.com, Tues.-Fri. noon-3pm, Tues.-Sat. 7pm-9:30pm, $26-40) is located in the Courtyard by Marriott, don't confuse it with generic chain hotel restaurant fare. The venerable French-influenced fine dining restaurant was located in this spot long before it was a Courtyard by Marriott. It is the place to go to don your evening finery, make a selection from the extensive wine list, and enjoy a leisurely meal. The foie gras and chocolate soufflé are highly recommended.

ISLA VERDE

Puerto Rican

Despite its location in an aging, nearly empty strip mall, ★ **Mi Casita** (La Plazoleta de Isla Verde, 6150 Ave. Isla Verde, 787/791-1777, daily 7:30am-10:30pm, $5-18) is a homey oasis of authentic Puerto Rican cuisine. The restaurant is designed to look like Mom's dining room, complete with china plates hanging on the green walls, and the menu features outstanding *criolla* cuisine, including a moist *mofongo, asopao, churrasco, chillo,* and mahimahi.

At **Don Jose Restaurant and Bar** (6475 Ave. Isla Verde, km 6.3, 787/253-1281, Mon.-Wed. 7am-11pm, Thurs.-Sun. 24 hours, $7-22), a large, fully stocked bar dominates the center of this long, narrow dining room serving traditional Puerto Rican dishes, including shrimp *asopao, bifstec encebollado, chuleta can can, churrasco,* and *mofongo.* It also serves a traditional American breakfast (eggs, oatmeal, pancakes) as well as burgers, sandwiches, and salads. Daily specials and free delivery are offered.

Platos Restaurant (below Coral by

the Sea hotel, 2 Calle Rosa, 787/791-7474 or 787/721-0396, www.platosrestaurant.com, Sun.-Thurs. 11:30am-11pm, Fri.-Sat. 11:30am-11:30pm, $17-23) is not named after the Greek philosopher but rather the Spanish word for "plates." This trendy, touristy restaurant is decorated in moss green and burnt orange with a large steel counter and big-screen TV in the bar. Tropical-drink specials are tall, but weak and pricey at $12 a pop. The formerly froufrou menu has been replaced with streamlined traditional dishes, including *mofongo,* steaks, pork chops, and fettuccine. Creativity reigns among the seafood dishes, which include mahimahi in coconut-passion fruit sauce.

Casa Dante (39 Ave. Isla Verde, 787/726-7310, Mon.-Thurs. 11:30am-1am, Fri.-Sat. 11:30am-midnight, Sun. 11:30am-10:30pm, $8-30) is a casual, low-key locals' restaurant serving authentic Puerto Rican cuisine, specializing in a variety of *mofongos* with choice of fish, seafood, beef, chicken, or pork. There are also a few pasta dishes available.

Breakfast

Piu Bello (2 Calle Rosa, 787/791-0091, Mon.-Thurs. 7am-11pm, Fri.-Sun. 7am-midnight, $7-13) is a large, modern, retro-style diner with indoor and outdoor dining. The enormous menu includes every sandwich imaginable, including wraps, Italian focaccia, flatbreads, panini, burgers, and clubs. It also serves breakfast, pasta dishes, and gelato. There is a second location (Ave. Ashford) in Condado. There's free wireless Internet.

Cuban

Decor is secondary at the crowded casual Cuban restaurant ★ **Metropol** (Ave. Isla Verde, beside Club Gallistico cockfight arena, 787/791-4046, www.metropolpr.com, daily 11am-10:30pm, $9-40, most dishes $10-15). The house specialty is *gallinita rellena de congri*—succulent roasted Cornish hen stuffed with a perfectly seasoned combination of rice and black beans. The presentation is no-nonsense and the service expedient, designed to get you in and out so the folks lining up outside can have your table. There are additional locations in Hato Rey (244 Ave. Roosevelt, 787/751-4022) and Guaynabo (Jardines Reales, Ave. Las Cumbres, 787/272-7000).

Italian

Despite its modest location on the busy thoroughfare, **Il Nonno** (41 Ave. Isla Verde, 787/728-8050, Sun.-Thurs. noon-10pm, Fri.-Sat. noon-11pm, $14-29) is a small fine-dining restaurant with a lovely setting. Pale green walls and walnut accents are complemented by an excellent selection of contemporary paintings. The restaurant serves Italian cuisine from gnocchi gorgonzola to osso buco.

The casual, modern, Argentine-Italian restaurant **Ferrari Gourmet** (3046 Ave. Isla Verde, 787/982-3115, www.ferrarigourmet.com, Sun.-Thurs. noon-10pm, Fri.-Sat. noon-11pm, delivery after 6pm, $10-22) specializes in a wide variety of tasty, creative pizzas. Selections include black olive and blue cheese; asparagus, Parmesan cheese, and fresh tomato; and ham, roasted red peppers, and green olives. Entrées include *churrasco,* veal saltimbocca, and lasagna.

Il Mulino New York (The Ritz-Carlton, 6961 Ave. of the Governors, 787/791-8632, www.ilmulino.com, Mon.-Wed. 6pm-10:30pm, Thurs.-Sat. 6pm-11pm, Sun. 6pm-10pm, Sun. brunch 11am-3pm, $24-48) is the Caribbean arm of the celebrated Italian restaurant, specializing in meat and seafood dishes with a menu that includes rack of lamb, osso buco, and scampi *fra diavolo.*

Pizza City (5950 Ave. Isla Verde, 787/726-0356, daily 24 hours, $3-20) is an open-air restaurant best known for its tasty thin-crust pizza sold by the slice or pie. It also serves breakfast, sandwiches, seafood salads, and *mofongo.* It has a full bar and offers free delivery.

Japanese

Catering to the late-night party crowd, **Kintaro** (5970 Ave. Isla Verde, 787/726-3096, Mon.-Thurs. and Sun. 5pm-3am, Fri.-Sat.

5pm-4am, $9-22) is a small, dark-red eatery serving sushi, tempura, and teriyaki into the wee hours. It offers free delivery.

Ikebana (Ave. Los Gobernadores, Pueblo Xtra Airport Plaza, 787/253-1705, www.ikebanasushibars.com, Mon.-Thurs. 5pm-11pm, Sat. 2pm-midnight, Sun. 2pm-10pm, $11-30) serves Caribbean-inspired sushi, like the Island Roll, stuffed with scallop, peach, and avocado, or the Tropical Roll, stuffed with shrimp tempura, cream cheese, cucumber, massago, and topped with passion fruit sauce. Entrées range from halibut steamed in soy daikon ginger broth over sweet potato pancake to grilled lamb cutlets in tamarind miso sauce.

Seafood and Steak

★ **Marisquería Atlantica** (2475 Calle Loiza, Punta Las Marías, 787/728-5444 or 787/728-5662, www.marisqueriaatlantica.com, Mon.-Thurs. noon-10pm, Fri.-Sat. noon-11pm, $18-49) is a longstanding, high-quality, upscale seafood restaurant, serving everything imaginable from the sea, including *asopao,* grilled lobster, fresh fish including *chillo* and dorado, and a variety of ceviches and paellas. It also has a market (Mon.-Sat. 9am-8pm, Sun. 10am-3pm) where you can pick up fresh seafood to prepare at home.

Locals and tourists alike flock to **Che's** (35 Calle Caoba at Calle Laurel, 787/726-7202 or 787/268-7507, www.chesrestaurant.com, Sun.-Thurs. 11:30am-10pm, Fri.-Sat. 11:30am-11pm, $13-48), a large casual restaurant serving excellent Argentine cuisine. Grilled meats are the specialty—veal, lamb, *churrasco,* veal kidneys, and so on. There are also some unexpected offerings—a Greek-style spinach pie with a whole boiled egg buried inside and an apple and celery salad. Che's has good service and a full bar.

At The Ritz-Carlton is **BLT Steak** (6961 Ave. of the Governors, 787/253-1700, www.e2hospitality.com, daily 6pm-11pm, $28-50), offering a contemporary interpretation of the classic American steakhouse in a casual setting.

If the restaurant didn't overlook the water, the ambiance of this casual, open-air restaurant would be just plain sad, with its plastic deck chairs and tattered tent awning, not to mention the view of the abandoned building next door. But **La Playita** (Hotel La Playa, 787/791-1115, www.hotellaplaya.com, daily 7am-11pm, $16-26) serves a diverse and tasty menu heavy on seafood, including mahimahi in mango chipotle sauce and salmon filet in spicy guava sauce. There is also an extensive appetizer menu, including ceviche and mini *alcapurrias* and empanadas, making it a great spot for drinks and appetizers. Salads, wraps, and burgers round out the menu.

Groceries

Supermax (1 Calle Venus, Isla Verde, 787/268-3084 or 787/728-2050, www.supermaxpr.com, daily 24 hours) is a modern, full-service grocery store with a bakery, deli, fresh meat counter, and produce section. It carries a large selection of spirits and a wide variety of local coffees, but you'll have to get a clerk to unlock the case for you.

CATAÑO

It's not necessarily worth a special trip, but if you take the ferry to Cataño to visit the Casa Bacardi Visitor Center, you might want to stop by **S.O.S. Burger** (36 Ave. Las Nereidas, Cataño, 787/788-3149, Wed.-Thurs. noon-7:30pm, Fri.-Sun. noon-11pm, $3-15). The psychedelic-colored structure with a palm-frond roof is the quirky domain of Sammy Ortega Santiago (his initials inform the establishment's name), who sports waist-length dreadlocks and an infectious smile. As the name implies, the short menu serves a variety of burgers. But the real reason to go here is to kick back with some ice-cold Medalla beers and to nosh on the variety of tasty *pastelillos,* thin, crisp turnovers stuffed with meat, cheese, or seafood. Here they come stuffed with everything from crab, lobster, and *chapín* (boxfish) to cheese, beef, and pepperoni with tomato sauce. There's live music on weekends.

Transportation and Services

GETTING THERE

Air

Luis Muñoz Marín International Airport (SJU, Isla Verde, 787/791-4670 or 787/791-3840) is nine miles east of San Juan. It is a full-service airport with three terminals. It has a bank, restaurants, bars, and shops on the second floor alongside the departure gates. A tourist information office (787/791-1014) is in Terminal C, and a ground-service desk is on the first level by the baggage claim.

Isla Grande Airport (Aeropuerto de Isla Grande, SIG, end of Ave. Lindberg, Miramar near Old San Juan, 787/729-8790) is a regional airport that services flights throughout the island and the Caribbean.

For transportation into the city from the airport, there are several car-rental agencies on the first level, including **Wheelchair Getaway Rent A Car** (787/726-4023), which provides vehicles for drivers with disabilities. The first level is also where you can catch a taxi or bus into town. From the airport, take Baldorioty de Castro Avenue west toward Isla Verde, Ocean Park, and Condado and into Old San Juan.

The airport also is the site of the **Luis Muñoz Marín International Airport Hotel** (787/791-1700), which can be found in Terminal D on the second level.

Airline ticket prices fluctuate throughout the year, but the cheapest rates can usually be secured during the off-season, May-September, which is the rainy season. Note that late summer through early fall is also hurricane season.

These airlines service San Juan from the United States:

- **American Airlines** (800/433-7300, www.aa.com)
- **Continental Airlines** (800/231-0856 or 800/523-3273, www.continental.com)
- **Delta Air Lines** (800/221-1212 or 800/325-1999, www.delta.com)
- **JetBlue Airways** (800/538-2583, www.jetblue.com)
- **Northwest** (800/225-2525, www.nwa.com)
- **Spirit Airlines** (800/772-7117, www.spiritairlines.com)
- **United** (800/864-8331, www.united.com)
- **U.S. Airways** (800/428-4322, www.usairways.com)

Cruise Ship

San Juan is the second-largest port in the western hemisphere, and it is a port of call or point of origin for nearly two dozen cruise-ship lines. The cruise-ship docks are at the piers along Calle La Marina in Old San Juan.

Some of the most popular cruise-ship lines serving San Juan include:

- **Carnival Cruise Lines** (866/299-5698 or 800/327-9501, www.carnival.com)
- **Celebrity Cruises** (800/647-2251, 800/722-5941, or 800/280-3423, www.celebritycruises.com)
- **Holland America Line** (877/724-5425, www.hollandamerica.com)
- **Norwegian Cruise Line** (800/327-7030, www.ncl.com)
- **Princess Cruises** (800/774-6237 or 800/421-0522, www.princess.com)
- **Radisson Seven Seas Cruises** (877/505-5370 or 800/285-1835, www.rssc.com)
- **Royal Caribbean International** (866/562-7625 or 800/327-6700, 305/539-6000, www.royalcaribbean.com)

GETTING AROUND

Taxi

Taxis are a terrific way to get around San Juan because you can catch them just about anywhere. In Old San Juan, there are taxi stands at Plaza de Colón, Plaza de Armas, and the Sheraton near the cruise-ship piers. In Condado, you can flag them down on Avenida Ashford or at the Marriott hotel. In Isla Verde, flag one down on Avenida Isla Verde or find them congregating at the InterContinental San Juan Resort. In outlying areas such as Santurce, Bayamón, Hato Rey, or Río Piedras, you can sometimes flag one down on the major thoroughfares, but you might be better off calling for one.

Licensed taxi services are well regulated. Operators include **Metro Taxi** (787/725-2870), **Rochdale Radio Taxi** (787/721-1900), and **Capetillo Taxi** (787/758-7000).

Fares between the airport and the piers in Old San Juan are fixed rates. From the airport, the rates are $10 to Isla Verde, $15 to Condado, $19 to Old San Juan, and $15 to Isla Grande Airport and the Puerto Rico Convention Center. From the piers, the rates are $12 to Condado and $19 to Isla Verde. There is a $1.50 gas surcharge, and each piece of luggage is $1. Metered fares are $3 minimum, $1.75 initial charge, and $0.10 every 19th of a mile. Customers pay all road tolls.

Bus

Autoridad Metropolitana de Autobuses (787/250-6064 or 787/294-0500, ext. 514, www.dtop.gov.pr/ama/mapaindex.htm, Mon.-Fri. 4:30am-10pm, Sat.-Sun. and holidays 5:30am-10pm) is an excellent public bus system that serves the entire metropolitan San Juan area. It's serviced by large air-conditioned vehicles with access for those with disabilities, and the cost is typically a low $0.75 per fare (exact change required). Bus stops are clearly marked along the routes with green signs that say "Parada," except in Old San Juan, where you have to catch the bus at **Covadonga Bus and Trolley Terminal** (corner of Calle la Marina and Calle J. A. Corretjer), the large terminal near the cruise-ship piers. When waiting for a bus at a *parada*, it is necessary to wave to get the driver to stop.

The most commonly used routes for tourists are B-21 and A-5. Route B-21 starts at the terminal in Old San Juan and travels down Avenida Ashford in Condado and then south along Avenida Muñoz Rivera through Hato Rey to Plaza Las Americas, the island's largest shopping mall. B-21 runs every 20 minutes Monday-Saturday and every 30 minutes on Sunday and holidays.

Route A-5 connects Old San Juan and Isla Verde. The route travels along Avenida Isla Verde, Calle Loíza, Avenida de Diego, and Avenida Ponce de León into Old San Juan. A-5 does not go to Condado. It is possible to get to Condado from this route by transferring to B-21 at Parada 18 by Avenida De Diego, but keep in mind this stop is near a public-housing project in Santurce, which has been the site of violent crime. A-5 runs every 7 minutes Monday-Friday, every 15 minutes Saturday, and every 30 minutes Sunday and holidays.

From the airport, visitors can take the C-45 bus to Isla Verde. To get to other parts of the city, it will be necessary to transfer to another route.

There are many other bus routes in San Juan. To obtain a free, detailed map of all routes, visit the bus terminal in Old San Juan. Riders should be aware, though, that buses serve tourist districts as well as housing projects, and some stops are in places where visitors who are unfamiliar with the lay of the land may not want to be. Make sure you know where you are before you disembark.

Trolley

Old San Juan Trolley (Mon.-Fri. 7am-7pm, Sat.-Sun. 9am-7pm, free) provides transportation from the cruise-ship piers throughout Old San Juan. You can catch the trolley at the Covadonga Bus and Trolley Terminal by Plaza de Colón, at La Puntilla parking lot on Calle Puntilla, or at marked stops throughout Old San Juan.

Ferry

The **AcuaExpreso San Juan** (Pier 2, Paseo Concepción de Gracia, Old San Juan, 787/729-8714 or 787/788-0940) ferry provides transportation across San Juan Bay from Old San Juan to the communities of Cataño ($0.50 one way) and Hato Rey ($0.75 one way). Even if you don't plan to get off and explore those neighborhoods, it's worth a ride to admire the view of Castillo San Felipe del Morro and Old San Juan on the return trip. The Cataño ferry takes about 10 minutes and operates daily 6am-9:40pm. The Hato Rey ferry, which takes about 15 minutes, operates weekdays only. Frequency is every 30 minutes except Monday-Friday 6am-10am and 3:45pm-7pm, when they run every 15 minutes with the exclusion of holidays.

AcuaExpreso Cataño (Ave. Las Nereidas, 787/729-8714 or 787/788-0940) ferry service is provided to Old San Juan for $0.50 each way. The 10-minute ride operates daily 6am-9:40pm. Frequency is every 30 minutes except Monday-Friday 6am-10am and 3:45pm-7pm, when they run every 15 minutes with the exclusion of holidays.

Train

In 2005, San Juan launched **Tren Urbano** (866/900-1284, www.dtop.gov.pr), its first, long-awaited commuter train service. The system runs 10.7 miles, mostly aboveground, and has 16 stations, many of which house a terrific collection of specially commissioned public art. The train connects the communities of Bayamón, the Universidad de Puerto Rico in Río Piedras, Hato Rey, and Santurce at Universidad del Sagrado Corazón. The train runs daily 5:30am-11:30pm. Round-trip fares are $1.50; daily passes start at $5.

Público

Públicos are privately owned transport services that operate passenger vans along regular routes from San Juan to areas around the island. This is a very slow but inexpensive way to see the island. Providers include **Blue Line** (787/765-7733) to Río Piedras, Aguadilla, Aguada, Moca, Isabela, and other areas; **Choferes Unidos de Ponce** (787/764-0540) to Ponce and other areas; **Lina Boricua** (787/765-1908) to Lares, Ponce, Jayuya, Utuado, San Sebastián, and other areas; **Linea Caborrojeña** (787/723-9155) to Cabo Rojo, San Germán, and other areas; **Linea Sultana** (787/765-9377) to Mayagüez and other areas; and **Terminal de Transportación Pública** (787/250-0717) to Fajardo and other areas.

Car

Driving a car in San Juan can be a nerve-rattling experience for drivers not accustomed to inner-city traffic. The sheer volume of cars on the road at any given time can be daunting, and parking on sidewalks and driving up expressway shoulders are not atypical habits of Puerto Rican drivers. But renting a car is one of the best ways to explore the city and its outlying areas. In addition to most major car-rental agencies, several local companies provide comparable services.

Charlie Car Rental (6050 Ave. Isla Verde, Isla Verde, 800/289-1227, 787/728-2418; 1100 Ave. Ashford, across from La Concha hotel, 800/289-1227, 787/728-6525, www.charliecars.com) is a cheap, reliable alternative to the national agencies. Drivers must be at least 21, and those younger than 25 must pay an additional $10 per day surcharge. Free pickup and drop-off at the airport, hotels, and cruise-ship port is available. There is also a location in Caguas (Carr. 183, km 2.4). Or try **Vias Car Rental** (Hotel Villa del Sol, 4 Calle Rosa, Isla Verde, 787/721-4120 or 787/791-2600; Carr. 693, km 8.2, Calle Marginal in Dorado, 787/796-6404 or 787/796-6882; and Carr. 3, km 88.8, Barrio Candelero in Humacao near Palmas del Mar, 787/852-1591 or 787/850-3070; www.viascarrental.com, daily 8am-5pm).

Bicycle

Rent the Bicycle (100 Calle del Muelle, Pier 6, Old San Juan, 787/602-9696 or 787/692-3200, www.rentthebicycle.net) will deliver bikes to your hotel. Rental rates are $17 for three hours, $27 a day. Bike tours of Old San Juan, Condado parks and beaches, and Piñones are $27 for three hours, with a two-person minimum.

SERVICES

Puerto Rico Tourism Company (500 Ochoa Bldg., Calle Tanca, Old San Juan, 787/721-2400 ext. 3901, www.seepuertorico.com, daily 9am-5:30pm) is located across the street from Pier 1.

Published five days a week, the ***San Juan Star*** (www.sanjuanweeklypr.com) is San Juan's only English language newspaper, featuring locally produced content and wire stories from *The New York Times*. ***El Nuevo Día*** (www.endi.com) is the island-wide Spanish-language daily newspaper. ***La Perla del Sur*** (www.periodicolaperla.com) is a daily paper serving Ponce.

The free bimonthly ***Qué Pasa?*** (www.qpsm.com) is an English language travel magazine published by Travel and Sports (www.travelandsports.com) for the Puerto Rico Tourism Company. The magazine's current issue is available online, and the publishing company's website is an exhaustive source of information about the entire island.

There is no shortage of banks and ATMs in San Juan, the most popular being **Banco Popular** (206 Calle Tetuán, Old San Juan, 787/725-2636; 1060 Ave. Ashford, Condado, 787/725-4197; 4790 Ave. Isla Verde, Isla Verde, 787/726-5600).

There are convenient **post office** facilities in Old San Juan (153 Calle Fortaleza, 787/723-1277) and Cordado (1108 Calle Magdalena, 787/723-8204).

Self-service laundries are available at 24-hour **Coin Laundry** (1950 Calle Magdalena, Condado, 787/726-5955) and **Isla Verde Laundromat** (corner of Calle Emma and Calle Rodríguez, Isla Verde, 787/728-5990).

Emergency Services

The central hospital serving San Juan's tourist areas is **Ashford Medical Center** (1451 Ave. Ashford, Condado, 787/721-2160, clinic Mon.-Fri. 7am-7pm, Sat. 7am-noon). The emergency room is open 24 hours a day. Call 911 for ambulance service. There's a pharmacy on the first floor.

There are several **Walgreens** pharmacies (201 Calle de la Cruz at Calle San Francisco, Old San Juan, 787/722-6290; 1130 Ave. Ashford, Condado, 787/725-1510; 5984 Ave. Isla Verde, Isla Verde, 787/982-0222). Another option is **Puerto Rico Pharmacy** (157 Calle San Francisco, Old San Juan, 787/725-2202).

Dial 911 to reach the fire or police department in case of emergency.

Vieques and Culebra

Look for ★ to find recommended sights, activities, dining, and lodging.

Highlights

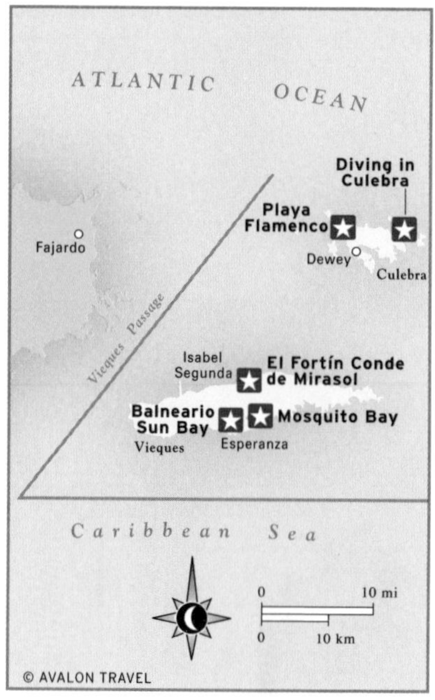

★ **El Fortín Conde de Mirasol:** Tour the last fort built by colonial Spain and see the 4,000-year-old remains of a man exhumed from an archaeological site in Vieques (page 93).

★ **Mosquito Bay:** Take a guided kayak or electric pontoon boat to Vieques's bioluminescent bay, which glows an electric blue at night (page 94).

★ **Balneario Sun Bay:** Vieques's mile-long, sandy, crescent-shaped beach borders crystal-blue waters (page 97).

★ **Playa Flamenco:** Puerto Rico's most celebrated stretch of white sand is considered one of the most beautiful beaches in the United States (page 112).

★ **Diving in Culebra:** Culebra is surrounded by 50 dive sites, and excellent snorkeling can be found right off its beaches (page 114).

Vieques and Culebra are two island municipalities a mere 8 and 17 miles, respectively, off the east coast of Puerto Rico, but the lifestyle there is light-years away from that of the main island.

Referred to as the Spanish Virgin Islands, Vieques and Culebra are often described as "the way Puerto Rico used to be." The pace of life doesn't just slow down, it comes to a screeching halt. There are no fast-food restaurants or high-rise hotels, no golf courses or casinos, virtually no nightlife, and few tourist sights. And the only way to reach the islands is by plane or ferry. But what they do have are stunning beaches, world-class water sports, and lots of opportunity for R&R.

The small Spanish fort and museum El Fortín Conde de Mirasol on Vieques and the Museo Histórico de Culebra are the closest things to cultural attractions the islands have to offer. Instead, one of the main reasons to go is the islands' wide sandy beaches, the most popular being Balneario Sun Bay in Vieques and Playa Flamenco in Culebra. In addition to its beaches, Culebra and Vieques offer fantastic opportunities for diving and snorkeling. If you don't want to go on a group tour, excellent snorkeling from the beach at Playa Carlos Rosario in Culebra is easily accessible. And visitors to Vieques would be remiss not to visit the bioluminescent Mosquito Bay, which requires an overnight stay.

HISTORY

Although details are sketchy, Vieques is believed to have been inhabited by a series of indigenous peoples possibly thousands of years before Christopher Columbus "discovered" Puerto Rico in 1493. Based on the discovery of remains found in Vieques, some historians date the earliest inhabitants to the Stone Age era more than 3,500 years ago.

Thanks to a few archaeological digs in Vieques, slightly more is known about the Saladoids, believed to have come from Venezuela around 250 BC. They were followed by the Ostionoids around 400 BC and eventually the Taínos, a highly developed society of agriculturalists who lived on both Vieques

Previous: Playa Flamenco in Culebra, the canal in Dewey, Culebra; **Above:** Vieques features miles of deserted beaches.

Vieques

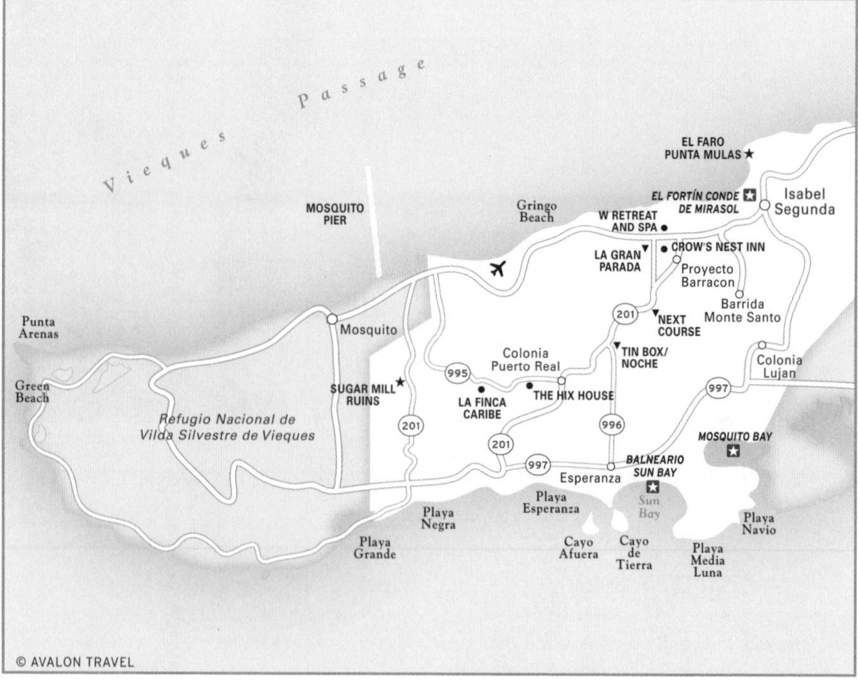

and Culebra. The Taínos ruled Puerto Rico from about AD 1200 until the Spanish colonists wiped them out in the 1500s.

In the early 1500s, two Taíno brothers in Vieques journeyed to mainland Puerto Rico to help their fellow natives fight the Spanish conquerors. As a result, the governor of Puerto Rico sent troops to Vieques, where all the Taínos were killed or enslaved. For a long time after that, the islands became lawless havens for pirates who sought refuge in the protected harbors and ambushed passing ships.

In 1832 a Frenchman named Le Guillou, known as the founder of Vieques, arrived on the island. Under Spanish authority, he restored order to the island and helped launch a golden era of prosperity. He brought over other Frenchmen from Guadeloupe and Martinique who established sugarcane plantations and processing plants that exported the products to Spain. The operations were manned by hundreds of slaves from Africa and thousands of free workers from surrounding islands. In the early 1800s, the area around Esperanza was a thriving community with an opera house, a movie theater, and a cultural center. But as the town tried to expand to accommodate its growing population, difficulty in clearing the thick vegetation led leaders to relocate the town center to Isabel Segunda in 1844. Vieques continued to enjoy its prosperity until around 1880, when the sugar industry began to decline because of the development of cheaper sources elsewhere.

It was around this time that Culebra was being settled in fits and starts. The first attempt was in 1875 by an Englishman named Stevens, who was named governor and given the task of protecting the island's waters from pirates. Later that same year he was

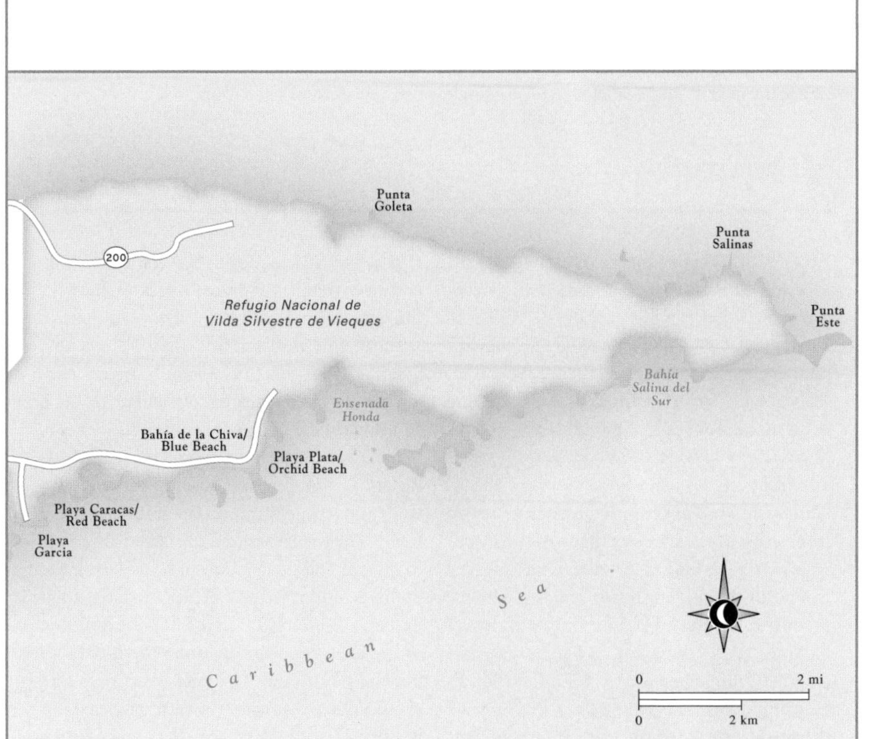

assassinated. He was followed in 1880 by a Spaniard, Cayetano Escudero Sanz, who established the first settlement, called San Ildefonso. The island's sole economy was agriculture.

Upon the ratification in 1898 of the Treaty of Paris, which ended the Spanish-American War, Vieques and Culebra came under the rule of the U.S. government. During World War II, the U.S. military became the major landholder on both islands and began to use them for bomb practice and defense-testing sites. Protests begun in Culebra in 1971 led the United States to abandon operations in 1975. But Vieques endured 24 more years until a civilian was accidentally killed by a bomb in 1999. Several years of persistent protesting followed, which captured international attention and led to the incarceration of many activists. In 2003, the Pentagon conceded and the Navy withdrew from Vieques. Its land—15,000 acres on the east side, along with 3,100 acres on the west side that was ceded two years earlier—was handed over to the federal Fish and Wildlife Service, which has classified the property a National Wildlife Refuge.

PLANNING YOUR TIME

To get to Vieques and Culebra, you can fly from Ceiba or San Juan or take a ferry from Fajardo. If you're visiting for only a day or two, spring for the airfare to save time.

Although it's possible to get to your hotel and some of the islands' beaches using *públicos* (shared vans that carry multiple fares at a time), to fully explore the islands' remote beaches a **rental car** is recommended. Book early though, because they go fast.

Vieques and Culebra are such small islands

that it's possible to **spend a day and a night on each** one to get a cursory feel for them both. But the reason most people go is to experience the islands' unparalleled natural beauty and soak up plenty of R&R. To do those things properly, it takes a few days to reset your internal clock to "island time" and achieve a blissful state of total relaxation.

Vieques

In a world where change is constant, it's nice to be reminded that some things stay the same. That is a big part of the charm of Vieques. Granted, a couple of new businesses have opened and a couple of them have closed. This hotel has changed names, and that one has a new coat of paint. But all in all, it's still just a sleepy little island where life moves at a snail's pace, cats and horses wander the island freely, and the only alarm clock you need is the crow of the roosters that run the place.

Just 21 miles long and 5 miles wide, Vieques is a natural wonderland. It is rimmed with primitive, fine-sand beaches, untouched by commercial development, and coral reefs that teem with undersea life. Among the island's mangrove forests is **Mosquito Bay,** one of the world's most spectacular bioluminescent bays. No visit to Vieques would be complete without a boat ride through luminescent blue waters. Inland Vieques is thickly forested hills and arid stretches of desert-like land. Bats are the only animal native to Vieques, but other wildlife commonly found includes geckos, iguanas, frogs, pelicans, seagulls, egrets, herons, doves, and horses, of course. Horses are a common mode of transportation in Vieques, and they can be seen following the same traffic laws as automobiles, stopping at four-way stops and so on. But they also graze and roam freely. The waters around the island are home to several endangered species, including the manatee and a variety of sea turtles, which nest on the beaches at night. The eastern side of the island is still off-limits to visitors, as the Navy continues to remove vestiges of its presence here. And 60 percent of the island is a protected wildlife sanctuary—**Refugio Nacional de Vida Silvestre de Vieques**—managed by the U.S. Fish and Wildlife

the *malecón* in Esperanza

Service. Some of the island's most beautiful primitive beaches are located here.

There are two primary communities on Vieques. On the north coast is **Isabel Segunda,** a.k.a. Isabel II, a traditional Puerto Rican town with a central plaza, an *alcaldía* (town hall), a post office, a grocery store, two banks—which contain the island's only ATMs—and the island's two gas stations. It is also where the ferry from Fajardo docks. There are a few shops, restaurants, and hotels here that cater to visitors, but Isabel Segunda is primarily a town where the island's residents conduct their daily business.

On the south coast is **Esperanza,** a funky, bohemian enclave where most tourists gravitate, thanks to the laid-back, "don't worry, be happy" atmosphere and the proximity of **Sun Bay,** one of the most gorgeous publicly maintained beaches in all of Puerto Rico. The main hub of Esperanza is along the oceanfront stretch of Calle Flamboyan, distinguished by the picturesque *malecón,* a boardwalk with balustrades, benches, and pavilions. From here you can also see Cayo Afuera, a small islet in spitting distance with excellent snorkeling on the western side. On the opposite side of the street is an inviting array of casual, open-air bars and restaurants that overlook the water and grow lively with tourists and locals—many of them "expats" from the mainland—as sundown approaches. There are also a handful of boutiques and a couple of guesthouses in the area, as well as the Vieques Conservation and Historical Trust, a modest institution but a great source of information on the island.

There are a few things travelers should know when visiting Vieques. The island has one of the highest unemployment rates in the United States, and petty theft from parked cars is a continuing problem. When in town, visitors are encouraged to keep their cars locked at all times and never to leave anything visible inside. The greatest threat to car break-ins is at the beach. Drivers are encouraged to leave all the windows rolled down and the sunroof and glove box open to avoid having to pay the cost of replacing a broken window. And always park your car as close to you as possible—preferably away from any bushes and within sight range.

For well-heeled travelers, there are some outstanding and unique guesthouses that provide plenty of luxurious amenities. But outside those plush environs, there is a rustic quality to life here. Restaurants tend to be open-air, even nice ones, so don't expect a respite from the heat and humidity at dinner. When using public facilities, plumbing issues require toilet paper be disposed of in trash receptacles instead of being flushed, which can make for an odorous experience. And if you think restaurant service is slow on the main island of Puerto Rico, you haven't seen anything yet. Many businesses close or curtail hours during low season. Just when "low season" is can be a topic of debate. To be safe, assume it's anything that isn't high season, which everyone seems to agree is mid-November through April. In fact, assume all hours of operation are more suggestions than fact. The secret to enjoying Vieques is to chill out and let things unfold in their own way and time.

SIGHTS

★ El Fortín Conde de Mirasol

Built between 1845 and 1855, **El Fortín Conde de Mirasol** was the last fort built by the Spanish in the New World. Never attacked or used in battle, it originally housed Spanish troops and later became a jail and execution site. Among those incarcerated here were fugitive slaves from local sugar plantations and political prisoners who sought Puerto Rico's independence from Spain. Later it was used as a municipal jail until the 1940s, when it was closed and fell into disrepair. In 1989 the Institute of Puerto Rico began restoration of the fort, which still has its original brick floors, exterior walls, and hardwood beams.

Today the fort is home to the **Vieques Museum of Art and History** (Fort Count Mirasol, Carr. 989, Isabel Segunda, 787/741-1717, www.enchanted-isle.com/elfortin/index.htm, Wed.-Sun. 10am-4pm, free). It houses

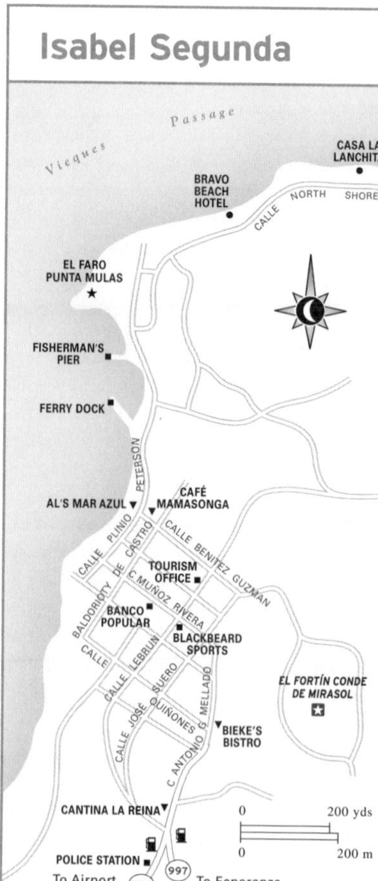

the Hombre de Puerto Ferro, the 4,000-year-old remains of a man whose body was discovered in an archaeological site near Esperanza. Other exhibits are dedicated to the island's indigenous people, its historic sugarcane industry, and local artists. It also contains the Vieques Historic Archives.

Often referred to as Vieques Stonehenge, the archaeological site of Hombre de Puerto Ferro is on the south side of the island off Carretera 997. About a quarter-mile east of the entrance to Sun Bay, turn inland onto a dirt road that takes you to the fenced-off site. Giant boulders mark the spot where the remains were excavated in 1990. Some believe the boulders were placed around the grave; others say it's a natural phenomenon.

★ Mosquito Bay

Mosquito Bay (off Carr. 997, near Esperanza, 787/741-0800) is a naturally occurring bioluminescent bay that attracts visitors to Vieques from around the world who paddle kayaks into the water at night to observe the bay's electric glow. Several outfitters in Vieques provide night excursions on kayaks or an electric pontoon boat for an up-close experience with the phenomenon. For best results, plan your trip during a new moon, when the bay glows brightest.

El Faro Punta Mulas

Built in the late 1800s, **El Faro Punta Mulas** (Calle Plinio Peterson, north of Isabel Segunda, 787/741-3141) looks less like a lighthouse and more like a modest, rectangular government building with a large light on top of it. It's still operational today but visitors can't enter the lighthouse.

Vieques Conservation and Historical Trust

Tucked between the bars and restaurants across from the *malecón* in Esperanza, **Vieques Conservation and Historical Trust** (138 Calle Flamboyan, Esperanza, 787/741-8850, www.vcht.org, daily 9am-5pm, free but donations accepted) is a small institution with a big mission to help protect and preserve the island's natural habitat. It has been involved in a research project with the Scripps Institute of Oceanography in San Diego, California on the effect of light pollution on Mosquito Bay. It also runs a children's summer camp and leads tours to the Sugar Mill Ruins. Stop in to take a look at the aquariums containing local sea creatures or pick up some information on the island.

Refugio Nacional de Vida Silvestre de Vieques/ National Wildlife Refuge

What was once the site of the U.S. Navy's

The Electric-Blue Waters of Mosquito Bay

In 2013, Vieques' world-renown bioluminescent Mosquito Bay went dark. It was a shocking turn of events that set the entire tourism industry—which constitutes the *only* industry on the island—on edge. Theories about what caused it included global warming, shifting tides, silt run-off, and pollution. In early 2014, the National Guard arrived and cleared debris from 10 acres around the lagoon, and by the end of the year, the glow had begun to return. It was a chilling reminder of the importance of protecting this remarkable natural phenomenon.

So just what is it that makes the bioluminescent lagoon in Mosquito Bay glow?

The mangrove bay's rich nutrients and clean, warm water create the perfect environment for sustaining the zillions of microscopic organisms called dinoflagellates that wash into the bay during high tide and remain trapped there when the tide recedes. The single-celled creature is unique in several ways. For one, it contains properties similar to both plants and animals. But more notably, when it senses motion, it experiences a chemical reaction that creates a burst of light not unlike that of a firefly.

Puerto Rico is said to have as many as seven bays rich in dinoflagellates, although only three are commonly known: Phosphorescent Bay in La Parguera on the southwest coast of Puerto Rico, Laguna Grande in Fajardo on the east coast, and Mosquito Bay in Vieques. Mosquito Bay is touted as one of the most spectacular bioluminescent bays in the world because of its high concentration of dinoflagellates and the absence of pollution and ambient light. Because darkness is required to see the glow, the best nights to tour the bay are when no moon is visible.

Before April 2007, when the Department of Natural Resources banned swimming in the island's bioluminescent bays, the highpoint of kayak trips into the bay came when visitors were permitted to jump in and frolic in the bathtub-warm water, where they could swim, turn flips, and create water angels in the electric-blue drink. Now visitors have to content themselves with watching the boat's blue wake and spotting brightly lit fish trails skim through the waters. It's not quite the same, but it's a small price to pay to help preserve the dinoflagellates. A visit to Mosquito Bay is still a magical experience unique to Puerto Rico.

Camp Garcia is now the **Refugio Nacional de Vida Silvestre de Vieques/National Wildlife Refuge** (Carr. 997, halfway between Isabel Segunda and Esperanza, 787/741-2138, www.fws.gov/caribbean/Refuges/Vieques, daily 6am-7:30pm May-Aug., daily 6am-6:30pm Sept.-Apr., free), the largest wildlife refuge in the Caribbean. Encompassing 60 percent of the island, the 17,770-acre refuge contains a variety of natural habitats, including beaches, mangrove forests, and subtropical dry forest. It is home to four endangered plants and 10 endangered animals, including the brown pelican and several species of sea turtles. Some of Vieques's finest primitive beaches are located in the refuge, including Playa Caracas/Red Beach, Playa Pata Prieta, Bahía de la Chiva/Blue Beach, and Playa Plata/Orchid Beach.

Sugar Mill Ruins

The **Sugar Mill Ruins** (off Carr. 201 near Playa Grande, west of Esperanza, 787/741-8850, free) are what is left of Playa Grande Mill, one of four sugar mills that operated in Vieques beginning in the 1830s. It was closed in the early 1940s when the Navy arrived, and much of what was left has begun to be reclaimed by Mother Nature, but there are still about a half-dozen buildings remaining. Long pants, hiking shoes, and bug spray are recommended. Much of the site is thick with vegetation. Look for the homemade sign marking the site.

SPORT AND RECREATION

Beaches

Aside from Mosquito Bay, the main reason to come to Vieques is to enjoy the staggering beauty of its miles of remote, pristine beaches and clear, turquoise waters. Each beach has its own unique characteristics—some are calm and shallow, others have big crashing waves, and still others offer spectacular snorkeling. Several are accessible only from dirt trails, off road or by foot, so bring sturdy shoes. And don't forget the bug spray.

Playa Negra is a black-sand beach containing minute particles of lava, a reminder of the island's volcanic origins millions of years ago. To get there from the *malecón* in Esperanza, go west on Carretera 996 and turn left on Carretera 201. When you reach the sign for Gallery Galleon, pull off the road and park. Look for the bridge in the road and hike down into the dry creek bed beneath it. Follow the creek bed through a thickly wooded forest to the ocean.

Playa Grande is a long, thin strip of beach that curves around the southwestern tip of the island and is a great spot for walking and hunting for shells. Go when it's breezy because it can be buggy with sand fleas. It's located west of Esperanza off Carretera 201.

Green Beach is on Punta Arenas at the farthest most southwestern tip of the island, and it features a shallow reef, making it ideal for snorkeling. Look for "flamingo tongues," a brightly colored sea snail that lives here. Nearby is Kiani Lagoon, a mangrove bay accessible by a wooden boardwalk that is rich with starfish. Green Beach is best visited early in the day or when it's breezy because it can be buggy with sand fleas. To access it take Carretera 200 as far west as possible, then follow the dirt road to the end. Look for the ancient ceiba tree with the massive trunk along the way.

Wilderness Refuge beaches are small, remote beaches tucked into the island's south central coastline, where the U.S. Navy's Camp Garcia was once located. From the entrance to the Refugio Nacional de Vida Silvestre de Vieques, located on Carretera 997 halfway between Isabel Segunda and Esperanza, there are four main wilderness beaches, and all of them are extraordinary.

Each one is a crescent of white, powdery sand, lapped by pale turquoise waters and rimmed with thick, lush vegetation. Measuring their distance from the entrance, they are **Playa Caracas/Red Beach** (2.4 miles), **Playa Pata Prieta** (2.7 miles), **Bahía de la Chiva/Blue Beach** (3 miles), and **Playa Plata/Orchid Beach** (4.4 miles). Note that the refuge closes at 6:30pm, except May-August when it closes

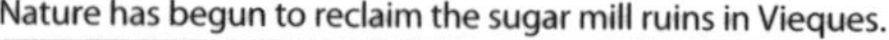
Nature has begun to reclaim the sugar mill ruins in Vieques.

at 7:30pm. No camping, fires, or alcohol are permitted.

Esperanza Beach is a fairly unremarkable beach along Esperanza's strip of restaurants and guesthouses. But it's within walking distance if you're staying in town and offers excellent snorkeling, especially around Cayo Afuera, a tiny islet just offshore.

A note of caution: Although violent crime is uncommon in Vieques, the island has a petty theft problem, which can be avoided if you use caution. Be vigilant around beaches with bushes where culprits may hide. Never take anything of value to the beach, including digital cameras or personal ID. If someone can't watch your things while you swim, bring a "dry bag," available at dive shops, to contain a car key and a photocopy of your driver's license. Don't leave anything inside your car and be sure to roll all your windows down and open the glove box so it's apparent nothing is inside.

★ BALNEARIO SUN BAY

The island's best beaches are on the southern coast. The most spectacular is the long white crescent and calm waters of **Balneario Sun Bay** (Sombé) (Carr. 997, east of Esperanza, 787/741-8198, Wed.-Sun. 8:30am-5pm, $2-5). It's the only publicly maintained beach in Vieques. Surrounded by a tall cyclone fence, it has plenty of modern, fairly clean facilities, including bathrooms, showers, changing rooms, a snack bar, and guards. Camping (787/741-8198) is permitted for $10 a day; reservations are required. Adding to the charm of the place is the herd of horses that grazes here.

The Balneario Sun Bay complex also encompasses two smaller, more secluded beaches farther eastward along a sandy road. The first one you'll encounter is **Media Luna,** a protective cove where the water is shallow. Farther eastward is **Navio Beach,** which sometimes has large waves and is popular with gay beachgoers.

Mosquito Bay Tours

Any trip to Vieques would be incomplete without a trip to the bioluminescent Mosquito Bay—unless, of course, you visit during a full moon, when the ambient light diminishes the visibility of the bioluminescent organisms that light up the water.

Island Adventures Bio-Bay Eco Tours (787/741-0720, www.biobay.com, $45) operates a tour of the bay on an electric pontoon boat that tools around the electric-blue water. Pick-up is provided along Calle Flamboyan in

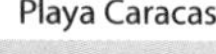

Playa Caracas

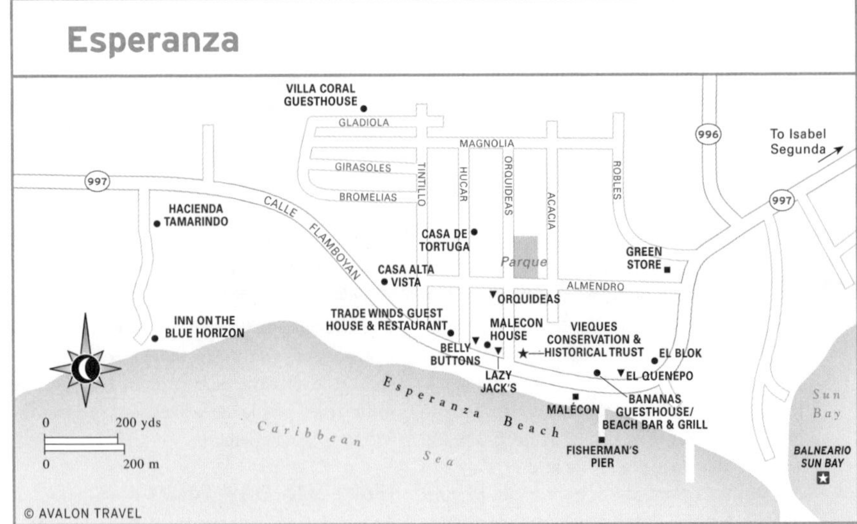

Esperanza. Unfortunately, guides are hit and miss. Some are chatty and informative, others barely acknowledge their guests.

If you want a more up-close and personal tour of the bay, **Blue Caribe Kayaks** (149 Calle Flamboyan, Esperanza, 787/741-2522) provides kayak tours of Mosquito Bay for $30 per person. Kayak rentals are also available for $10-15 per hour, $25-35 for four hours, and $45-55 all day. Snorkel-equipment rentals are also available.

Abe's Snorkeling & Bio-Bay Tours (787/741-2134 or 787/436-2686, www.abessnorkeling.com, reservations required, $45-125) offers a variety of kayak, bio-bay, snorkeling, and beach tours.

Snorkel, Dive, and Kayak

The best diving in Vieques can be found along the fringe reefs on the southern side of the island. **Vieques Island Powercat** (787/980-9978, www.viequesislandpowercat.com) offers half-day ($900) and full-day ($1,100) charters aboard a 47-foot power Catamaran for up to six people. Meals, beverages, and gear for snorkeling, kayaking, and paddleboarding are provided. Sunset cruises ($900) are also available.

Combine a day of sailing and snorkeling with **Sail Vieques** (787/508-7245, billwillo@yahoo.com) in Isabel Segunda. A half-day trip with snorkeling is $50, and a daylong trip to the southern tip of the Bermuda Triangle with snorkeling is $110. Captain Bill also offers a two-hour sunset cruise for $30.

Vieques Adventure Company (69 Calle Orquideas, Esperanza, 787/692-9162, www.bikevieques.com) offers kayak rentals ($45) and tours, as well as individual kayak fishing tours ($150).

Abe's Snorkeling & Bio-Bay Tours (787/741-2134 or 787/436-2686, www.abessnorkeling.com, reservations required) offers a variety of kayak tours, ideal for exploring beaches, mangrove bays, the bio-bay, or undersea life. The Cayo Afuera kayak and snorkel tour is $35 adults, $17.50 children. A Mosquito Pier snorkeling excursion designed for beginners costs $30 adults, $15 children. Custom tours are available.

Fun Brothers Hut (grass hut on the *malecón* across from El Quenepo, 787/435-9372, www.funbrothers-vieques.com) rents scooters, Jet Skis, and snorkel equipment. Take a guided kayak and snorkeling tour, with or without water scooters, or charter a

21-foot boat and captain for a custom outing to fish, ski, snorkel, wakeboard, or sightsee. Two-passenger scooters rent for $50 a day. Jet Skis and Waverunners are $60 for a half hour, $100 for an hour. Snorkel gear rents for $10 a day. A guided kayak and snorkel tour costs $35, or $50 with water scooter. Boat charters are $400 half day, $750 full day.

Blackbeard Sports (101 Calle Muñoz Rivera, Isabel Segunda, 787/741-1892, www.blackbeardsports.com, Mon.-Tues. 8am-5pm, Wed. 8am-5:30pm, Thurs.-Fri. 8am-5pm, Sat. 8am-4:30pm, Sun. 9am-3pm) is the place to go to buy or rent mountain bikes or gear for snorkeling, diving, camping, and kayaking. You can also pick up all your needs for the beach. Kayak tours cost $75.

Paddleboarding

The stand-up paddleboard is a great way to explore the island. At **Vieques Paddleboarding** (787/366-5202, www.viequespaddleboarding.com), the four-hour downwind tour ($85) travels 2-4 miles, depending on wind conditions, along the north and south shores. Or take a three-hour tour ($65) across the bay, through a mangrove forest, ending at a beach with a snorkel. Kids 11 and younger can ride with adults for $20.

Fishing

Go inshore fishing for kingfish, amberjack, barracuda, pompano, and tarpon on a 21-foot Ranger bay boat with Captain Franco Gonzalez of **Caribbean Fly Fishing** (61 Calle Orquideas, Esperanza, 787/741-1337 or 787/450-3744, www.caribbeanflyfishingco.com, $375 half day, $650 full day, including gear and tackle, two-person maximum).

Fun Brothers Hut (grass hut on the *malecón* across from El Quenepo, 787/435-9372, www.funbrothers-vieques.com) charters a 21-foot boat and captain for custom outings to fish, ski, snorkel, wakeboard, or sightsee ($400 half day, $750 full day).

Horseback Riding

Explore the island atop a locally bred Paso Fino horse with **Esperanza Riding Company** (787/435-0073, www.esperanzaridingcompany.com, cash only, reservations required). Two-hour guided tours through hills, meadows, riverbeds, and beaches cost $80. A private guided tour is $110. Children 7 and younger can take a 20-minute, hand-led pony trail ride for $15. Due to the small stature of the breed, there is a weight limit of 225 pounds for riders. Long pants and closed-toe shoes are recommended.

Taxi Horses (787/206-0122, www.taxihorses.com) offers guided trail rides in the mornings and afternoons for $75 for guided tours and $90 for private tours. American Express is not accepted.

Mountain Biking

Landlubbers looking to explore inland Vieques can get a guided, off-the-beaten-path mountain-bike tour with **Vieques Adventure Company** (69 Calle Orquideas, Esperanza, 787/692-9162, www.bikevieques.com). Bikes rent for $25 a day, two-day minimum, and include a helmet, a lock, and a trail repair kit. Half-day tours are $95. Combination bike-kayak-snorkel tours are also available.

ENTERTAINMENT AND EVENTS

Bars

If partying into the wee hours is your idea of the perfect vacation, Vieques may not be the place for you. There are no nightclubs, discos, or casinos on the island, and many of the restaurants close by 10pm. There are a couple of watering holes that stay open late, though. Salty sea dogs gravitate to the no-frills **Bananas Guesthouse, Beach Bar & Grill** (Calle Flamboyan, Esperanza, 787/741-8700, www.bananasguesthouse.com, daily 11am-10pm, bar stays open later). A sign behind the bar proudly proclaims: "This Is A Gin-u-wine Sleazy Waterfront Bar." Ask the bartender what the drink special is, and she's likely to respond: "A beer and a shot." But it also serves a potent rum punch made with three kinds of rum. There are eight small guest rooms on-site if you drink too much and can't drive home.

Apologies to Bananas, but the real "gin-u-wine sleazy waterfront bar" in Vieques is **Al's Mar Azul** (577 Calle Plinio Peterson, Isabel Segunda, 787/741-3400, Sun.-Thurs. 11am-1am, Fri.-Sat. 11am-2:30am). Hanging right over the water, this pleasant dive bar is cluttered with a random collection of junk that looks as if it has been sitting around the place for decades: old lifesaving rings, an inflated blowfish, paper lanterns, the grill off a jeep, a huge plastic turtle, a carved coconut head. There are some worn pool tables and video poker games if you're compelled to do something besides drink and chat up the locals who hang here. And if you really get bored, there's a dusty bookshelf filled with tattered paperbacks. The deck out back is the perfect place to watch the sunset or nurse a hangover with a spicy Bloody Mary.

Lazy Jack's Pub (61A Calle Orquideas, corner of Calle Flamboyan, Esperanza, 787/741-1447, www.lazyjacksvieques.com, daily noon-late, $8-14) serves food, but the reason to come is the well-stocked bar, the entertainment, and the convivial patrons. Beginning at 9pm, there's entertainment every night, ranging from live bands to DJs to karaoke to Wii competitions. The menu features pub fare like jalapeño poppers and chicken fingers, as well as a selection of hand-rolled thin-crust pizzas.

Duffy's Esperanza (on the *malecón*, 787/741-7600, daily 11am-11pm, bar closes 2:30am Fri.-Sat., $6-13) is primarily a great bar where you can down a few cold ones, rub elbows with the locals, and watch the ocean waves roll in. The bar serves artisan beers from Abita, Anchor, Goose Island, North Coast, and Old Harbour in San Juan, as well as a menu of creative cocktails, including the Viequense, a combination of vodka, passion fruit liqueur, orange juice, and cranberry juice. The menu features pub fare such as nachos, burritos, burgers, and an Italian hoagie. For something more substantial, try the Caribbean crab cakes or curry chicken *pastelillos.* Brunch is served 10am-2pm Sunday and features a Bloody Mary bar.

No pubcrawl in Esperanza is complete without a stop at **La Nasa** (Calle Flamboyan, Esperanza, daily noon-late, $1-6, cash only), a rustic, seaside, open-air Latin dance spot popular with locals, young and old. Loud, dark, crowded, and a whole lot of fun, come to watch the dancers in action or join in. The

Al's Mar Azul

music is recorded, but nobody cares. A small menu of local fritters is served, but most people just drink the $1.50 Medalla beers or $1 *chichaitos,* a shot made of rum and anise.

If you're looking for something upscale and chic, **Living Room Bar** (W Retreat & Spa, Carr. 200, km 3.2, 787/741-4100, www.wvieques.com) is a cool, sleek oceanfront lounge serving creative cocktails and tapas.

Cockfights

If there is such a thing as politically correct cockfighting, it exists in Vieques, where the birds do not fight until death. Winners are proclaimed by judges before the birds are seriously harmed. Fights are held at **Gallera Puerto Real** (Carr. 200, about three miles west of Isabel Segunda, no telephone), typically on Friday nights and Sunday afternoons, although the schedule changes. Admission is $10 for men; women are admitted for free. Food and alcohol are served.

Festivals and Events

There are two major festivals in Vieques. The biggest one is **Fiestas Patronales de Nuestra Señora del Carmen** (787/741-5000), which is held on the plaza of Isabel Segunda Wednesday-Sunday during the third weekend of July. Attractions include parades, religious processions, a small carnival, and lots of live Latin music and dancing. Entertainment usually starts around 9pm and lasts until the wee hours of the morning. Festivities are fueled by *bili,* a traditional beverage made from a local fruit called *quenepa* mixed with white rum, cinnamon, and sugar.

The other big event is the **Cultural Festival** (787/741-1717), sponsored by the Institute of Puerto Rican Culture at El Fortín Conde de Mirasol in Isabel Segunda after Easter. Festivities include folk music and dance performances, a craft fair, and a book fair.

SHOPPING

Arts and Crafts

At first glance you might think **Vieques Flower and Gifts** (134 Calle Flamboyan, Esperanza, 787/741-4197, daily 9am-6pm Nov.-May, daily 10am-5pm summer) is another souvenir shop selling T-shirts and tchotchkes, but you'll also find artisan-made *vejigante* masks and pottery made by local artists.

Vibrant original paintings and prints on canvas of tropical flowers, fish, palm trees, and jungle scenes by local artist Siddhia

Dance into the wee hours at La Nasa in Esperanza, Vieques.

Hutchinson can be found at **Siddhia Hutchinson Fine Art Design Studio and Gallery** (Carmen Hotel, Calle Muñoz Rivera, 787/741-1343, http://siddhiahutchinsongallery.com, Mon.-Sat. 10am-4pm). The artwork has also been tastefully reproduced on ceramics, dinnerware, rugs, and pillows.

Gallery Galleon (Carr. 201, west of Esperanza, south of Carr. 197, 787/741-3078, www.gallerygalleon.com, Tues.-Sun. 11am-5pm) is a large and beautiful fine-art gallery that hosts changing exhibitions. Local and regional artists exhibit work in a variety of mediums—from photography and painting to sculpture and metalwork. The gallery also hosts lively artist receptions and dance performances.

Clothing and Jewelry

For your hip, floaty, natural fiber tropical-wear needs, **Funky Beehive** (359 Calle Antonia G. Mellado, Isabel Segunda, 787/741-3192, Mon.-Sat. 10am-4pm) has you covered. Also on-hand are lots of artisan-made jewelry and gift items, such as candles, cards, and locally made soaps.

Vieques Yacht Club Shopping Court (Calle Orquideas, Esperanza, 787/741-1447, daily noon-5pm) boasts a quartet of tiny shops situated around a gravel courtyard. A variety of vendors sell jewelry, handbags, resort wear, shoes, housewares, books, cigars, and more.

Diva's Closet (134 Calle Flamboyan, Esperanza, 787/741-7595, daily 10am-5pm) is the place to go for funky, chunky jewelry, floral print bathing suits, and a variety of resort wear.

Kim's Cabin Clothing Boutique and Gifts (136 Calle Flamboyan, Esperanza, 787/741-3145, daily 9:30am-5pm) sells Haitian metal art, sea-glass earrings, and cotton beach wear.

Sol Creation (370 Calle Antonio G. Mellado, Isabel Segunda, 787/741-1694 or 808/280-6223, www.solcreationclothing.com, Mon.-Sat. 10:30am-4:30pm) is a clothing boutique specializing in floaty, bohemian styles in silk and cotton, plus jewelry, bags, and more.

Markets

Buen Provecho (353 Calle Antonio G. Mellado, Isabel Segunda, 787/529-7316, Tues.-Sat. 10am-6pm) is a gourmet market selling organic goods, fresh produce, and specialty foods, including artisan cheeses and live lobsters. **The Green Store/La Tienda Verde** (corner of Calle Flamboyan/Carr. 996 and Calle Robles, 787/741-8711, daily 9am-9pm) is a small market selling everything you need to set up house for a week—coffee, toilet paper, bug spray, beer, etc.

ACCOMMODATIONS

$50-100

Villa Coral Guesthouse (485 Calle Gladiolas, Esperanza, 787/741-1967, www.villacoralguesthouse.com, $80-85 s/d, $160-185 two-bedroom apartment) is a clean, comfortable six-room guesthouse in a residential neighborhood several blocks from the *malecón*. Rooms come with a queen bed, window air-conditioning unit, ceiling fan, a mini-refrigerator, and a coffeepot—but alas, no coffee. There's a covered porch with wireless Internet, board games, magazines, and a microwave, plus a rooftop terrace with a view of the ocean. The owners also have a one-bedroom cottage with a full kitchen and satellite TV a couple blocks away that rents for $795-895 a week.

Trade Winds Guest House and Restaurant (Calle Flamboyan, Esperanza, 787/741-8666, www.tradewindsvieques.com, $80-115 s/d, $220 apartment, $260 two bedroom house, plus tax) is a very simple, basic guesthouse conveniently situated in the middle of Esperanza and across the street from the *malécon* (sea walk). The 10 rooms are small, windowless, and spartan, but they're clean and have firm mattresses. Rooms come with mini refrigerators, wireless Internet, and continental breakfast. There's no TV or telephone, but some rooms have air-conditioning. The rooms open onto a scrappy courtyard with plastic patio furniture, and there's a decent restaurant and bar upstairs. The oceanfront apartment and two-bedroom house located nearby come with free wireless Internet, continental breakfast, and maid service.

Just want a cheap place to crash? If you don't plan to spend much time in your room, **Bananas Guesthouse, Beach Bar & Grill** (Calle Flamboyan, Esperanza, 787/741-8700, www.bananasguesthouse.com, $70-90 s/d, $100 d with private terrace, plus tax) may meet your needs. In the back of the popular Bananas bar and restaurant, this barebones guesthouse has eight small, rustic, dimly lit rooms with deck flooring. There's no TV or telephone, but some rooms have air-conditioning, screened porches, and mini-refrigerators.

$100-150

★ **Casa de Tortuga** (6 Calle Hucar, Esperanza, 787/741-2852, www.casadetortuga.com, $85 s/d casitas, $170-255 apartments with two or three bedrooms) is a welcome addition to the island. Located just a block from the *malecón* in Esperanza, this clean, modest guesthouse has eight units. Amenities include a small swimming pool, multiple patios, barbecue grills, and beach gear. Each room has a kitchenette or full kitchen, air-conditioning, and free wireless Internet. Some rooms have flat-screen TVs and satellite service.

It fell onto hard times for a while, but in 2015 new management took over **Casa Alta Vista** (297 Calle Flamboyan, Esperanza, 787/741-3296, www.casaaltavista.net, $80 s, $120 d, $140-160 for four people, plus tax), a small, 10-room guesthouse. There's no TV, telephone, or pool, but the air-conditioning and mini-refrigerator keep things cool. A rooftop sundeck offers a 360-degree view of the island, three-quarters of it ocean. If it's available, ask for room 12—it has the best view of the ocean and hillsides. Registration is in the small market on the first floor. Scooter, bicycle, snorkeling gear, beach chair, umbrella, and cooler rentals are available on-site. There is also a one-bedroom apartment, and some rooms are wheelchair-accessible.

For a unique, rustic experience, **La Finca Caribe** (Carr. 995, km 2.2, 787/741-0495, www.lafinca.com, rooms $97-135, casitas $125-205, plus tax) is a three-acre farm sitting in the island's interior, featuring stripped-down casitas with kitchenettes and private outdoor showers, and dorm-style rooms that sleep as many as six people in the main villa. Amenities include a salt-water pool, an eclectic lending library, fruit trees, and hammocks. There is no air-conditioning or TVs.

$150-250

Luxury has many different definitions, and Vieques seems to have a unique hotel to match each one. The ultramodern boutique hotel **Bravo Beach Hotel** (1 N. Shore Rd., Isabel Segunda, 787/741-1128, www.bravobeachhotel.com, $110-125 s/d economy, $200-225 s/d ocean view, $380 two-bedroom, two-bath apartment with private terrace, plus tax; no children under 18 permitted; two-night minimum stay) is a study in glamorous minimalism. Nine rooms and a two-bedroom villa are located in a cluster of small bungalows painted pastel shades of green, blue, and yellow. Each room is different, but the spacious interiors all feature stark white walls that create a dramatic contrast to the dark mahogany platform beds and modular furnishings made of wood and glass. Some rooms have ocean-view balconies and floor-to-ceiling windows. One room has 180-degree windows and a king-size canopy bed. Each room has satellite TV, air-conditioning, a mini-refrigerator, wireless Internet, a DVD player, and a PlayStation. Although it's on the ocean, the hotel doesn't have a swimmable beach. Instead there are two swimming pools, one ocean side.

Perched on an inland hillside is **Crow's Nest Inn** (Carr. 201, km 1.1, Isabel Segunda, 787/741-0033 or 877/276-9763, www.crowsnestvieques.com, $152 s/d, $283 two-bedroom terrace suite, $261 two connecting rooms, plus tax, includes continental breakfast). The Spanish hacienda-style inn has 16 modern rooms, all with air-conditioning, TV, and a kitchen or kitchenette.

There's something positively Mediterranean about the exterior appearance of **Casa La Lanchita** (374 N. Shore Rd., Isabel Segunda, 787/741-8449 or 800/774-4717, www.viequeslalanchita.com, $125-195, four-night minimum stay). The bright white four-story structure with archways and balustrades is built right on the sandy beach of a brilliant blue sea and is surrounded by flowering bougainvillea. Despite the posh exterior, the rooms are modestly appointed with budget rattan and metal furnishings, but each room has a private terrace and full-size kitchen.

★ **Malecón House** (105 Calle Flamboyan, Esperanza, 787/741-0663, www.maleconhouse.com, $175-265 s/d, $265 t/q, plus tax; two-night minimum required) is a modern two-story guesthouse overlooking the *malecón*. It was built in 2010 and has brought a new level of sophistication to the area. Rooms come with air-conditioning and ceiling fans; some rooms have mini refrigerators and balconies. Amenities include a small pool, rooftop deck, wireless Internet in common areas, and continental breakfast.

Victorian elegance is the theme at **Hacienda Tamarindo** (Calle Flamboyan, just west of Esperanza, 787/741-8525, www.haciendatamarindo.com, $185-255 s, $199-265 d, $250-310 suites, $375 two-bedroom villa, plus tax and service charge). Built around a 200-year-old tamarind tree that's rooted in the lobby and shades the second-floor breakfast room, this beautifully appointed hotel is furnished in a tasteful combination of antique Caribbean and Victorian styles. Folk art, wall murals, and vintage circus posters provide playful touches. There are 13 rooms and three suites. Each one is different, but they all contain basket-weave furnishings, brightly colored bedspreads, and air-conditioning. Rooms have neither TVs nor telephones, but each one comes with folding chairs, oversize towels, and coolers for the beach or pool. The hotel doesn't have a restaurant per se, but it does serve a free breakfast, and a box lunch can be prepared if requested the night before. There's a 24-hour honor bar and a swimming pool. No guests under age 15 are permitted during high season.

A romantic getaway doesn't get any more lovely or secluded than ★ **Inn on the Blue Horizon** (Calle Flamboyan, west of Esperanza, 787/741-3318 or 787/741-0527, www.innonthebluehorizon.com, $240-390 s/d, plus tax and service fee; no children 16 or younger). The small, 10-room inn perched on a cliff overlooking the ocean hosts many weddings and is geared primarily toward couples. Rooms are exquisitely furnished with poster beds, antiques, and original artwork. Amenities include a small gym, pool, lighted tennis courts, and an inviting pavilion bar. Rooms have air-conditioning but no TV or telephone. **Carambola** restaurant serves upscale Caribbean fusion cuisine, and the **Blue Moon Bar and Grill** serves breakfast and lunch in a lovely, open-air, pavilion-style restaurant overlooking the ocean.

Avant-garde architecture in a thickly wooded setting distinguishes the most unusual hotel in Puerto Rico, **The Hix House** (Carr. 995, km 1.6, 787/741-2302, www.hixislandhouse.com, $175-315 s/d, $450 two-bedroom suite, plus tax and service charge). Five unpainted concrete buildings house 16 "lofts," many with open sides, outdoor showers, and ocean views. Designed by architect John Hix to have as little impact on its 13 acres as possible, the property uses solar energy and recycles used water to replenish the vegetation. There's no TV or telephone, but the linens are Frette, the pool is spectacular, and each morning the kitchen is stocked with juices, cereal, breads, and coffee. Yoga classes are conducted in the pavilion, and in-room or garden massages are available. New to the property is Casa Solaris, an all-solar guesthouse with six lofts.

Over $250

In 2014, ★ **El Blok** (Calle Flamboyan, Esperanza, www.elblok.com, s/d $330-410 plus tax; no children under 16 permitted), a new 22-room luxury boutique hotel, opened and brought a fresh, retro-modern style of glamour to the funky seaside strip in Esperanza. Featuring a stunning architectural design by Fuster+Architects, the four-story boasts a striking curved shape and lacy concrete facade that recalls the mid-century modern design of some of San Juan's grand hotels, such as Caribe Hilton. The rooms are designed in a minimalist style featuring industrial-chic plaster walls and tile floors. All rooms have forest or ocean views, terraces, flat-screen TVs, and Wi-Fi. There's a rooftop pool and a lobby bar.

An anomaly in every way, **W Retreat & Spa** (Carr 200, km 3.2, 787/741-4100, www.wvieques.com, $408-1,310 s/d, plus resort fee and taxes) is a mega-resort that brings chic style and plush luxury to the rustic environs of Vieques. Located on a low cliff right on the beach, the resort has 156 accommodations ranging from standard rooms with garden views to high design "retreats" with direct access to the ocean. Amenities include chef Alain Ducasse's MiX on the Beach plus two other restaurants, a lounge, a spa, tennis courts, a fitness room, a business center, and infinity pool. Rooms come with air-conditioning, flat-screen TVs, coffeemakers, hair dryers, and balconies.

FOOD

Puerto Rican

La Gran Parada (Corner of Carr. 200 and Carr. 201, Isabel Segunda, 787/529-3272, Mon.-Fri. 7am-9pm, Sat.-Sun. 9am-9pm, $11-30 cash only) is a casual, open-air roadside spot serving simple, delicious, traditional cuisine, including *mofongo, arepas,* and fried snapper.

For breakfast sandwiches, *mofongo,* rice and beans, and other traditional Puerto Rican fare, ★ **El Resuelve** (Carr. 997, km 1, Isabel Segunda, 787/741-1427, Thurs.-Sat. 9am-9pm, Sun. 9am-6pm, $2-12, cash only) serves it fresh and cheap in a small, modest spot with patio dining in a residential neighborhood. Stop by and pick up a bag of empanadas for $2 apiece on your way to the beach.

Restaurante Bili (144 Calle Flamboyan, 787/741-1382 or 787/402-0357, http://bilirestaurant.com, daily 11am-11pm, lunch $8-16, dinner $10-29) is a veteran restaurant that must be doing something right because it has been in business for many years. I heartily recommend the fresh and tasty mojitos; however, meal service can be slow to nonexistent.

Bieke's Bistro (787/741-6381, 34001 Calle Antonio Mellado, Isabel Segunda, www.biekesbistro.com, Tues.-Sat. 10:30am-9:30pm, $18-29) serves a slightly upscale version of *criolla* cuisine, featuring *churrasco, mofongo,* fried snapper, and lobster tail.

Nueva Criolla

★ **El Quenepo** (148 Calle Flamboyan, Esperanza, 787/741-1215, reservations@elquenepovieques.com, Wed.-Sun. 5:30pm-9:30pm June-Aug., Tues.-Sun. 5:30pm-10pm Thanksgiving-May, closed Sept. to mid-Nov., $20-32, no American Express) is hands-down the finest restaurant in Vieques. Owner-chef Scott Cole is creating sublime new interpretations of *criolla* cuisine, and his wife Kate, who runs the front of the house, knows how to provide the kind of service diners expect from a top-dollar establishment. Together they have created a casually elegant oasis of fine dining. Open to the sea on one side, the interior is hung with long white sheers, and wall sconces provide just enough lighting to make everyone look more attractive than they really are. Soft jazz noodles in the background. The effect is instantly calming. And then there is the food. The menu includes calabaza gnocchi pan-seared in brown butter and served with toasted pumpkin seeds, goat cheese, and pomegranate molasses; jasmine rice-crusted calamari, Peking duck pad Thai; and breadfruit *mofongo* stuffed with lobster. And that's just the regular menu. There are usually several daily specials to choose from as well.

James Beard Award nominee (and *Food & Wine* magazine's Best New Chef of 2013) José Enrique is the owner of ★ **El Blok Vieques Restaurant** (158 Calle Flamboyan, Esperanza, 787/741-6020, www.elblok.com, Sun.-Wed. 6pm-10pm, Thurs.-Sat. 6pm-10:30pm, $31-50), located on the first floor of El Blok hotel. The industrial-chic dining room provides a sophisticated backdrop to Enrique's fresh, simple translations of traditional dishes that pop with flavor. The constantly changing menu offers small plates and full entrées; recent offerings include lobster ceviche, lobster sausage, and passion fruit bread pudding. There are lots of vegetarian options, too.

At W Retreat & Spa, **Sorcé** (Carr. 200, km 3.2, 787/741-7022, www.sorcevieques.com, daily 7am-11am, 1pm-3pm, and 6pm-10pm, $22-38) serves inspired interpretations of local dishes with locally sourced produce, including gazpacho *de bacalao,* grilled tenderloin, lobster macaroni, and vegetarian *pastelón.*

Breakfast

You can't miss **Belly Buttons** (62 Calle Flamboyan, Esperanza, 787/741-3336, daily 7:30am-2pm, Thurs. and Sun. 5pm-9pm, breakfast $4-8, lunch $6-9); just look for two tin-roofed shacks trimmed in neon green with brightly colored picnic tables and umbrellas out front. That's the place to go for a cheap lunch or breakfast. In addition to typical breakfast fare, check out the specials. If you're lucky, the thick, tasty banana pancakes will be on the menu. Lunch includes burgers, hot wings, fish and chips, and tuna salad. Thursday night is Mexican night and Sunday night is rib night.

American

Tucked behind Lazy Jack's on the *malecón,* **Orquideas** (61 Calle Orquideas, Esperanza, 787/741-1864 or 337/739-2311, www.orquideasvqs.com, daily 6pm-midnight, Thanksgiving-Easter, $8-15) is a quaint little open-air spot draped dramatically with curtains that sway in the breeze. The menu specializes in tapas and small plates, including baby octopus salad and mahi ceviche, as well as sushi and a selection of creative confections for dessert, such as chocolate cherry ganache and mojito fried ice cream. The bar excels at classic cocktails. Reservations are accepted.

Bananas Guesthouse, Beach Bar & Grill (Calle Flamboyan, Esperanza, 787/741-8700, www.bananasguesthouse.com, daily 11am-10pm, bar stays open later, $5-17) is a casual drinking hole serving mostly American pub fare, including burgers, wings, and hot dogs, as well as jerk chicken, ribs, and grilled fish. There are eight small guest rooms in the back.

Once a breakfast spot, **Café Mamasonga** (566 German Rieckehoff, Isabel Segunda, 787/741-0103, Wed.-Mon. 11am-9pm, $9-16)

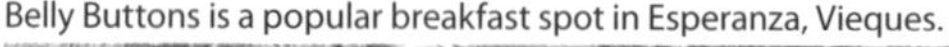
Belly Buttons is a popular breakfast spot in Esperanza, Vieques.

now just serves lunch, dinner, and cocktails, but there's still a fried egg and bacon sandwich on the menu that hits the spot. Offerings run the gamut from coconut shrimp with orange marmalade and fettucine Alfredo to seafood stew and crab cakes, but burgers, quesadillas, and other simple fare are your best bests. Be sure to sit on the deck upstairs and check out the massive iguanas that sleep on the rails.

International

Meson del Pilar (Carr. 200, 787/556-3271, Thurs.-Sun. 5pm-10pm, $8-20) serves traditional Spanish tapas, including Serrano ham, spicy potatoes, and shrimp in brandy sauce. On Sunday only, enjoy paella and sangria.

Coqui Fire is the name of a popular, locally made hot sauce found in gift shops across the island. Now you can enjoy the sauce prepared in meals by its creator at his restaurant **Coqui Fire Café** (421 Calle Carlos Lebrum, Isabel Segunda, 787/741-0401, www.coquifire.com, Mon.-Fri. 5pm-9pm, $8-30). Located in a small yellow house, the casual eatery serves Caribbean-inspired Mexican cuisine. The golden margarita is highly recommended.

★ **Next Course** (Carr. 201, just north of Carr. 995, 787/741-1028, Fri.-Wed. 5:30pm-10pm, $20-40) is a romantic restaurant serving dishes inspired by international cuisines. Specialties include lobster tail and asparagus with risotto, crab salad, and ice cream sandwiches. The indoor dining room is nice, but the deck is the place you want to be to get the most from the ambience.

Decorated with vintage pictures of banditos and revolutionaries, **Cantina La Reina** (351 Calle Antonio G. Mellado, Isabel Segunda, 787/741-2700, www.cantina-lareina.com, Tues.-Sat. 5pm-10pm, Sun. brunch 11am-2pm, $13-20) serves typical Mexican fare with flair, including fish tacos, fajitas, burritos, and the catch of the day served with mango salsa. And the bar serves a long list of tequilas, as well as a variety of margaritas, specialty cocktails, sangria, and a short list of beers and wines. Reservations are accepted.

Steak and Seafood

★ **Tin Box** (Carr. 996 at Carr. 201, 787/741-7700, Tues.-Sat. 2pm-10pm, Sun. 11am-3pm, closed Sept.-Oct., $8-20) is an open-air spot also decked out in corrugated metal, but the best part is the deck out back overlooking the forest. The menu specializes in smoked ribs, a raw seafood bar, and an elaborate Sunday brunch featuring lobster Benedict and a build-your-own Bloody Mary bar. Save room for the

Barbecue is on the menu at Tin Box in Vieques.

chocolate bacon crème brûlée. Reservations are accepted.

Next door to Tin Box is ★ **Noche** (Carr. 996 at Carr. 201, 787/741-7700, Wed.-Sun. 5:30pm-10pm, closed Sept.-Oct., $20-30), an upscale fine-dining restaurant with a romantic, atmospheric deck, especially at night when the mood lighting kicks in. Specialties include scallop sashimi, lobster *mofongo,* filet mignon, and chocolate pot de crème. Be sure to ask the sommelier to recommend a wine from the restaurant's extensive selection. Reservations are accepted.

Carambola (Inn at the Blue Horizon, Calle Flamboyan, west of Esperanza, 787/741-3318, www.innonthebluehorizon.com, daily 8am-3pm and 5pm-10pm, $18-29, reservations recommended for dinner) serves Caribbean cuisine in an elegant setting overlooking the sea. Menu includes conch ceviche, grilled mahimahi with *amarillos* and chorizo salad, and whole fried snapper.

Trade Winds Restaurant (Calle Flamboyan, Esperanza, 787/741-8666, www.tradewindsvieques.com, Thurs.-Mon. 7:30am-2pm and 6pm-9:30pm, $14-34) is a casual open-air restaurant that overlooks the water and serves grilled fish, steak, lobster, pork loin, pasta, *mofongo,* and coconut curry. For dessert, try the piña colada bread pudding with warm rum sauce. There are 10 small guest rooms behind the restaurant.

French chef Alain Ducasse brings his impressive pedigree to **MiX on the Beach** (W Retreat & Spa, Carr. 200, km 3.2, 787/741-4100, www.wvieques.com/mix, daily 7:30am-11am and 6pm-10pm, $22-39), an elegant, ocean-side restaurant specializing in Caribbean cuisine. Breakfast includes short-rib hash served with poached egg and hollandaise sauce, and MiX Benedict, served with choice of crab or lobster and a spicy hollandaise. Dinner options include roasted lobster curry, salted cod, and pineapple tart.

TRANSPORTATION

Air

As almost anyone who's taken the ferry from Fajardo to Vieques will tell you, the best way to get to the island is by air. Several small airlines fly to Vieques from the main island, and the flights are fairly inexpensive and speedy.

In San Juan, flights can be arranged from Luis Muñoz Marín International Airport near Isla Verde or from the smaller Isla Grande Airport near Old San Juan. But the shortest, cheapest flight is from the newly opened José Aponte de la Torre Airport on the former Roosevelt Roads Naval Base in Ceiba on the east coast. Round-trip flights are about $125 from San Juan and $60 from Ceiba. Flights between Vieques and Culebra are about $70.

Vieques Air Link (787/534-4221, 787/534-4222, or 787/741-8331) offers flights to Vieques from San Juan International, Isla Grande, St. Croix, and Ceiba.

Seaborne Airlines (340/773-6442 or 866/359-8784, www.seaborneairlines.com) flies to Vieques from San Juan International, Isla Grande, St. Thomas, and St. Croix.

Air Flamenco (787/724-1818, 787/721-7332, 877/535-2636, www.airflamenco.net) offers flights from San Juan International and Ceiba. Charter flights are available.

Air Sunshine (787/741-7900 or 800/327-8900, www.airsunshine.com) has flights to Vieques from San Juan International.

Cape Air (787/741-7734 or 800/352-0714, www.capeair.net) offers flights to Vieques from San Juan International and St. Croix.

Ferry

The **Puerto Rico Port Authority** (in Vieques 787/741-4761 or 787/863-0705, or 800/981-2005, daily 8am-11am and 1pm-3pm) operates a ferry service between Vieques and Fajardo. But save yourself a headache—don't take the ferry. The operation has been plagued with scheduling irregularities and overcrowding due to ferries being out of commission for repairs.

Car rental agencies in Puerto Rico do not permit their automobiles to leave the main island. The best option is to leave your car in Fajardo and rent another car in Vieques. The trip takes about two hours. The fare is $4.50 per person round-trip, $26 for vehicles.

The ferry schedule is subject to change. For updates follow @PRFerryWatch on Twitter.

- **Fajardo to Vieques:** Monday-Friday 4am, 9am, 1pm, 4:45pm, 8:15pm; Saturday-Sunday 9am, 1pm, 4:45 pm, 8:15pm
- **Vieques to Fajardo:** Monday-Friday 6am, 6:30am, 11am, 3pm, 6:30pm; Saturday-Sunday 6:30am, 11am, 3pm, 6:30pm

Car

Unless you plan to park yourself at one of the island's full-service hotels and never leave it, you're going to need a rental car to get around, especially if you want to explore the island's remote beaches. There are now two taxi companies offering service, and *públicos* are a great way to get from the ferry or airport to your hotel, but beyond that, neither service is as reliable as the taxi service mainland Americans may be accustomed to.

If you do rent a car, book it well in advance of your arrival. They get snapped up quickly. Rental fees start around $80 per day, and penalties can be accrued if you return it with excessive sand inside, damp seats, or less gas in the tank than when you got it. Most vehicles are four-wheel drive because many of the beaches require off-roading to reach them. Blowouts are not unusual, so make sure your car has a full-size replacement tire and the tools necessary to change it. If you need assistance changing the tire, the rental-car agency may send someone to help, but again, it will cost you. The seatbelt law is enforced, as are speed limits, which are mostly 35 miles per hour, except in town and on beach roads, where it's 10-15 miles per hour.

There are only two gas stations on the island, and they're both on Carretera 200 in Isabel Segunda, just west of the plaza. Because gas is shipped from San Juan on weekdays only, gas shortages are not unusual, and sometimes gas stations close early on Sundays, since that's the day everyone goes to the beach, including the gas-station operators.

Car rental agencies include **Martineau Car Rental** (787/741-0078, 787/741-1666, airport office 787/741-0700, www.maritzas-carrental.co, $50-100 per day, scooters $50), **Vieques Car** (787/741-1037, http://viequescarrental.com), and **Steve's Car Rental** (787/741-8135, www.enchanted-isle.com/steves). Remember that horses roam freely on Vieques. Because many roads in Vieques are unlit, it's nearly impossible to see the horses in the dark, so take extra care when driving at night.

Público

Públicos typically can be found waiting for fares at the airport or ferry. They can also be called randomly throughout the day for pickup service, although some travelers report that they are not always reliable or timely. Fares are typically $5 in town and $8 to various sites and beaches on the island.

You can usually pick up a list of *público* operators at the airport or your hotel. Here is a partial list: **Lolo Felix** (787/485-5447), **Coqui Ayala** (787/741-3214 or 787/374-6820), **Fast Eddie** (787/741-0082), and **Angel** (787/484-8796).

For travelers seeking transportation from San Juan to Fajardo to catch the ferry to Vieques, **Travel with Rivera** (787/644-3091, http://enchanted-isle.com/rivera) operates 24-hour *público* service between Fajardo and the Luis Muñoz Marín International Airport in San Juan. Rates are $70 for up to four people, $80 up to six, $85 up to nine, and $12 per person for more than nine people. Reservations must be made at least 24 hours in advance.

Taxi

Vieques Taxi (787/741-8294) typically provides transportation until 10pm, but late-night service may be arranged in advance. Daytime taxi service is provided by **Ana** (787/313-0599) and **Rafael** (787/385-2318).

SERVICES

All of the services on Vieques are in Isabel Segunda. The **tourism office** (787/741-0800,

Mon.-Fri. 9am-4pm) is on the plaza in Casa Alcaldía (town hall). For the most comprehensive and up-to-date information, visit www.enchanted-isle.com and www.viequestravelguide.com.

To stay abreast of local goings-on, pick up a copy of ***Vieques Insider*** (787/435-3172, www.viequesinsider.com). It's available online and in print (in English and Spanish) quarterly in low season, and every two months during high season.

The island's only bank, with an ATM, is **Banco Popular** (115 Calle Muñoz Rivera, 787/741-2071). Nearby, on the same street, is the **post office** (787/741-3891). You'll find the **police station** (Carr. 200, km 0.2, 787/741-2020 or 787/741-2121) at the corner of Carretera 200 and Carretera 997, and the **fire department** (787/741-2111) can be reached by phone.

For health services, **Centro de Salud de Familia** (Carr. 997) is open Monday-Friday 7am-3:30pm, and the emergency room is open 24 hours. Serving visitors' pharmacy needs is **Farmacia San Antonio** (Calle Benitez Guzman across from Casa Alcaldía, 787/741-8397).

There is a self-serve laundry **Familia Ríos** (Calle Benítez Castaño, 787/438-1846, Sun.-Mon. and Wed.-Fri. 6am-7pm, Sat. 6am-5pm) on the island.

Culebra

As laid-back as Vieques is, it's practically Las Vegas compared to Culebra. Halfway between mainland Puerto Rico and St. Thomas, the tiny amoeba-shaped archipelago with 23 surrounding cays is just four miles by seven miles. The island is home to 3,000 residents and has one small community—**Dewey** (commonly called "Pueblo" or "Town")—on **Ensenada Honda harbor,** where the ferry docks.

Culebra has yet to be discovered by the tourism industry, but experienced divers know it as one of the best diving spots in the Caribbean. The clear, clean waters are practically untouched by people and their polluting by-products, thanks in part to the arid island's absence of rivers or streams. The result is superb underwater visibility and healthy, intact coral systems that support a wide variety of sea life.

In 1909, recognizing the island's vital role as a natural wildlife habitat, President Theodore Roosevelt proclaimed much of the island a National Wildlife Refuge, which today encompasses 1,568 acres. Nonetheless, in 1939, the U.S. Navy made Culebra its primary gunnery and bomb practice site and continued its operations here until 1975, when it turned its focus to Vieques.

The island is a combination of hilly terrain with dry subtropical forest and a highly irregular coastline punctuated by cliffs, mangrove forests, and spectacular sandy coral beaches. Because it is so sparsely inhabited, Culebra is home to many endangered species and is an important nesting site for birds and sea turtles. Playa Flamenco is celebrated as one of the best beaches in the United States. But there are many other smaller beaches to discover, some completely deserted much of the time.

Accommodations in Culebra are mostly small mom-and-pop guesthouses, some little more than spare bedrooms. The operations here are mostly self-serve. In fact, it's not unusual for visitors to have the run of the place when owners decide to head to the beach or bar to while away the day. But a handful of small luxury hotels and condo rental units service travelers who want more modern-day amenities. At the dozen or so restaurants, service typically moves at a snail's pace, and there are a couple of bars, but little real nightlife.

Because water is shipped from San Juan, shortages are not unusual, and pressure is

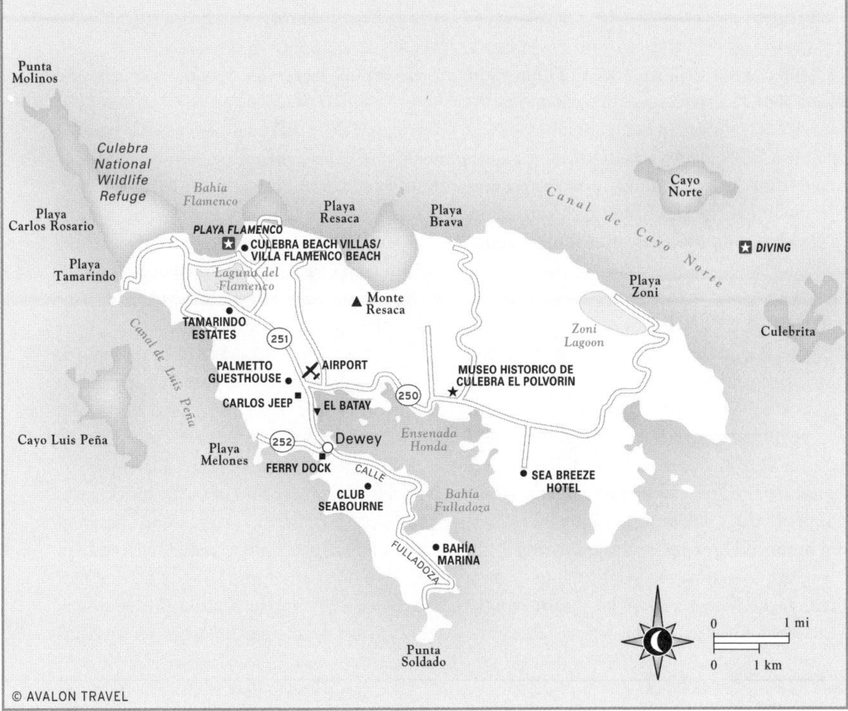

often low. Some smaller properties have limited hot water or none at all. Plumbing in general can be problematic—the standard practice is to discard toilet paper in the trash instead of flushing it. And alarm clocks are never necessary, because you're sure to be woken by one of the roosters that roam the island. An anomaly in the world, Culebra is virtually crime-free. Instead of petty theft, visitors need only brace themselves against the voracious mosquitoes and sand gnats that tend to invade around dusk.

Culebra is one of the last vestiges of pre-tourism Puerto Rico. Nobody is in a hurry, modern conveniences are few, and all anybody really wants to do is go to the beach. That's the way people in Culebra like it, and most of them want to keep it that way. Visitors are advised to embrace the island's quirky inconveniences and sleepy pace of life to fully appreciate its many rare charms.

SIGHTS

If you spend any time in Culebra, you're bound to enter the **Culebra National Wildlife Refuge** (787/742-0115, Mon.-Fri. 7:30am-4pm, free). It encompasses 1,568 acres, including much of Flamenco Peninsula, where 60,000 sooty terns nest, as well as mangrove forests, wetlands, coastline, surrounding cays (except Cayo Norte), and **Monte Resaca,** the island's highest point at 650 feet, which contains forested canyons, ravines, and a unique habitat known as the boulder forest. The refuge contains excellent beaches, diving, bird-watching, and hiking. Culebrita, Cayo Luis Peña, and Monte Resaca are open daily sunrise-sunset. Other areas are off-limits to visitors. For maps and information, visit the refuge office, east on Carretera 250, just past the cemetery.

Museo Histórico de Culebra El Polvorin (off Carr. 250 toward Playa Brava, 787/405-3768 or 787/742-3832, Thurs.-Sun. 10am-3pm, free) is a museum of history on the island that features old maps and photographs of Culebra, Taíno artifacts, traditional canoes made from the zinc plant, and Navy artifacts. It's located at the site of the first settlement in Culebra, in a 1905-era stone building that once stored ammunition for the Navy.

Turtle-Watching

Culebra is one of three nesting grounds for hawksbill and leatherback turtles, the latter of which is the largest species of turtle in the world, weighing between 500 and 1,600 pounds. From April to early June, the sea turtles spend the evenings trudging up the beach at **Playa Resaca** and **Playa Brava** to dig holes and lay eggs before returning to the sea in grand displays of sand-tossing to cover their tracks. Visitors are not permitted on the beaches at night during nesting season.

SPORTS AND RECREATION

Beaches

Once you see Culebra's craggy coastline of hidden coves, private beaches, coral outcroppings, and cays, it's easy to imagine why pirates liked to hide out here. Playa Flamenco is the island's most celebrated beach, and rightly so. But there are many less populated and more remote beaches to be found for those willing to hike in.

If Playa Flamenco is too crowded, take a 20-minute hike over the ridge and bypass the first small beach you encounter to reach the more private **Playa Carlos Rosario,** a pleasant, narrow beach flanked by coral reef and boulders. It offers excellent snorkeling around the long, vibrant stretch of coral reef not too far offshore. Other great snorkeling and diving beaches are **Punta Soldado** (south of Dewey, at the end of Calle Fulladoza), which also has beautiful coral reefs; **Playa Melones,** a rocky beach and subtropical forest within walking distance of Dewey; and **Playa Tamarindo,** where you'll find a diversity of soft corals and sea anemones.

Excellent deserted beaches can also be found on two of Culebra's cays—**Cayo Luis Peña** and **Culebrita,** which is distinguished by a lovely but crumbling abandoned lighthouse and several tidal pools. To gain access, it is necessary to either rent a boat or arrange a water taxi. And be sure to bring water, sunscreen, and other provisions; there are no facilities or services on the islands.

At the far eastern side of the island at the end of Carretera 250 is **Playa Zoni,** which features a frequently deserted sandy beach and great views of Culebrita, Cayo Norte, and St. Thomas.

Playa Brava has the biggest surf on the island, but it requires a bit of a hike to get there. To reach the trailhead, travel east on Carretera 250 and turn left after the cemetery, and then hike downhill and fork to the left. Note that Playa Brava is a turtle-nesting site, so it may be off-limits during nesting season from April to June.

Like Playa Brava, **Playa Resaca** is an important nesting site for sea turtles, but it is ill-suited for swimming because of the coral reef along the beach. The hike to Playa Resaca is fairly arduous, but it traverses a fascinating topography through a mangrove and boulder forest. To get there, turn on the road just east of the airport off Carretera 250, drive to the end, and hike the rest of the way in.

★ PLAYA FLAMENCO

Named one of "America's Best Beaches" by the Travel Channel, **Playa Flamenco** (north on Carr. 251 at dead-end) is one of the main reasons people come to Culebra. It's a wide, mile-long, horseshoe-shaped beach with calm, shallow waters and fine white sand. The island's only publicly maintained beach, it has bathroom facilities, picnic tables, lounge-chair and umbrella rentals, and a camping area. You can buy sandwiches and alcoholic

Sea Turtles

One of the most magnificent sights you can witness in the waters around Vieques and Culebra is a sea turtle. A chance encounter is reason enough to go diving or snorkeling in the area. Three species of sea turtles can be found in the area, all of them are endangered and protected.

The **leatherback sea turtle** is the largest species of sea turtle, weighing between 500 and 1,600 pounds and reaching lengths from four to eight feet. It is distinguished by seven pronounced ridges that run down the length of the shell, which has a rubbery texture and is primarily black with white spots. Leatherback sea turtles feed mostly on jellyfish, but they also like to eat sea urchins, squids, crustaceans, fish, seaweed, and algae. They dive as deep as 4,200 feet and can stay submerged for up to 85 minutes.

The **green sea turtle** has a hard, smooth shell mottled in shades of black, gray, green, brown, and yellow. Its head is small and its lower jaw is hooked. It tops out at 350 pounds, is around three feet long, and is the only sea turtle that just eats plants.

The **hawksbill sea turtle** is the smallest species at 180 pounds and three feet long. It is distinguished by the serrated edges of its shell, its beak-shaped mouth, and the brown and white pattern of its shell and skin. The hawksbill lives in coral reefs and primarily eats sea sponges but also sea anemones, jellyfish, and Portuguese Man o' War.

Sea turtles mate every couple of years, and the females return to the beaches of their birth to lay their eggs in pits they dig in the sand. When they hatch, the tiny turtles crawl to the water where they swim to offshore feeding sites. This is a vulnerable time in their life cycle because birds and lizards feed on the eggs and hatchlings. Nesting may occur anytime between March and October, depending on the species, during which time beaches may be closed to the public unless they are part of a turtle watch program, approved by the Puerto Rico Department of Natural and Environmental Resources.

For more information about the turtles and conservation efforts, visit the **Wider Caribbean Coastal Sea Turtle Conservation Network**'s website at www.widecast.org.

beverages at Coconuts Beach Grill in front of Culebra Beach Villa, as well as from vendors who set up grills and blenders in the ample parking lot. An abandoned, graffiti-covered tank remains as a reminder of the Navy's presence. It can get crowded on summer weekends and holidays—especially Easter and Christmas.

★ Diving

Culebra more than makes up for its dearth of entertainment options with a wealth of diving opportunities. There are reportedly 50 dive sites surrounding the island. They're mostly along the island's fringe reefs and around the cays. In addition to huge diverse coral formations, divers commonly spot sea turtles, stingrays, puffer fish, angel fish, nurse sharks, and more.

Among the most popular dive sites are **Carlos Rosario (Impact)**, which features a long, healthy coral reef teeming with sea life, including huge sea fans, and **Shipwreck**, the site of *The Wit Power*, a tugboat sunk in 1984. Here you can play out your *Titanic* fantasies and witness how the sea has claimed the boat for its habitat.

Many of the best dive sites are around Culebra's many cays. **Cayo Agua Rock** is a single, 45-foot-tall rock surrounded by sand and has been known to attract barracudas, nurse sharks, and sea turtles. **Cayo Ballena** provides a 120-foot wall dive with spectacular coral. **Cayo Raton** is said to attract an inordinate number and variety of fish. And **Cayo Yerba** features an underwater arch covered in yellow cup coral, best seen at night when they "bloom," and a good chance to see stingrays.

The island's sole diving and snorkeling source, **Culebra Divers** (across from the ferry terminal in Dewey, 787/742-0803, www.culebradivers.com), offers daily snorkeling trips for $60. One-tank dives are $85, and two-tank dives are $125, including tanks and weights. Snorkeling and dive gear is available for rent. It's also a good place to go for advice on snorkeling from the beach.

Kayaking and Snorkeling

Aquafari Culebra (787/245-4545, http://kayakingpuertorico.com) offers a kayaking and snorkeling tour of Culebra for $55-75 per person, including ferry fare from Fajardo. **Culebra Island Adventures** (www.culebraislandadventures.com, Wed.-Sun.) leads kayak and snorkel tours of Culebra for $75 per person. Ferry and air packages from Fajardo,

Playa Zoni in Culebra

Ceiba, and San Juan's Isla Grande airport are available. Turtles tours are $29.

Seabreeze Culebra Water Sports (Carr. 250, km 1.8, 855/285-3272, www.seabreeze-culebra.com) rents kayaks ($25-35 an hour), stand-up paddleboards ($25), a Sunfish sailboat ($65 an hour), and an inflatable mini powerboat ($125 an hour). Daylong sailing, snorkeling, and hiking tours run $125 per person.

Day & Night Boat Tours (787/435-4498) offers daylong snorkeling trips to Culebrita for $75 per person, including drinks, snacks, and gear. Custom fishing, snorkeling, and sightseeing tours can be arranged.

Culebra Bike Shop & Kayak Culebra (Hotel Kokomo on the Ferry Dock, 787/742-0589, http://culebrabikeshop.com, daily 9am-6pm) rents kayaks for $50 a day.

Bicycling

Culebra Bike Shop & Kayak Culebra (Hotel Kokomo on the Ferry Dock, 787/742-0589, http://culebrabikeshop.com, daily 9am-6pm) rents bikes for $15 for 24 hours and $20 a day.

ENTERTAINMENT

Nightlife is limited on Culebra, but sometimes even nature lovers and beachcombers need to cut loose. **El Batey** (Carr. 250, km 1.1, 787/742-3828, Sun.-Thurs. 11am-midnight, Fri.-Sat. 11am-2am) provides that opportunity. Dancing is the primary attraction at this large, no-frills establishment, where DJs spin salsa, merengue, and disco on Friday and Saturday nights. It also serves deli sandwiches and burgers ($3-5) during the day.

Everybody who goes to Culebra ends up at **Mamacita's** (64 Calle Castelar, 787/742-0090, www.mamacitasguesthouse.com, Sun.-Thurs. 4pm-10pm, Fri.-Sat. 4pm-11pm) at some point. The popular open-air watering hole right on the canal in Dewey attracts both locals and visitors. Two side-by-side tin-roofed pavilions provide shade for the cozy oasis appointed with brightly painted tables and chairs surrounded by potted palms. The blue tiled bar is tricked out with colorful folk art touches painted in shades of turquoise, lime green, and lavender. Behind the bar you can buy cigarettes and condoms, and you can get a spritz of bug spray free of charge when the sand gnats attack. Happy hour is 3pm-6pm daily. Try the house special cocktail, the Bushwhacker, a frozen concoction of Kahlúa, Bailey's Irish Cream, coconut cream, rum, and amaretto. Check the chalkboard for excellent daily dinner specials.

The Sandbar (ferry dock, 787/742-3112, Sun.-Thurs. 10am-midnight, Fri.-Sat. 10am-2am) is a pleasant dive bar serving a variety of beers and cocktails in a small, cool spot with colorful paintings of sea creatures on the walls and ceilings.

SHOPPING

Colmado Milka (Calle Escudero, 787/742-2253, Mon.-Sat. 7am-9pm, Sun. 7am-noon) is a general store selling a good selection of dry goods, meats, produce, and frozen foods. **Culebra Gift Shop La Cava** (Dewey, 787/742-0655, daily 10am-1pm and 3pm-5pm) is a small shop selling tourist trinkets, T-shirts, jewelry, sundresses, floppy hats, and postcards.

ACCOMMODATIONS

Some properties require a minimum stay, although exceptions may be made for a surcharge. It's worth asking if you don't mind the extra cost.

Under $50

Playa Flamenco Campground (Playa Flamenco, 787/742-7000, $20, cash only) is not necessarily the place to go if you want a quiet spot to commune with nature. It's more like party central on weekends, holidays, and in summer, when the grounds can get crowded. Facilities include toilets, outdoor showers, and picnic tables. Reservations are required. If you can't get through by phone, write to Autoridad de Conservación y Desarrollo de Culebra (Attn.: Playa Flamenco, Apartado 217, Culebra, PR 00775).

Dewey

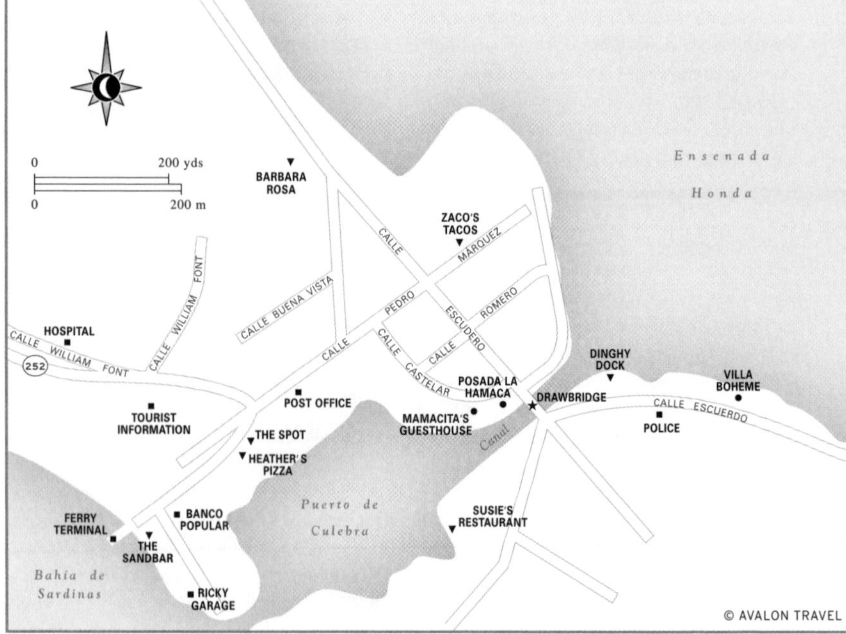

$50-100

The Spanish-style guesthouse ★ **Posada La Hamaca** (68 Calle Castelar, Dewey, 787/742-3516, www.posada.com, $90-103 s/d, $123 studio, $160 one-bedroom that sleeps eight, plus tax) has 10 rooms that are light, airy, and tidy; each comes with satellite TV, air-conditioning, mini-refrigerators, free Internet, and hot water. There's a large shady deck overlooking the canal out back with two gas grills. Beach towels, coolers, and free ice are provided for trips to the beach. It's within walking distance of the ferry dock.

$100-150

In town on Ensenada Honda is **Casa Ensenada** (142 Calle Escudero, 787/241-4441 or 866/210-00709, www.casaensenada.com, $125 s/d, $150 studio, $175 one-bedroom, plus tax). Despite its small size and modest aesthetics, this three-room guesthouse has everything you could need. Rooms are outfitted with air-conditioning, satellite TV, VCRs, hot showers, and kitchenettes, and a telephone, high-speed Internet, and copier are on-site. For trips to the beach, towels, chairs, coolers, umbrellas, and ice are available.

Mamacita's Guesthouse (64 Calle Castelar, 787/742-0090, www.mamacitasguesthouse.com, $102 s, $115 d, including tax) is a pastel-colored hodgepodge of balconies and archways squeezed between Calle Castelar and the canal. The hostel-like accommodations are strictly functional and feature air-conditioning and satellite TV in the bedrooms. It's best suited for those just looking for a place to crash and a hopping bar and excellent restaurant on-site. Laundry facilities and boat dockage are available for guests. Internet access is available for a fee.

Palmetto Guesthouse (128 Manuel Vasquez, two blocks behind Carlos Jeep, 787/742-0257 or 787/235-6736, www.

palmettoculebra.com, $100-130 s/d) is a modest six-unit property in the residential part of Dewey, within walking distance of the airport. One of the few properties that don't boast a view of the water, it makes up for its location with the "we aim to please" attitude of its owners, former Peace Corps volunteers Mark and Terrie Hayward. The small, tidy rooms are appointed with modern furnishings, air-conditioning, and mini-refrigerators. Common areas include two kitchens, a computer with Internet access, and a TV with a DVD/VCR player (but no cable or satellite access). Beach chairs, umbrellas, boogie boards, and coolers are provided free of charge for a small deposit. The shady backyard has a deck and gas grill. Co-owner Mark Hayward also operates an informational website on Culebra at http://culebrablog.com.

Vista Bella Apartments (on Ensenada Honda, 787/644-6300 or 787/742-0549, www.islaculebra.com, $120 studio, $163 one-bedroom that sleeps four, $218 two-bedroom that sleeps six) has four modern and spacious apartments that come with kitchens, air-conditioning, large covered balconies, and a spectacular view of Ensenada Honda.

An option right on Playa Flamenco is **Villa Flamenco Beach** (Playa Flamenco, 787/742-0023, Jan.-Apr., $125-135 studio, $150 one-bedroom, plus tax). The two-story pink-and-green concrete structure contains six tidy, basic units. There are four studio apartments with kitchenettes, air-conditioning, and hot water, which sleep two, and two efficiency apartments with full kitchens, hot water in the shower only, and no air-conditioning, which sleep four. A couple of rooms have beachfront balconies. The place is low-key and self-serve. Bring insect repellent.

★ **Villa Boheme** (368 Calle Fulladoza, 787/742-3508, www.villaboheme.com, $115-170 s/d, $170-220 family suites with kitchens, plus tax) has a lovely Spanish hacienda-style exterior and landscaped grounds right on Fulladoza Bay. Inside are 11 cheerfully appointed rooms with air-conditioning and hot water. Some rooms have private balconies and small kitchens; others share a communal kitchen in the patio area, which also contains satellite TV. A large terrace spans the length of the rambling property and overlooks the bay. Guests may use the dock, equipped with water and electricity, for $2 per foot per night. Moorings are also available for rent.

$150-250

Right on Playa Flamenco, **Culebra Beach Villas** (Playa Flamenco, 787/767-7575, 787/754-6236, or 877/767-7575, www.culebrabeachrental.com, www.culebrabeach.com, $125 studio, $175-195 one-bedroom, $215-225 two-bedroom, $300 three-bedroom, plus tax) offers 33 individually owned cottages and rooms with air-conditioning and kitchens, some with TVs but no Internet or telephones. The rooms are fairly spartan, but the cottages have decks and covered porches. The service is minimal, although linens and towels are provided. Request a newer unit in the back of the complex if available. Basic pub fare can be had at the open-air waterside Coconuts Beach Grill. Just be sure to bring your insect repellent—it gets buggy.

★ **Club Seabourne** (Carr. 252, Calle Fulladoza on Ensenada Honda, 787/742-3169 or 800/981-4435, www.clubseabourne.com, $185 pool cabana room, $279 one-bedroom villa, $339 two-bedroom, including tax) is a charming property with 14 units overlooking Fulladoza Bay. There is a New England vibe to the gray clapboard villas with pitched tin roofs dotted around the wooded property. The rooms are quite luxe, with super plush canopy beds and balconies. Rooms have air-conditioning but no TV or telephone. A lovely landscaped pool surrounded by umbrella tables overlooks the bay, as does the poolside bar. Fine dining can be had at Club Seabourne Restaurant, serving Caribbean cuisine on a screened porch on Fridays and Saturdays. Rates include breakfast, courtesy cocktails, one hour of free kayak rental, and transportation to and from the airport and ferry. Kayaks, snorkeling equipment, bikes, beach chairs, and umbrellas are available for rent, and picnic lunches are available by request.

Even more modern amenities can also be found at **Bahía Marina** (Punta Soldado Rd., km 2.4, 787/742-0535 or 866/285-3272, www.bahiamarina.net, $151-179 one-bedroom apartment, $295 two-bedroom, plus tax). This hilltop row of 16 corporate-looking apartments with sleeper sofas in the sitting rooms comes with kitchenettes, air-conditioning, cable TV, and ocean-view balconies. There's also a large pool and an open-air bar and restaurant.

For total seclusion, you can't do much better than **Tamarindo Estates** (off Carr. 251 just south of Playa Flamenco, 787/742-3343, www.tamarindoestates.com, $166-186 one-bedroom, $260 two-bedroom, two-bath, plus tax). The property is on the wildlife refuge and features 12 simply furnished, hillside cottages on 60 acres overlooking the water and Cayo Luis Peña. Units are three or six to a building, and they look like they were furnished by a flea market, which gives them a quaint homespun vibe. Each one contains a TV, a VCR, air-conditioning in the bedroom, a fully equipped kitchen, a screened porch, and a rooftop veranda. Internet access is available in the common computer room. The rocky beach directly in front of the property offers great snorkeling, and a short hike north is a sandy beach for swimming. There's also a small pool on-site, but no restaurant or bar.

Over $250

Sea Breeze Hotel (Carr. 250, km 1.8, 855/285-3272, www.seabreezeculebra.com, $149 advance purchase, $249 rack rate) is a large complex overlooking the bay featuring 160 units; more than half are privately owned condominium units. Suites and junior suites come with microwaves, mini refrigerators, air-conditioning, and balconies. There are no TVs or daily housekeeping services. Amenities include a swimming pool and a pool-side bar and grill.

FOOD

The concept of service is very different here from what stateside dwellers may be accustomed to. Things move at a slow, casual pace, so it's best to be patient and prepared to linger for a while. Also, note that operating hours can change unexpectedly, and some restaurants close up shop completely for weeks at a time.

Puerto Rican

★ **Barbara Rosa** (Carr. 250, 787/742-0073, Thurs.-Mon. 5pm-9pm, $8-16) is located between the airport and the school in a modest house with a large front porch. When the Christmas lights are on and the bed sheet has been removed from the sign, Barbara Rosa is in business. Diners place their orders at the kitchen, pick up their plates when their names are called, and clear their own dishes when they're done. Dining is alfresco on the front porch and the food is homey and filling. The menu includes grilled kingfish, plantain-crusted mahi, fried shrimp, and *churrasco.* The pumpkin soup and red beans are especially good. Note that Barbara Rosa is probably the only restaurant in all of Puerto Rico that doesn't have a bar, but you're welcome to bring your own bottle. And be prepared to wait. The restaurant gets crowded and it is a one-woman operation.

The name says it all. At **Dinghy Dock** (Calle Fulladoza, south of the drawbridge, on Ensenada Honda, 787/742-0233 or 787/742-0518, daily 8am-2:30pm and 6pm-9:30pm, dinner $9-30) boats literally dock beside your table at this casual waterfront spot. Plastic patio chairs line a narrow dock under a hanging roof. The cuisine is standard Puerto Rican, featuring Angus steaks, tuna, and lobster. Breakfast includes waffles and French toast. Check out the huge tarpon swimming below waiting for a handout. There is a full bar, which is a good thing because service takes forever.

Breakfast and Lunch

Vibra Verde (Calle Pedro Marquez,

787/909-4094, Thurs.-Sat. 8am-5pm, Sun. 8am-1pm, $3-10) is a quick, casual spot for a healthy and delicious breakfast or light lunch, including fruit smoothies, fruit bowls, soups, salads, and sandwiches.

Pandeli Bakery (17 Calle Pedro Marquez at the corner of Calle Escudero, Carr. 250, 787/402-3510, Mon.-Sat. 5:30am-5pm, Sun. 6:30am-5pm, $2-6) is a cool, modern, cozy bakery serving breakfast, sandwiches, burgers, empanadas, and pastries. There's also a small selection of dry goods and wines.

Heather's Pizza & Sports Bar (14 Calle Pedro Marquez, 787/742-3175, Mon.-Tues and Thurs.-Sun. 5pm-10pm, bar open until 11pm, $2-15) is a friendly spot where locals gather to watch the game, have a drink, and chow down on pizza, served by the slice or pie. Options include unusual combinations such as the Boricua Pizza, featuring ground beef, garlic, sweet plantains, and cilantro. Panini and pasta round out the menu.

International

Located in a brightly colored house on a dead-end street in town, ★ **Zaco's Tacos** (21 Calle Pedro Marquez, 787/742-0243, www.zacostacos.com, Sat.-Wed. noon-8pm, $3-9) is a happy new addition to the dining scene serving fresh fruit cocktails and creative tacos and burritos stuffed with goodies like pork belly or blackened tofu. Order and pick up at the bar and take a seat on the covered deck out back. It also serves milkshakes and smoothies.

The Spot (16 Calle Pedro Marquez, Culebra, 787/742-0203, Sun.-Tues. and Thurs. 6:30pm-midnight, Fri.-Sat. 6:30pm-2am, $6-18) serves Middle Eastern-inspired dishes, including couscous with curry chicken, gyros, and a burger made from hummus, olives, and feta cheese.

Steak and Seafood

Coconut Pizza Bar & Grill (990 Calle Luis Muñoz Marin, 787/742-0264, Wed.-Sun. 5pm-10pm, $11-30) is oddly named for a restaurant better known for dishes such as grilled mahi, marinated skirt steak, and lobster mac and cheese. But you can get pizza, too.

★ **Mamacita's Restaurant** (64 Calle Castelar, by the canal south of the drawbridge, 787/742-0322, www.mamacitasguesthouse.com, daily 8am-3pm and 6pm-9pm, bar Sun.-Thurs. 10am-10pm, Fri. 10am-11pm, $14-20, plus 15 percent gratuity) is a colorful open-air restaurant and bar serving excellent Caribbean-American-style dishes featuring dorado, *churrasco,* pork, and pasta, as well as

Zaco's Tacos in Culebra

a few pub-style appetizers. The dinner menu changes nightly and recently included a terrific dish of grilled dorado in cilantro lime aioli. Mamacita's doubles as a popular watering hole at night and rents rooms too.

Susie's Restaurant (on the canal, Dewey, 787/742-0574 or 787/340-7058, www.susiesculebra.com, Tues.-Sun. 6pm-10pm, reservations recommended, $18-25) serves creative Caribbean cuisine inside this modest concrete restaurant located at the end of a nameless road on the canal in Dewey. The seasonal menu may include such delicacies as coriander-crusted tuna loin, shrimp glazed in a tamarind coconut sauce, and whole fried snapper.

Shipwreck Bar and Grill (at Bahía Marina, Calle Punta Soldado, km 2.4, 787/742-0535, www.bahiamarina.net, daily 4pm-10pm, $10-24) is a casual open-air eatery at Bahía Marina hotel, high up on a hill overlooking the water. The menu serves everything from burgers and conch fritters to whole snapper, *mofongo,* and New York strips.

Mamacita's is a popular guesthouse, restaurant, and bar in Culebra.

TRANSPORTATION AND SERVICES

Air

Several small airlines fly to Culebra from the main island, and the flights are fairly inexpensive and speedy. The only catch is that it's not for the faint of heart. Landing on the tiny island requires a steep descent over a mountaintop that takes your breath away.

In San Juan, flights can be arranged from Isla Grande Airport for about $190 round-trip, or from the José Aponte de la Torre Airport in Ceiba, on the east coast of the big island, for about $66 round-trip.

Vieques Air Link (787/534-4221, 787/534-4222, or 787/741-8331; for service to Culebra, call 888/901-9247) flies to and from Ceiba.

Air Flamenco (787/724-1818, 787/721-7332 or 877/535-2636, www.airflamenco.net) offers flights from Ceiba and Isla Grande. Charter flights are available.

Ferry

The **Puerto Rico Port Authority** (in Culebra 787/742-3161 or 787/863-0705, or 800/981-2005, daily 8am-11am and 1pm-3pm) operates a ferry service between Culebra and Fajardo. But save yourself a headache, and don't take the ferry. At publication time, all passenger ferries were out of service and had been for months. Passengers are now required to take the cargo ferry, which has limited passenger space and often does not run on time.

Car rental agencies in Puerto Rico do not permit their automobiles to leave the main island. The best option is to leave your car in Fajardo and rent another car in Culebra. The trip takes about 2.5 hours. The fare is $4.50 per person round-trip, $26 for vehicles.

The ferry schedule is subject to change. For updates follow @PRFerryWatch on Twitter.

- **Fajardo to Culebra:** Daily 9am, 3pm, 7pm
- **Culebra to Fajardo:** Daily 6:30am, 1pm, 5pm

Car

It is possible to get around Culebra without

Ferry Riding Tips

the car ferry in Vieques

Ferry service to Vieques and Culebra has become increasingly unreliable. At time of publication, there were no passenger ferries in use, just cargo ferries. If you plan to take a ferry to Vieques or Culebra, here are a few things worth noting.

- Tickets may be bought in advance, but they do not guarantee space on the ferry.
- Ferries often sell out, especially on weekends and holidays. Therefore, passengers typically line up hours in advance.
- If a ferry is oversold, ticket holders with a Puerto Rico Permanent Resident Card get priority over visitors.
- If you are prone to motion sickness, take preventive medication. The ride is sometimes choppy.
- Ferries do not always arrive or depart on time.
- There is an additional $2 charge for camping or beach equipment.
- Rental cars may not be transported on the car ferry.

renting a vehicle, but it is not advisable. If you want to explore the island, jeeps, scooters, and golf carts are available for rent. Just be sure to book early—2-3 months in advance is recommended.

There are few roads on Culebra, but they can be narrow, steep, and riddled with potholes. Parking and seatbelt laws are strictly enforced, and for some odd reason, driving bare-chested can get you a ticket.

Note that many places don't have traditional addresses with street names and numbers. If you ask people for an address, they're more likely to describe its physical location in relation to something else, as in "beside El Batey," or "across from the ferry." Also, nobody who lives in Culebra calls Dewey by its name; it's usually just referred to as "Pueblo" or "Town."

CAR RENTALS

Several agencies provide jeep rentals for about $65 per day, although some travelers report success at negotiating a better rate. Bring a copy of your insurance policy to avoid steep insurance charges.

Carlos Jeep Rental (office 787/742-3514, airport 787/742-1111, cell 787/613-7049, www.carlosjeeprental.com) is conveniently located at the airport and has a well-maintained fleet of 2011 jeeps for $65 a day. Golf carts are $40 a day. Other options include **Jerry's Jeeps** (787/742-0587 or 787/742-0526, www.jerrys-jeeprental.com) and **Dick and Cathie's Jeep Rental** (787/742-0062, cash only).

For gassing up your vehicle, **Garage Ricky** (ferry dock, 787/742-3174, daily 8am-6pm) has the only gas pump in Culebra, so allow plenty of time to wait in line to use it. The small store sells soft drinks, cigarettes, bug spray, and liquor.

Público

If you arrive at the airport and there aren't any *públicos* waiting, strike out walking a short distance to Willys. From the airport turn left and go one block past the stop sign; he's on the right. Otherwise, you can give one a call. Operators include **Willys** (787/742-3537 or 787/396-0076), **Kiko** (787/514-0453, 787/361-7453, or 787/363-2183), **Adrianos** (787/590-1375), **Isla Bonita** (787/223-3428), **Natas** (787/510-0736), and **Pichi** (787/455-5569). It costs about $4 to go from the airport to "downtown" Dewey or from Dewey to Flamenco Bay.

For travelers seeking transportation from San Juan to Fajardo to catch the ferry to Culebra, **Travel with Rivera** (787/644-3091, http://enchanted-isle.com/rivera) operates 24-hour *público* service between Fajardo and the Luis Muñoz Marín International Airport in San Juan. Rates are $70 for up to four people, $80 up to six, $85 up to nine, and $12 per person for more than nine people. Reservations must be made at least 24 hours in advance.

Services

The **Culebra Tourism Department** (787/742-3521 or 787/742-3116, ext. 441 or 442, Mon.-Fri. 8am-4:30pm) is in the yellow concrete building on Calle William Font in Dewey. For the most up-to-date information on the island, visit www.culebra-island.com, www.islaculebra.com, and www.culebra.org.

Because many businesses accept only cash, it's important to know where the island's ATM is. **Banco Popular** (787/742-3572, Mon.-Fri. 8:30am-3:30pm) is across from the ferry terminal on Calle Pedro Marquez. You'll find the **post office** (787/742-3862, Mon.-Fri. 8am-4:30pm) at 26 Calle Pedro Marquez, and **laundry facilities** (64 Calle Castelar, 787/742-0090) can be found at Mamacita's Guesthouse.

The **police department** (787/742-3501) is on Calle Fulladoza just past Dinghy Dock. For medical services, **Hospital de Culebra** (Calle William Font, 787/742-3511 or 787/742-0001, ambulance 787/742-0208) operates a clinic Monday-Friday 7am-4:30pm, as well as 24-hour emergency service and the island's only pharmacy.

Background

The Landscape

GEOGRAPHY

Puerto Rico is a rectangular island, situated roughly in the middle of the **Antilles,** a chain of islands that stretches from Florida to Venezuela and forms the dividing line between the Atlantic Ocean and the Caribbean Sea. The Antilles are divided into two regions—Greater Antilles and Lesser Antilles. Puerto Rico is the smallest and easternmost island of the Greater Antilles, which include Cuba, Hispañola (Dominican Republic and Haiti), and Jamaica.

In addition to the main island, which is 111 miles east to west and 36 miles north to south, Puerto Rico comprises several tiny islands or *cayos,* including Mona and Desecheo off the west coast and Vieques, Culebra, Palomino, Icacos, and others off the east coast. The northern and eastern shores of Puerto Rico are on the Atlantic Ocean, and the southern shores are on the Caribbean Sea. To the west is Mona Passage, an important shipping lane that is 75 miles wide and 3,300 feet deep.

The island was believed to have been formed between 135 million and 185 million years ago when a massive shift of tectonic plates crumpled the earth's surface, pushing parts of it down into deep recesses below the ocean floor and pushing parts of it up to create the island. This tectonic activity resulted in volcanic eruptions, both underwater and above it.

Two significant things happened as a result of all this geologic activity. The **Puerto Rico Trench** was formed off the island's north coast. At its greatest depth, it is 28,000 feet below sea level, making it the deepest point known in the Atlantic Ocean. Secondly, it formed the mountainous core of Puerto Rico that spans nearly the entire island from east to west and reaches heights of 4,390 feet above sea level. Volcanic activity is believed to have been dormant in Puerto Rico for 45 million years, but the earth is always changing. The Caribbean plate is shifting eastward against the westward-shifting North American plate, which has resulted in occasional earth tremors through the years. Although this activity is suspected to have led to the volcanic activity in Montserrat in recent years, its danger to Puerto Rico is its potential to cause earthquakes, not volcanic activity.

Puerto Rico has three main geographic regions: mountains, coastal lowlands, and karst country. More than 60 percent of the island is mountainous. The island's mountains, which dominate the island's interior, comprise four ranges: **Cordillera Central, Sierra de Cayey, Sierra de Luquillo,** and **Sierra de Bermeja.** The largest and highest range is Cordillera Central, which spans from Caguas in the east to Lares in the west. Its highest point is Cerro Punta (4,390 feet above sea level), in the Bosque Estatal de Toro Negro near Jayuya. Sierra de Luquillo is in the northeast and contains the Caribbean National Forest, home to El Yunque rainforest. These two mountain ranges feature dramatic pointed peaks and lush tropical vegetation. Sierra de Cayey, in the southeast between Cayey and Humacao, and Sierra de Bermeja, in the southwest between Guánica and the island's southwestern tip, are smaller in area and height, drier, and less forested.

The **coastal lowlands** span more than 300 miles around the rim of the island, 8-12 miles inland in the north and 2-8 miles inland

---

Previous: Taíno petroglyphs carved into La Piedra Escrita in Jayuya; a reminder of the U.S. Navy's presence on Playa Flamenco in Culebra.

in the south. Formed through time by erosion of the mountains, the coastal lowlands are important agricultural areas that benefit from the rich soil and water that wash down from the mountains. Much of the area is defined by sandy or rocky beaches and mangrove swamps, although the mangrove forests are being whittled away by development.

The island's third region is unique. The **karst region** spans the island's northern interior, from San Juan in the east to Aguadilla in the west, and the southern interior, from Ponce in the east to San Germán in the west. It can also be found in isolated pockets throughout the island, as well as on Mona Island off the west coast. The karst region is distinguished by a fascinating landscape of sinkholes, cliffs, caves, and conical, haystack-shaped hills called *mogotes*. More than 27 percent of Puerto Rico's surface is made up of limestone, and its erosion from rain helped create the beguiling patchwork of hills and holes. One of limestone's unique properties is that it re-precipitates and forms case rock that is impervious to chemical and climatic change, which has basically frozen the odd formations in time. In addition, water produced by re-precipitation bubbles up to hydrate the earth's surface, and drips down, creating subterranean rivers and caves.

As a result of its karst region, Puerto Rico has some of the most significant cave systems in the western hemisphere and the third-largest underground river, Río Camuy. The public can tour part of the massive cave system at **Las Cavernas del Río Camuy** in the municipality of Camuy.

In addition to Río Camuy, Puerto Rico's other major rivers include the north-running **Grande de Arecibo,** the island's longest; **La Plata, Cibuco, Loíza,** and **Bayamón,** which run north; and **Grande de Añasco,** which runs west. There are no natural lakes in Puerto Rico, although 15 reservoirs have been created by damming rivers. But there are several natural lagoons, including **Condado** and **San José** in San Juan, **Piñones** and **Torrecilla** in Loíza, **Joyuda** in Cabo Rojo, **Tortuguero** in Vega Baja, and **Grande** in Fajardo.

CLIMATE

Puerto Rico's climate is classified as **tropical marine,** which means it's typically sunny, hot, and humid year-round. The temperature fluctuates between 76°F and 88°F in the coastal plains and 73-78°F in the mountains. Humidity is a steady 80 percent, but a northeasterly wind keeps things pretty breezy, particularly on the northeast side of the island.

Nobody wants rain during a tropical vacation, but precipitation is very much a part of life in Puerto Rico. Although there are periods when the deluge is so heavy that you might think it's time to build an ark, rains are generally brief and occur in the afternoons. The average annual rainfall is 62 inches. Although it rains throughout the year, the heaviest precipitation is from May to October, which is also hurricane season. The driest period is January to April, which coincides with the tourism industry's high season. Keep in mind that the north coast receives twice as much rain as the south coast, so if the outlook is rainy in San Juan, head south.

Hurricanes are a very real threat to Puerto Rico. It is estimated that the island will be hit by a major hurricane every 30 years. The most devastating storm in recent history was Hurricane Georges, a category 3 storm that struck in September 1998 and rendered $2 billion of damage.

For the latest information on weather conditions in Puerto Rico, visit the National Weather Service at www.srh.noaa.gov/sju.

ENVIRONMENTAL ISSUES

Because Puerto Rico is part of the United States, local industry is subject to the same federal environmental regulations and restrictions as in the United States.

Puerto Rico's greatest environmental threats concern its vanishing natural habitat and the resulting impact on soil erosion and wildlife. Reforestation efforts are under way in many of the island's national parks and forest reserves, and organized efforts are under way to protect and rebuild endangered wildlife populations, especially the Puerto Rican parrot, the manatee, and the leatherback sea turtle.

Many of the island's environmental protection efforts are overseen by the Conservation Trust of Puerto Rico, whose headquarters is based in **Casa de Ramón Power y Girault** (155 Calle Tetuán, San Juan, 787/722-5834, www.fideicomiso.org, Tues.-Sat. 10am-4pm), where visitors can peruse exhibits and pick up printed information on its projects.

In Vieques, the biggest environmental concern surrounds the ongoing cleanup of the grounds once occupied by the U.S. Navy, which stored munitions and performed bombing practice on the island. After years of protest by local residents, the Navy withdrew in 2003, but much of its land (18,000 acres) is still off-limits to the public while efforts to clear it of contaminants and the live artillery that still litters the ocean floor are under way. The cancer rate in Vieques is 27 percent higher than that of the main island, and many blame it on the presence of unexploded artillery leaking chemicals into the water and the release of chemicals into the air when the artillery is detonated, which is the Navy's way of disposing of it.

Plants and Animals

For such a small island, Puerto Rico has a wide diversity of biological environments.

For instance, Bosque Estatal de Guánica in the southwestern corner of the island is classified as a subtropical dry forest, where cacti, grasses, and evergreen trees hosting Spanish moss and mistletoe compete for water and nutrients from sun-bleached rocky soil. On the opposite end of the island is the Caribbean National Forest, which contains subtropical moist forest, also called rainforest. Palm trees, a multitude of ferns, *tabonuco* trees, orchids, and bromeliads grow here. And along the coast are mangrove forests, where the mighty land-building trees flourish in the salty water and provide vital habitat to marine life.

The first extensive study of Puerto Rico's diverse flora was undertaken in the early 1900s, thanks to American botanists Nathaniel and Elizabeth Britton, founders of the New York Botanical Gardens. Their annual trips to the Caribbean, beginning in 1906, led to the publication in 1933 of *The Scientific Survey of Puerto Rico and the Virgin Islands,* the first systematic natural history survey in the Caribbean region.

TREES

The official tree of Puerto Rico is the **ceiba,** also called silk-cotton tree or kapok tree. Often the tallest tree in the forest, the ceiba attains heights of 150 feet and has a ridged columnar trunk and a massive umbrella-shaped canopy. Its far-reaching limbs often host aerial plants, such as moss and bromeliads.

The ceiba was important to the island's indigenous Taínos because its thick trunks were perfect for carving into canoes. Its flowers are small and inconspicuous, but it produces a large ellipsoid fruit that, when split open, reveals an abundance of fluffy fibers, called kapok.

Arguably Puerto Rico's most beautiful tree, though, is the ***flamboyan,*** also known as royal poinciana. If you visit the island between June and August, you're sure to notice the abundance of reddish-orange blooms that cover the umbrella-shaped canopy of the *flamboyan*. It is a gorgeous sight to behold. The tree is also distinguished by fern-like leaves and the long brown seedpods it produces.

Probably the most plentiful and easily identifiable tree in Puerto Rico is the mighty palm,

Flamboyan trees blossom throughout the island in summer months.

which grows throughout the island. There are actually many varieties of palm in Puerto Rico. Among them are the **coconut palm,** which has a smooth gray bark marked by ring scars from fallen fronds and which bears the beloved coconut in abundance; the **royal palm,** distinguished by its tall, thin, straight trunk, which grows to 25 feet and sports a crown of leaves that are silver on the underside; the **Puerto Rican hat palm,** featuring a fat tubular trunk and fan-shaped frond; and the **sierra palm,** which has a thin straight trunk and thick thatch.

Puerto Rico's **mangrove** forests are found in swampy coastal areas throughout the island. Much of the island's coast was once covered in mangrove, but a lot of it has been destroyed to make way for commercial development. Fortunately efforts are under way to preserve many of the island's last remaining mangrove forests in parks in Piñones, Boquerón, Fajardo, Vieques, and elsewhere.

The mangrove tree is a unique plant. For one thing, it is able to grow along the ocean's shallow edges, absorbing, processing, and secreting salt from the water. But what's truly amazing about the mangrove, and what makes it so vital to marine life, is its adaptive root system. Because the trees grow in thick, oxygen-deprived mud, they sprout aerial roots to absorb oxygen from the air and nutrients from the surface of the water. The aerial roots take many different forms, including thousands of tiny pencil-shaped roots sticking up from shallow waters; big knee-shaped roots that emerge from the ground and loop back down; and roots that sprout from branches.

Between its complex tangle of roots and its low-lying compact canopy, the mangrove forest plays several important roles in the environment, primarily by providing habitat to local wildlife. Its branches are a haven to nesting birds, and its underwater root systems protect crabs, snails, crustaceans, and small fish from predators. Mangrove forests also help protect the coastal plains from violent storms, reduce erosion, and filter the ocean waters. And finally, mangrove forests actually build land by providing nooks and crannies within their root systems that capture soil, aerate it, and create conditions where other plants can grow.

Puerto Rico is rich in plants that have edible, medicinal, or other practical uses. For the Taíno Indians, the island's forests served as their pharmacy and grocery store.

The **mamey** is prized not only for the delicious fruit it bears but also for its fragrant flowers and lovely appearance. Resembling a Southern magnolia, the mamey grows to 60 feet high and features a short stout trunk and dense foliage with long, glossy, leathery dark-green leaves. The flowers feature 4-6 white petals and have a lovely fragrance. The fruit is brown and leathery on the outside, and inside can be sweet and tender or crisp and sour, depending on the variety. Another popular tree that bears edible fruit is the **mango.** The ubiquitous leafy tree grows in forests, backyards, and alongside roadways, and in the summer each tree bears what appear to be hundreds of mangoes. When ripe, the fruit is covered with a thick yellow and brown skin, but inside is a soft succulent fruit similar to a peach. You'll often see locals on the side of the road selling bags of them out of their trucks.

The curious **calabash tree** served an entirely different purpose in Taíno culture. Its greatest value was in the large, round, gourd-like fruit that sprouts directly from the tree's trunk. After the fruit was cleansed of its pulp, the remaining shell was dried and used as a bowl for food preparation and storage. Sometimes the bowls were decorated with elaborate carvings etched into the sides before the shell dried. Carved calabash bowls are popular souvenir items today.

FLOWERING PLANTS

Like any good tropical island, Puerto Rico has a bounty of flowering plants. Probably the one most commonly encountered, particularly in gardens but also in the wild, is the beautiful sun-loving **bougainvillea.** The plant produces great clusters of blossoms with thin papery petals, which come in an assortment of colors, including pink, magenta, purple, red, orange, white, and yellow. The plant is actually a vine, but in Puerto Rico bougainvillea often grows freestanding, with its long thin branches hanging heavy with blooms.

The mountains are home to many varieties of flowering plants, including one that home gardeners in the States may recognize—the shade-loving **impatiens,** a lovely ground-covering plant with white blooms. They can be seen blooming in great drifts along mountain banks. Other mountain flowering plants include more than 50 varieties of **orchids,** but don't look for corsage-sized blossoms—Puerto Rico's orchids tend to be small, some the size of a fingernail. Where you find orchids, you can usually find **bromeliads,** which, like orchids, grow on other plants that serve as hosts. Bromeliads are typically distinguished by overlapping spirals of leaves with a tubular punch of color in the center, but the family includes some atypical variations, including **Spanish moss** and the **pineapple,** both of which grow on the island.

Gourds produced by the calabash tree were used for storage by the Taíno.

Other plants found commonly in Puerto Rico are a large variety of ferns, large and small, in the mountains. Along the beaches, the sea grape, a low-lying compact shrub that grows in clusters, creates a cave-like reprieve from the sun. Several varieties of cactus grow in the subtropical dry forest along the southwestern coast and on the islands of Vieques and Culebra.

MAMMALS

The only mammal native to Puerto Rico is the bat. Eleven species live on the island, including the **red fig-eating bat,** which roosts in the forest canopy in the Caribbean National Forest, and the **Greater Antillean long-tongued bat,** which lives in caves and feeds on fruits and nectar from flowers.

Thanks to colonial trade ships, **rats** were introduced to the island in the late 1400s. They thrived here in great abundance, causing havoc on sugar plantations. Then someone had the brilliant idea of introducing **mongooses** from India to keep the rat population down. Unfortunately, mongooses are active during the day, and rats are active at night, so the effort failed, and now there's a mongoose problem. They have no natural predators on the island, and they live up to 40 years. Mongooses are to be avoided at all costs as they are major carriers of rabies.

Paso Fino horses are a common form of transportation in rural areas of Puerto Rico, especially in Vieques and Culebra, where they roam the island freely.

Some parts of Puerto Rico also have a **feral dog** problem. It's not uncommon to see roving packs of mangy, skeletal canines rummaging for scraps in small towns and rural areas.

BIRDS AND INSECTS

Puerto Rico is a bird-watcher's paradise, but the one endemic bird you probably won't see is the **Puerto Rican parrot.** Although once prolific throughout the island, the endangered bird's population is a mere 35 or so that live in the wild today because of the loss of habitat to development. They are found in the Caribbean National Forest.

In 1987 the U.S. Fish and Wildlife Service initiated a program to raise Puerto Rican parrots in captivity and release them into the Caribbean National Forest in hopes of building up the population. Unfortunately, success has been stymied by hurricanes and predators (primarily the red-tailed hawk). But the efforts continue, and today there are about 150 living in captivity in aviaries in Luquillo and Bosque Estatal Río Abajo.

It's highly unlikely a visitor to El Yunque will see a Puerto Rican parrot, but just in case, keep your eyes peeled for a foot-long, bright green Amazon parrot with blue wingtips, white eye rings, and a red band above its beak. When in flight, it emits a repetitive call that sounds like a bugle.

Other species of birds found in more plentiful numbers in Puerto Rico include **sharp-skinned hawks, broad-wing hawks, bananaquits, Puerto Rican todies, red-legged thrushes, stripe-headed tanagers, brown pelicans, lizard cuckoos, elfin woods warblers, hummingbirds,** and **nightjars,** which nest silently on the ground by day and fly in search of prey at night.

At dusk, many of Puerto Rico's wilderness beaches come under attack by **sand fleas,** also called no-see-ums: vicious, minuscule buggers that have a fierce bite. If they attack, your best defense is to pack up as quickly as possible and call it a day.

Pelicans are commonly spotted along the west coast.

The Coqui Tree Frog

There is one sweet sound unlike any other that you can hear throughout the island of Puerto Rico at night, and that is the song of the coqui tree frog. Rarely seen but often heard, these tiny translucent amphibians are the beloved mascot of the island. The scientific name is *Eleutherodactylus,* and they differ from other frogs in two key ways: First, instead of webbed feet, they have tiny pads on their feet that facilitate climbing to the tops of trees, where they like to gather at night to mate and feed on insects, including mosquitoes, termites, and centipedes. Second, they do not begin life as tadpoles but hatch fully formed from eggs. There are 17 varieties of coquis in Puerto Rico, but only two of them sing the famous songs: the *coqui comun* and the *coqui de la montaña,* also known as the *coqui puertorriqueño.* And only the male sings the "co-QUI!" call after dusk. Coquis can be found throughout the Caribbean and Latin America, but only those in Puerto Rico sing the song. In recent years the coqui inadvertently has been introduced to Hawaii, hidden in plants shipped there from Puerto Rico. But while Puerto Ricans love the sound of their coquis, many people in Hawaii do not. In fact, they consider the frogs to be a scourge to the island and the state government is trying to have them eradicated. Meanwhile, in Puerto Rico, some species of coquis have been put on the endangered list, including the tiniest one, the *coqui llanero,* which was only discovered in 2005 and whose song is so high-pitched it is barely perceivable by humans.

REPTILES AND AMPHIBIANS

Of all the creatures that call Puerto Rico home, none are as beloved as the tiny **coqui tree frog,** the island's national symbol. A mere 1-1.5 inches long fully grown, the coqui is difficult to spot, but you can definitely hear the male's distinctive "co-QUI" call at dusk or after a rain. Despite the ubiquity of their cheerful chirp, of the 16 varieties that live in Puerto Rico, only two make the eponymous sound, which serves to attract a mate and repel reproductive competitors.

Unlike many frogs, the coqui does not have webbed appendages and does not require water to live or reproduce. In fact, coquis are never tadpoles. The female coqui lays its eggs on leaves, and tiny little froglets emerge fully formed from the eggs. Although they're born with tails, they lose them posthaste.

It is considered good luck to spot a coqui, and there are many other legends surrounding them. One is that a little boy was transformed into a frog because he misbehaved, and now he comes out and sings at sunset. Another involves a bird that was stripped of its wings but was later turned into a frog so it could climb back into the trees where it once lived.

The one creature visitors to Puerto Rico are sure to spot is a **lizard.** The island is literally crawling with them, varying in species from the ubiquitous four-inch **emerald anoli,** which is sure to slip inside the house if a window is left open, to the **Puerto Rican giant green lizard,** an imposing reptile that can grow up to 16 inches long and lives mostly in the limestone hills.

But Puerto Rico's mack-daddy lizard is the prehistoric-looking **Mona iguana,** which grows up to four feet long. Mona Island off the west coast of Puerto Rico is the only natural habitat for the Mona iguana, but there is a tiny mangrove *cayo* in the bay at La Parguera where a small population is kept for research purposes and which can be seen by boat. Although an herbivore, the Mona iguana has an intimidating appearance because of its horned snout and the jagged bony crest down its back. The Mona iguana lives up to 50 years.

Snakes are few in Puerto Rico, but they do exist. Fortunately, they are all nonpoisonous. The **Puerto Rican boa** is an endangered species. The longest snake on the island, it grows up to six feet and is quite elusive.

MARINE LIFE

Unlike on many islands in the Caribbean, Puerto Rico's underwater coral reef systems are still mostly healthy and intact. And where there's a healthy reef system, there is an abundance of marine life.

Among Puerto Rico's endangered marine creatures is the **manatee,** a 1,000-pound submarine-shaped mammal with a tail, two small flippers, and a wrinkled, whiskered face. The slow-moving herbivore lives in shallow, still waters, such as lagoons and bays. Their only natural predators are humans, and because they often float near the water's surface, they are particularly susceptible to collision with watercraft. The U.S. Fish and Wildlife Service operates a recovery program for the manatee, and if you spot one, you're likely to see its tracking device, which looks like a walkie-talkie attached to its back.

Also endangered are the **hawksbill** and **leatherback sea turtles,** the latter of which is the world's largest species of sea turtle. There are several important turtle nesting sites in Puerto Rico, along the north shore and on the islands of Mona and Culebra. The turtles nest between April and June by climbing up on the beach at night and burying their eggs in the sand before returning to the sea. Unfortunately, turtle nests are vulnerable to animals and poachers, who prize the eggs. Several government agencies are involved in protected the nesting sites. If visitors want to help out, they should contact the Puerto Rico Department of Natural and Environmental Resources (787/556-6234 or 877/772-6725, fax 530/618-4605, www.coralations.org/turtles), which accepts volunteers to catalog the turtles during nesting season.

Besides its endangered species, Puerto Rico has numerous other varieties of thriving marine life, from **rays** and **nurse sharks** to **puffer fish** and **parrot fish.** The reefs themselves are sights to behold, with their **brain coral, sea fans,** and **yellow cup coral,** which blooms at night.

And although typically associated with colder waters, migrating **humpback whales** can be spotted along the island's west coast between January and March.

History

INDIGENOUS CULTURES

The earliest known inhabitants of Puerto Rico were the **Archaic** or **Pre-Ceramic** cultures, which are believed to have lived on the island from 3000 BC until AD 150. They were loosely organized in small nomadic groups of about 30 who occupied encampments for brief periods. What little is known about this culture has been deduced from a couple of burial sites and a few excavated stone and shell artifacts, such as flint chips, scrapers, and pestles. They are believed to have been primarily hunters and gatherers who did not cultivate crops or make pottery. There are two main theories about the origins of the Archaic culture. It is believed they either originated in South America and migrated to Puerto Rico by way of the Lesser Antilles or they originated in the Yucatán Peninsula and crossed from Cuba and Hispañola.

The Archaic were followed by the **Arawak,** who migrated from Venezuela. The earliest Arawak were classified as **Igneri** or **Saladoid,** and they lived in Puerto Rico from 300 BC to AD 600. The Igneri were superb potters, whose ceramics were distinguished by white paint on a red background. They also produced small *cemies,* three-sided amulets believed to have religious significance. Their society was organized in villages of extended-family houses situated around a central plaza, under which the dead were buried. In addition to hunting and gathering, the Igneri cultivated crops.

Around AD 600, the Igneri culture evolved into two separate cultures that are grouped together under the name **Pre-Taíno.** The

Elenoid lived on the eastern two-thirds of the island while the **Ostionoid** lived on the western third of the island. The Elenoid culture is distinguished by a coarse, thick style of unpainted ceramics. The Ostionoid produced pottery similar to the Igneri's, except that it was painted in shades of pink and lilac. Little is known about Pre-Taíno culture. Both cultures continued to hunt, fish, gather, and farm. Although they had centralized villages, there is evidence that many Pre-Taíno split into nuclear families and lived in houses separate from one another scattered throughout the island. It is during this time that many Taíno customs began to appear. The Pre-Taíno were the first to construct *bateyes* (rectangular ball courts) and central plazas, which were square or round. They produced larger *cemí* amulets than found in Igneri culture, and they began carving petroglyphs—typically human or animal faces—into stones.

The most significant Igneri and Pre-Taíno archaeological site in Puerto Rico is **Centro Ceremonial Indígena de Tibes** near Ponce. In addition to seven *bateyes* and two plazas, a cemetery containing the remains of 187 people was discovered here.

Around AD 1200, the Pre-Taíno evolved into the **Taíno** culture. Of all the indigenous groups that lived in Puerto Rico, the most is known about the Taíno, perhaps because they were the ones to greet Christopher Columbus when he arrived in 1493, and several Spanish settlers wrote historical accounts about their culture.

The Taíno society was highly organized and hierarchal. They lived in self-governing villages called *yucayeques.* Commoners lived in conical wood-and-thatch huts called *bohios,* while the chief, or cacique, lived in a rectangular hut called a *caney.* They were a highly spiritual culture and would gather on sacred grounds, distinguished by plazas and *bateyes* (ball courts), to perform their religious ceremonies and compete in ball games.

The Taínos produced highly complex ceramics, as well as wood and stone implements, such as axes, daggers, *dujos* (ceremonial stools), and stone collars, the purpose of which is unknown. In addition to hunting, fishing, and gathering, they were highly developed farmers. The Taínos were also highly spiritual, and they created many *cemí* amulets, which were much more complex than those of past cultures, and stone carvings.

The Taínos were a peaceful culture, a fact that was severely challenged by the arrival of the Spanish conquistadors as well as the marauding Caribs, a highly aggressive, warrior culture that originated in Venezuela and roamed the Antilles plundering goods and capturing women. A hotly debated topic in scholarly discussions about the Caribs is whether or not they practiced cannibalism. The Taíno culture vanished around 1500 after the arrival of the Spanish conquistadors. Those not killed and enslaved by the Spanish died from a smallpox epidemic.

When Taíno Indians Ruled Boriken

The Taínos were an indigenous group of people who ruled the island of Puerto Rico (which they called Boriken) when Christopher Columbus and his expedition arrived in 1493. A little more than two decades later, they were virtually wiped out.

But surprising developments have recently revealed that the Taínos may live on in Puerto Rico, and not just in the vestiges of their customs, cuisine, and language that are still prevalent today. Preliminary results from DNA studies recently conducted at the Universidad de Puerto Rico in Mayagüez indicate that nearly half the island's Puerto Rican residents may contain indigenous DNA.

The study of Taíno history and culture is a fairly recent academic undertaking. Previously, what little was known of the peaceful, agrarian society was derived from written accounts by Spanish settlers. But the ongoing study of archaeological sites has uncovered new details about the highly politicized and spiritual society.

The Taínos are thought to have originated in South America before migrating to the

Caribbean, where they settled in Puerto Rico, Haiti, the Dominican Republic, and Cuba. Taíno society in Puerto Rico is believed to have developed between AD 1100 and 1500. By the time of Columbus's arrival, the island comprised about 20 political chiefdoms, each one ruled by a cacique (chief). Unlike the laboring class, who mostly wore nothing, the cacique wore a resplendent headdress made of parrot feathers, a gold amulet, and a *mao,* a white cotton shawl-like garment that protected the shoulders and chest from the sun.

Second in power to the caciques were the *bohiques* (shamans). Ornamenting their faces with paint and charcoal, they led spiritual rituals and ceremonies, using herbs, chants, maracas, and tobacco to heal the sick. To communicate with the gods and see visions of the future, *bohiques* and caciques inhaled a hallucinogenic powder made from the bright red seeds of the *cohoba* tree. It was ingested in a ceremony that began with a ritual cleansing that involved inducing vomiting with ornately carved spatulas. The powder was then inhaled through tubes created from tubers or bones.

Of special spiritual importance to the Taínos was the enigmatic *cemí,* a three-pointed object carved from stone or wood. Its significance is a mystery, but some believe it was thought to contain the spirit of the god Yocahu. *Cemies* were plentiful, powerful objects, believed to control everything from weather and crops to health and childbirth. Most *cemies,* which were kept in shrine rooms, were representations of animals and men with froglike legs. Some were ornamented with semiprecious stones and gold and are believed to represent the *cohoba*-fueled visions of the caciques and *bohiques.*

The Taínos saw spirituality in every natural thing, even death. Laborers were buried under their houses, called *bohios*—conical huts made from cane, straw, and palm leaves. But chiefs and shamans had special funerary rites. Their bodies were left to decompose in the open, and then their bones and skulls were cleaned and preserved in wooden urns or gourds, which were hung from the rafters. Pity the poor wives of the caciques, who were polygamists. Their favorite wives were buried alive when their husbands died.

Religious ceremonies, called *areytos,* were held in ceremonial plazas or rectangular ball courts, called *bateyes.* Lining its perimeter were monoliths adorned with petroglyphs—carvings of faces, animals, and the sun. This is where feasts, celebrations, sporting events, and ritual dances were held. Music was performed on conch trumpets, bone flutes, wooden drums, maracas, and *güiros,* a washboard-type percussion instrument made from gourds. Sometimes neighboring villagers would join in the festivities, participating in mock fights, footraces, or ball games similar to soccer, played with a heavy bouncing ball made from rubber plants and reeds. As in our modern-day ball games, the consumption of alcoholic beverages—corn beer in Taíno times—was also a highlight of the activities.

When they weren't whooping it up at the *batey,* the Taínos were hard at work growing, gathering, and hunting food. Luckily for them, the island was rich in resources. Peanuts, guavas, pineapples, sea grapes, black-eyed peas, and lima beans grew wild. Fields were cleared for the cultivation of corn, sweet potatoes, yams, squashes, papayas, and yucas, a staple that was processed into a type of flour used to make cassava bread. Cotton was also grown for the making of hammocks. Iguanas, snakes, birds, and manatees were hunted. The sea provided fish, conchs, oysters, and crabs. Canoes, carved from tree trunks, were used to fish and conduct trade with nearby islands. Some canoes were so huge that they could hold 100 men.

The Taínos were a matrilineal society. Women held a special place in the culture because nobility was passed down through their families. The only commoners to don clothing, married women wore a cotton *nagua* (apron); the longer the *nagua,* the higher the social rank of the wearer. Women spent their time making pottery, weaving hammocks, and processing yuca, a time-consuming and complicated procedure. Babies were carried on their mothers' backs on boards that were tied to the babies' foreheads, a practice that produced the flat heads that Taínos found attractive.

Columbus's arrival marked the beginning of the end for Taíno society. They were already weakened from attacks by the Caribs, an aggressive, possibly cannibalistic indigenous group from South America who captured Taíno women and forced them into slavery. The Spanish followed suit by enslaving many of the remaining Taínos.

It didn't take long for unrest to grow among the Taínos. In 1510, Cacique Urayoan ordered his warriors to capture and drown a Spanish settler to determine if the colonists were mortal. Upon Diego Salcedo's death, the Taínos revolted against the Spanish, but they were quickly overpowered by the Spaniards' firearms. Thousands of Taínos were shot to death, many are believed to have committed mass suicide, and others fled to the mountains.

Several devastating hurricanes hit the island during the next several years, which killed many more Taínos. It has been reported that by 1514, there were fewer than 4,000 Taínos left, and in 1519 a smallpox epidemic is said to have virtually wiped out the rest of the remaining population.

In the last decade, interest in learning more about the Taínos has increased. As pride in the legacy of Taíno society grows, so do efforts to preserve its heritage.

In 2007, what experts are calling the largest and most significant pre-Columbian site in the Caribbean was discovered during the construction of a dam in Jacana near Ponce. The five-acre site contains plazas, *bateyes*, burial grounds, residences, and a midden mound—a pile of ritual refuse. After a preliminary four-month investigation that included the removal of 75 boxes of skeletons, ceramics, and petroglyphs, the site has been covered back up to preserve it until a full-scale excavation can begin. It is expected to take 15 to 20 years to unearth all the secrets the site contains.

There are two archaeological sites open to the public: **Centro Ceremonial Indígena de Caguana** (Carr. 111, km 12.5, 787/894-7325 or 787/894-7310, www.icp.gobierno.pr) in Utuado and **Centro Ceremonial Indígena de Tibes** (Carr. 503, km 2.5, 787/840-2255, www.nps.gov/nr/travel/prvi/pr15.htm) in Ponce.

And for a taste of Taíno culture, visit Jayuya in November for the Festival Nacional Indígena, featuring traditional music, dance, food, and crafts.

To learn more about Taíno history and culture, visit the websites of the United Federation of Taíno People (www.uctp.org) and the Jatibonicu Taíno Tribal Nation of Boriken (www.taino-tribe.org).

COLONIZATION

Christopher Columbus was on his second voyage in his quest to "discover" the New World when he arrived in Puerto Rico in 1493. There is debate as to where exactly Columbus, called Cristóbal Colón by the Spanish, first disembarked on the island. That momentous occasion is claimed by Aguada, on the northwest coast of the Atlantic, and Guánica, on the southwest coast of the Caribbean. Either way, he didn't stick around long enough to do much more than christen the island San Juan Bautista, after John the Baptist.

It wasn't until 1508 that Juan Ponce de León, who had been on the voyage with Columbus, returned to the island to establish a settlement. The Taíno provided no resistance to his arrival. In fact, Taíno cacique Agueybana allowed Ponce de León to pick any spot he wanted for a settlement so long as the Spanish would help defend the Taíno against the Caribs. His choice of Caparra, a marshy, mosquito-ridden spot just west of what is now San Juan, was a poor one.

Around 1521 the settlement was relocated to what is now Old San Juan, and in 1523 Casa Blanca was built to house Ponce de León and his family, although by that time the explorer had left for Florida, where he met his demise. Originally the new settlement was called

Puerto Rico for its "rich port." It's not clear why—possibly a cartographer's mistake—but soon after it was founded, the name of the settlement was switched with the name of the island.

San Juan quickly became a vital port to the Spanish empire. An important stopover for ships transporting goods from the New World to Europe, it soon became a target for foreign powers. To protect its interests, Spain began a centuries-long effort to construct a formidable series of fortresses to defend the harbor and the city.

Construction of the island's first Spanish fort, La Fortaleza, began in 1533. The small structure, which to this day serves as home to the island's governor, was built to store gold and protect it from Carib attacks. The port quickly grew in importance, and Spain's enemies—England, Holland, and France—began to threaten it with attacks. More elaborate defense systems were needed. To protect the city's all-important harbor, construction of Castillo San Felipe del Morro began in 1539, forming the nucleus of the city's fortifications. Through the years it was expanded to four levels and five acres before completion in 1787.

To protect the city from attack by land, San Cristóbal castle was begun in 1634. By the time it was completed in 1783, it was the city's largest fort, spanning 27 acres. That same year began the 200-year construction of La Muralla, the massive stone wall that once encircled the city and much of which still stands. It contained five gates, which were closed at night and guarded at all times.

The English were the first to significantly damage the city. In 1595, Sir Francis Drake led 26 vessels in an attack that partially burned the city but was successfully repelled. The next English attack proved more fruitful. Led by George Clifford, the earl of Cumberland, troops landed in Santurce in 1598 and occupied the city for several months before illness and exhaustion forced them to abandon their stronghold.

The most devastating attack to date came when 17 Dutch ships led by Boudoin Hendricks attacked in 1625. And in 1797 the British, led by Sir Ralph Abercrombie, attacked again.

Meanwhile, other settlements were being established throughout the island. The area now known as Aguada was established as Villa de Sotomayor in 1508, but it was destroyed by Indians in 1511. In 1516, Franciscan friars built a monastery nearby, which was destroyed by Indians 12 years later. A new monastery was built in 1590, followed by a chapel in 1639. Also an important stopover for ships on their way to Spain from South America, it suffered attacks by the English, French, and Dutch. San Germán was founded in 1573 and was attacked by pirates, the English, and the Dutch. Arecibo followed in 1606.

Attack by foreign powers waned in the 1800s, and the island's sugarcane and coffee plantations flourished because of the slave labor that was brought in from Africa. But by the 1860s, a new challenge to Spanish rule arose in the form of an independence rebellion that was brewing among the island's rural class.

On September 23, 1868, about 500 Puerto Ricans organized a revolt, proclaiming the mountain town of Lares free of Spanish rule. Local stores and offices owned by Spanish merchants were looted, slaves were declared free, and city hall was stormed. The revolt was quickly squelched the next day, when rebel forces attempted to take over a neighboring town. The revolutionaries, including leaders Manuel Rojas and Juan Rius Rivera, were taken prisoner, found guilty of treason and sedition, and sentenced to death. But to ease the political tension that was brewing on the island at that time, the revolutionaries were eventually released. Although the revolt, referred to as **Grito de Lares,** was unsuccessful, it did result in Spain's giving the island more autonomy.

Colonial reforms were made, national political parties were established, and slavery was abolished. But at the same time, restrictions were imposed on human rights, such as freedom of the press and the right to gather. Meanwhile, the Spanish empire was beginning to crumble. It eventually lost all its Caribbean colonies except Cuba and Puerto Rico, and increased tariffs and taxes were imposed on imports and exports to help fund Spain's efforts to regain control of the nearby Dominican Republic. Living conditions in Puerto Rico deteriorated as the economy declined. Illiteracy was high; malnutrition and poverty were rampant. Violent clashes broke out between desperate residents and Spanish merchants, who monopolized trade on the island.

SPANISH-AMERICAN WAR

As the 19th century drew to a close, tensions had grown between Spain's declining empire and the rising world power of the United States, which had set its sights on the Caribbean islands to protect its growing sea trade. Under pressure from the United States, Spain granted Puerto Rico constitutional autonomy, and the island was preparing to hold its first self-governing elections when the Spanish-American War was declared in April 1898.

The war was fought mostly in the waters around Cuba and the Philippines, but in May San Juan was pounded with artillery for three hours from U.S. warships led by Admiral William T. Sampson. The attack was a misguided effort to flush out a Spanish squadron commander who was not in San Juan at the time. Both of San Juan's major forts sustained damage. The top of Castillo San Felipe del Morro's lighthouse was destroyed, and several residences and government buildings were damaged.

In July, 18,000 U.S. troops were sent to secure Puerto Rico. Landing in Guánica, ground troops began working their way northwest to San Juan, but before they could arrive, Spain agreed to relinquish sovereignty over the West Indies. With the signing of the Treaty of Paris in December 1898, Puerto Rico was ceded to the United States.

U.S. RULE AND THE FIGHT FOR INDEPENDENCE

For two years after the Spanish-American War, the United States operated a military government in Puerto Rico until 1900, when the first civilian government was established. The governor, his cabinet, and the senate-like Higher House of Delegates were appointed by the U.S. president. A 35-member Local House of Delegates and a resident commissioner, who represented Puerto Rico in the U.S. House of Representatives but had no vote, were elected by popular vote. In 1917, Puerto Ricans were granted U.S. citizenship by President Woodrow Wilson.

Living conditions in Puerto Rico advanced very little in the first 30 years under U.S. rule. A couple of hurricanes between 1928 and 1932 left the economy—dependent solely on agriculture—in ruins. Homelessness and poverty were rife. The unhappy state of affairs fueled the organization of another independence movement led by the Harvard-educated nationalist leader Pedro Albizu Campos. The doctor chafed against U.S. rule and asserted it had no claims to the island because it had been given its independence from Spain before the Spanish-American War broke out. Campos was named president of the island's Nationalist Party, which had formed in 1922. In 1936, Campos was arrested for his suspected role in the death of Colonel E. Francis Riggs in retaliation for the Río Piedras Massacre. After two trials, he was found guilty and sentenced to prison.

On Palm Sunday in 1937, a Nationalist Party demonstration was organized in Ponce, Campos's hometown, to protest the independence leader's incarceration. Just as the march was getting under way, police fired on the crowd, killing 19 people and injuring 200 in what went down in history as the Ponce Massacre. It was a huge blow to the independence movement, and with Campos imprisoned, it seemed as though the fight for freedom had been quelled. Instead, the incident merely drove the movement underground and possibly fueled its embrace of violent tactics.

To quell the brewing unrest, protect its interests, and benefit from the island's resources, the United States took several momentous steps beginning in the 1940s that had far-reaching effects on Puerto Rico's culture. During World War II, several large military bases were established on the island—Fort Buchanan Army Base in Guaynabo, Ramey Air Force Base in Aguadilla, Roosevelt Roads Naval Station in Ceiba, and Vieques Navy Base—which significantly boosted the economy. In 1940 a major hydroelectric-power expansion program was undertaken, providing electrical power throughout the island and attracting U.S. industry. In 1947, President Harry S. Truman agreed to give Puerto Rico more control of its local government, and the next year the island chose its first self-elected governor, Luis Muñoz Marín, a member of the Popular Democratic Party.

But by this time, Campos had finished serving his time and returned to Puerto Rico, where he reinvigorated efforts to achieve independence—this time, at any cost.

On November 1, 1950, two Puerto Rican nationalists—Oscar Collazo and Griselio Torresola—attempted to assassinate President Truman at the Blair House, where the president and his family were living while the White House was being renovated. Approaching the house from opposite sides, they attempted but failed to shoot their way in. After the gunfire ended, Torresola and one police officer were dead, and two police officers were wounded. Collazo was sentenced to death, but Truman commuted the sentence to life. Campos was again arrested and found guilty of his role in planning the assassination attempt. He spent the remainder of his life in and out of prison until his death in 1965.

In 1952, Puerto Rico adopted a new constitution, and commonwealth status was established. The island had more self-governing powers than ever before. This was the beginning of the long debate that still rages today over Puerto Rico's political status. While roughly half the population is content with commonwealth status, an equal number of residents have worked steadily toward trying to achieve statehood.

Puerto Rico's first self-elected governor, Luis Muñoz Marín, was a New Deal-style reformist with progressive ideas who served four terms as governor of Puerto Rico. In partnership with the United States, he initiated many programs that advanced economic and cultural development throughout the island and significantly improved the infrastructure. Under his leadership, an economic development program called Operation Bootstrap was successfully launched to entice global industry to the island with federal and local tax exemptions. *The Economist* described it as "one century of economic development... achieved in a decade." The standard of living leapt to new heights, and the tourist trade soon exploded. The next three decades, from the 1950s through the 1970s, were a huge period of growth and development for the island. But some believed Operation Bootstrap was a throwback to colonial ideals in which the island's resources were exploited without fair compensation, rendering the island increasingly more dependent on the United States.

The island suffered several setbacks in the 1980s. The energy crisis and U.S. recession sent the tourist trade into decline, and many of San Juan's glamorous high-rise hotels fell into disrepair, some shuttering altogether. Hurricane Hugo in 1989 dealt a devastating blow, and Operation Bootstrap was discontinued, which sent many manufacturers packing.

Meanwhile, the independence movement was quietly gaining momentum, and peaceful protest was not part of the agenda. Two pro-independence organizations formed in the 1970s. The Popular Boricua Army, commonly known as Los Macheteros, primarily operated in Puerto Rico. The Armed Forces of Puerto Rican National Liberation (FALN) operated in the United States. The two organizations communicated their desire for independence with terrorist attacks.

One of FALN's most notorious attacks was setting off a briefcase bomb in 1975 in New

Nationalist Hero

Dr. Pedro Albizu Campos has been dead since 1965, but the beloved nationalist leader lives on in the memory of Puerto Ricans everywhere. Nearly every town in Puerto Rico has a street or school named after him, and on the side of a building on Calle San Sebastián in Old San Juan, local artist Dennis Mario Rivera has memorialized him with a stunning graffiti portrait, helping make Campos a pop-culture icon among Puerto Ricans akin to Che Guevara in other Latin American countries.

Born in Ponce in 1891, Campos was a brilliant man who was fluent in eight languages and earned five degrees at Harvard University—in law, literature, philosophy, chemical engineering, and military sciences. So how did a man with such a promising future end up spending the last 25 years of his life in and out of prison? By leading the charge for Puerto Rico's independence from the United States.

Campos was reportedly not anti-American, nor was he communist. But he passionately believed that the 1898 Treaty of Paris, which ended the Spanish-American War, wrongfully gave the United States sovereignty over Puerto Rico. After all, Spain had granted autonomy to Puerto Rico in 1897. The island had established its own currency, postal service, and customs department. It's hard to deny Campos's belief that Spain had no authority to bequeath the island to the United States.

Nevertheless, the island did become a property of the United States, and Campos even went on to serve as a first lieutenant in the U.S. Infantry during World War I. After he was discharged, he completed his studies at Harvard and returned to Puerto Rico, where he joined the Nationalist Party in 1924.

A gifted orator, Campos traveled throughout the island, as well as the Caribbean and Latin America, seeking support for the independence movement with such eloquent speeches that he was nicknamed El Maestro. And he was eventually elected president of the Nationalist Party. Although the Nationalist Party fared poorly in local elections, during the next six years Campos kept the movement in the forefront of political discourse by staging a protest at the San Juan capitol, implicating the U.S.-based Rockefeller Institute in the deaths of patients who were the subject of medical testing without their consent, and by serving as legal representation for striking sugarcane workers.

The beginning of Campos's downfall came in 1935, when four nationalists were killed by po-

York City's Fraunces Tavern, a historic landmark where George Washington delivered his farewell speech to colonial troops during the Revolutionary War. Four patrons were killed. Other bombs were detonated in a Harlem tenement, Penn Station, and JFK airport. All told, FALN set off 72 bombs in New York City and Chicago, killing 5 people and injuring 83.

In 1981, Los Macheteros infiltrated the Puerto Rican Air National Guard base and blew up 11 military planes, causing $45 million in damage. In 1983 members of Los Macheteros raided a Wells Fargo depot in Hartford, Connecticut, wounding a policeman and making off with $7.2 million, ostensibly to fund the organization's efforts.

Sixteen instigators from both organizations were eventually captured and sentenced to federal prison, bringing the terrorist acts to a halt. In 1999, President Clinton granted them clemency.

CONTEMPORARY TIMES

The dawn of a new century found Puerto Rico in a heated contest with the U.S. military over its naval base in Vieques. For years the military had been using the island for bombing practice and ammunitions storage. But in 1999, civilian David Sanes was accidentally killed by a bomb in Vieques, which set off an organized protest effort that raged for several years and grew stronger in numbers through time. The military finally relented, pulling out of Vieques in 2003. Without the base in

lice under the command of Colonel E. Francis Riggs in an event referred to as the Río Piedras Massacre. The next year, two nationalists killed Riggs, a crime that resulted in their being arrested and executed without trial. That same year, the federal court in San Juan ordered the arrest of Campos and several other nationalists on the grounds of seditious conspiracy to overthrow the U.S. government in Puerto Rico. A jury trial found him innocent, but a new jury was ordered and Campos was found guilty. The verdict was upheld on appeal, and Campos was sent to the federal penitentiary in Atlanta.

Graffiti portrait of Don Pedro Albizu Campos by local artist Dennis Mario Rivera on Calle San Sebastián

Campos returned to Puerto Rico in 1947 and is believed to have become involved in a plot to incite armed struggle against the United States. Three years later, two nationalist attacks—one on La Fortaleza, the governor's residence in San Juan, and one on Blair House, the temporary home of President Harry Truman—led to Campos's rearrest, conviction, and imprisonment for sedition. His imprisonment at La Princesa in Old San Juan was marked by a serious decline in his health, which he attributed to radiation experiments performed on him without his consent.

Governor Luis Muñoz Marín pardoned Campos in 1953, but the pardon was overthrown when there was another attempted attack made on the U.S. House of Representatives. In 1964, Marín successfully pardoned Campos, who was by then a sick and broken man. A year later he died of a stroke in Hato Rey. More than 75,000 Puerto Ricans reportedly joined the procession that carried Campos's body to his burial in Cementerio de Santa María Magdalena de Pazzis, Old San Juan's historic cemetery.

Although the independence movement still has little political clout in Puerto Rico today, Campos is revered as a man who gave his life for liberty—an ideal the island has never fully achieved.

Vieques, the U.S. Navy decided it didn't need the Roosevelt Roads Naval Station in Ceiba, and it was closed in 2004, taking with it its estimated $250 million-a-year infusion into the local economy. With Ramey Air Force Base having closed in the mid-1970s, Fort Buchanan is the last remaining U.S. military base on the island.

The independence movement in Puerto Rico has long since abandoned its violent ways, and in truth, only 5 percent of the population wants independence. But every once in a while, something occurs that reminds islanders of the movement's presence and its bloody history. As recently as 2005, the FBI killed—some say ambushed—Los Macheteros organizer Filiberto Ojeda Ríos in a shoot-out at his home in Hormigueros. The 72-year-old man was the ringleader in the 1983 Wells Fargo attack and had evaded authorities ever since. To some, the fact that Ojeda was killed on September 23—a holiday honoring the independence movement's 1868 uprising against Spain—seemed to send a clear reminder to *independistas* that their past activities had not been forgotten.

The single most defining characteristic of Puerto Rico's political climate today is the decades-old debate over whether it should remain a territory of the United States or become a state. In 2012, 61 percent of the voters chose statehood in a historic, non-binding referendum. Whether the island actually attains statehood remains to be seen.

Government and Economy

GOVERNMENT ORGANIZATION

Puerto Rico is a self-governing commonwealth of the United States. Its residents are U.S. citizens, but they can't vote for members of Congress or the president. A resident commissioner represents the island's interests in Washington but cannot vote on legislative matters. Businesses pay federal taxes, but individuals do not, although they do contribute to federal programs such as Social Security and Medicare. Individuals also pay about 32 percent of their income in local taxes.

Ever since Puerto Rico became a commonwealth in the early 1950s, its residents have debated the best course for the island's political future. A small but fervent number want independence, but the rest of the island is evenly divided between pro-statehood and pro-commonwealth factions. Statehood would mean more federal funding and a voice in national decisions. Those opposed to statehood fear losing their Spanish language and heritage in the rush toward Americanization.

In some ways, Puerto Rico is already like a state. The United States oversees all federal affairs, including interstate trade, foreign relations, customs, immigration, currency, military service, judicial procedures, transportation, communications, agriculture, mining, and the postal service. The local Puerto Rican government oversees internal affairs. The head of government is an elected governor, and there are two legislative chambers—the House and the Senate. The island's capital is based in San Juan. The island is divided into 78 municipalities, and each one is governed by a popularly elected mayor and municipal assembly.

For the first time since the United States claimed the island as a territory in 1898, Puerto Rico may be in the position to help decide its own fate. In 2012, voters overwhelmingly approved statehood in a referendum; however, no other action has been taken. Ultimately, whether Puerto Rico becomes the 51st state or not is up to the U.S. Congress. But for the first time ever, the majority of Puerto Ricans want statehood.

POLITICAL PARTIES

Puerto Ricans are passionate about politics. Political rallies are frequent, and during election years, political alliances are proclaimed by flag-waving caravans that drive through towns honking their horns and broadcasting speeches from loudspeakers. Puerto Rico has one of the highest percentages of voter turnout in the United States.

There are three political parties in Puerto Rico. The **Popular Democratic Party** is pro-commonwealth, the **New Progressive Party** is pro-statehood, and the **Puerto Rican Independence Party** is pro-independence. Those who embrace independence represent only 5 percent of the population. For decades the island was fairly evenly divided between pro-statehood and pro-commonwealth factions. But a 2012 referendum indicates statehood is gaining in popularity.

JUDICIAL SYSTEM

The judicial system in Puerto Rico is structured the same as in the United States. The highest local court is the Supreme Court, consisting of a chief justice and six associate justices appointed by the governor. There is a Court of Appeals, Superior Court, a civil and criminal District Court, and Municipal Court. The U.S. Federal Court, based in San Juan, has final authority.

ECONOMY

Puerto Rico has one of the best economies in the Caribbean, but it's still well below U.S. standards. Approximately 41 percent of the population lives below the poverty level. In 2012 the unemployment rate was 14 percent, and the median household income was $23,168. The island is heavily dependent on U.S. aid, and the government is the largest employer.

From colonial times until the 1940s, the island's largest industry was sugar production. But that industry went into decline when sugar prices plummeted as other sources became available.

In 1948, the federal and local governments came together to introduce an economic development program called Operation Bootstrap. In addition to bringing land reforms, roads, and schools to neglected parts of the island, it stimulated industrial growth by giving federal and local tax exemptions to U.S. corporations that established operations in Puerto Rico. Many major manufacturing firms set up shop, and before long the production of pharmaceuticals and electronics far eclipsed agriculture on the island. The period from the 1950s through the 1970s was a huge period of growth and development. The standard of living achieved new heights very quickly, and the tourism industry began to blossom.

But in the latter part of the 20th century, Puerto Rico's economy suffered a series of setbacks. First the energy crisis and U.S. recession put a damper on the tourist trade in the 1980s. Then in the 1990s, Operation Bootstrap's tax incentives were discontinued and the North American Free Trade Agreement (NAFTA) was enacted, which sent industries packing to Mexico, where labor was cheaper. Adding insult to injury, in 2004 the United States closed the Roosevelt Roads Naval Station, which had contributed $250 million a year to the local economy.

But there is a new vigor fueling the economy of Puerto Rico today, and it's apparent in the many cranes and construction projects under way throughout the island. Economic development has turned its attention aggressively toward tourism during a time, especially after 9/11, when U.S. travelers are seeking destinations closer to home. Port Authority improvements to San Juan's 12 ship docks and seven piers have made it the largest port in the Caribbean. The 113-acre Puerto Rico Convention Center beside the Isla Grande Airport near Old San Juan was completed in late 2005, making it the largest convention center in the Caribbean. New road construction projects are under way, and seemingly every town is renovating its central plaza. An estimated five million tourists visit the island each year.

People and Culture

POPULATION

Today more Puerto Ricans live on the U.S. mainland than in Puerto Rico, and the island's population is continuing to shrink as the high unemployment rate sends residents—mostly educated professionals—stateside in pursuit of work. Per a July 2014 estimate, the population dropped 120,000 to 3.6 million. About 45 percent of the island's residents live below the poverty level and at least 10 municipalities (primarily those in the Cordillera Central) have poverty rates greater than 60 percent.

NATIONAL IDENTITY

There is a saying on the island that Puerto Ricans are like porpoises: They can barely keep their heads above water, but they're always smiling. It's an apt description. In 2005, Puerto Ricans were proclaimed the happiest people on earth, according to a highly reported study by the Stockholm-based organization World Values Survey. Despite high poverty and unemployment rates, it seems nothing can put a damper on the lively, fun-loving Puerto Rican spirit. Most Puerto Ricans like to celebrate big and often.

Puerto Rico Municipalities

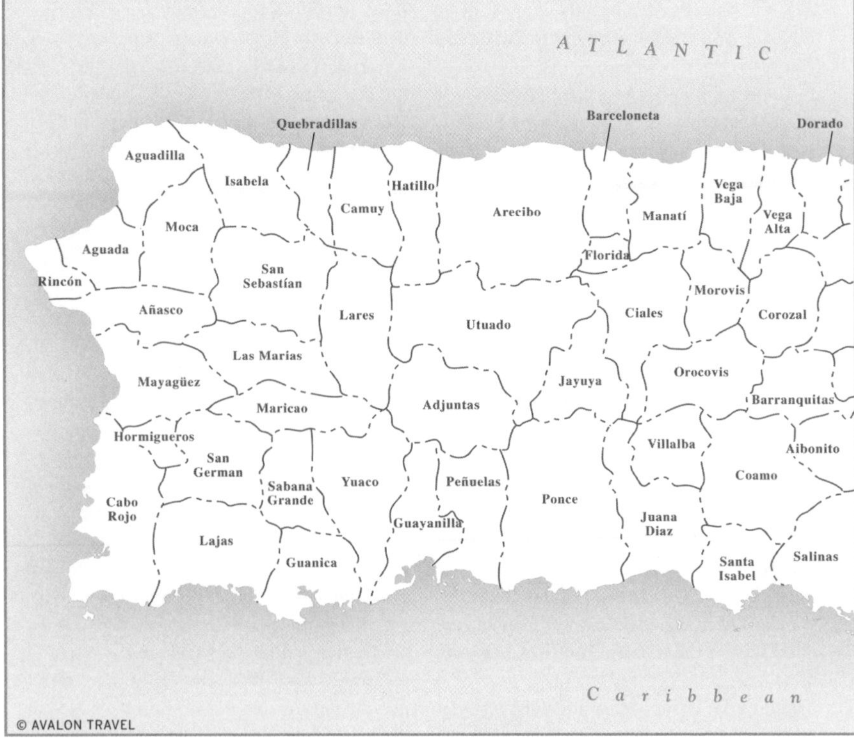

In fact, there are reportedly more than 500 festivals a year on the island, and everything is a family affair involving multiple generations of relatives. Music is usually at the heart of most gatherings, and Puerto Ricans are passionate about their opinions and love few things more than to debate politics or sports for hours.

The culture of Puerto Rican life has been significantly shaped by its history. It was originally inhabited by a society of peaceful, agriculturally based indigenous people who migrated to the island from South America. But beginning in 1508, the island became a Spanish colony, and for the next four centuries European influence reigned. Towns were developed according to Spanish custom around central plazas and churches. The church spread Catholicism, and Spanish became the official language.

Because the majority of colonists were men, the Spanish Crown officially supported marriage between Spanish men and Taíno women, leading to a population of mixed offspring. The Spanish also brought in slaves from Africa to work the island's many coffee and sugar plantations, and they too produced offspring with the Taíno and Spanish colonists, producing what for years was called a population of mulattoes.

Perhaps because of this historic mixing of races, racial tensions are relatively minimal in Puerto Rico. There are some levels of society that proudly claim to be of pure European blood, and darker-skinned populations are sometimes discriminated against.

But in general, Puerto Rico is a true melting pot of races in which skin comes in all shades of white and brown, and the general population is fairly accepting of everyone else.

When the United States took control of Puerto Rico in 1898, the island underwent another enormous cultural transformation. Suddenly U.S. customs and practices were imposed. English became a common second language, and has at times been proclaimed the official language. The U.S. dollar became the legal tender. American corporations set up shop, bringing with them an influx of American expatriates whose ways of dress, cuisine, and art were integrated into the existing culture. Much of this influence came in the form of the military, due to the many military bases that were established on the island. Some people credit that influence on the relative stability and orderliness of public life, particularly as compared to other Caribbean islands. The island's governmental and judicial systems are organized similarly to the United States, and many U.S. social services are offered on the island.

Inroads of contemporary American culture have been made into much of island life, but Puerto Ricans are fiercely proud of their Spanish heritage. Since becoming a U.S. territory a little more than 100 years ago, Puerto Rico has undergone a seismic shift in its national identity that has divided the island politically. Puerto Ricans are U.S. citizens, and they enjoy many—but not all—the privileges

Jíbaro Culture

After the Taíno Indians succumbed to the Spanish conquistadors, an agrarian culture developed in the mountains of Puerto Rico. By the 19th century, wealthy Europeans arrived by ship to establish grand haciendas. Along with slaves, locals were employed to work the land, growing coffee and sugar. Isolated from developing port cities by unnavigable forest, dependent upon their own two hands to feed and shelter their families, and governed by a strict moral code informed by both Catholicism and Taíno spiritual beliefs, the early Puerto Rican men and women were poor, hard-working people who made up for their lack of formal education with common sense. When they did venture into the cities, townspeople jeered at them for their straw hats, their neckerchiefs, and their country ways, calling them *jíbaros,* a word similar in meaning to hillbilly.

The word *jíbaro* first appeared in a song and poem in 1820, but it gained widespread acceptance in 1849 when Dr. Manuel Alonzo published his book *El Gíbaro,* a collection of folktales about rustic life. Because they had to create their own entertainment, a big part of *jíbaro* culture was music. Steeped in Spanish roots, *jíbaro* music emphasizes stringed instruments, particularly the four-string *cuatro.* It is similar in sound to the *guajiro* sound from Cuba, and is often likened to the folk music of the Appalachian region of the United States. *Jíbaro* music is still quite popular in Puerto Rico and is performed at weddings and Christmas celebrations.

Once a source of embarrassment, the *jíbaro* identity has evolved over time to become a source of Puerto Rican pride. The symbol for the Popular Democratic Party formed in 1938 is the *jíbaro's* straw hat. A monument in Salinas, depicting a man, woman, and child, pays tribute to the *jíbaro* culture. And popular restaurants, such as Raíces Resturante in Old San Juan, dress their servers as *jíbaros* in straw hats and neckerchiefs. To be called a *jíbaro* today is to be called a true Puerto Rican, and that's a good reason to feel proud.

that entails. The issue of Puerto Rico's future political status has been an ongoing debate for more than 50 years, and it is as much a part of the island's national identity as its Spanish language and customs. Roughly half the island's population wants to remain a U.S. commonwealth, in large part because they believe that status ensures the preservation of their Spanish culture. The other half wants to become a U.S. state so they can have full privileges of citizenship, including the ability to vote for the U.S. president and have full representation in Congress.

Puerto Rico held a referendum in 2012 that voted in favor of becoming the 51st state of the United States, but no other action has been taken. So far, the island's political status remains status quo.

GENDER ROLES

When it comes to gender roles, Puerto Ricans are fairly traditional. However, as in the rest of the industrial world, women have made inroads into the formerly male world of business and sports, particularly in urban areas. At one time it was common practice among the island's most traditional families for young women to be accompanied by chaperones in the form of an aunt or older sister when they began dating, but that practice is quickly vanishing.

Vestiges of machismo still exist. Attractive young women may attract unwanted catcalls, usually expressed with a "s-s-s" sound, or calls of *"Mira, mami!"* ("Look, mama!"). But in general, Puerto Rican men can be quite chivalrous in ways American women may be unaccustomed to. Having a bus seat relinquished for their comfort and the holding of doors are courtesies commonly encountered.

RELIGION

Before the arrival of Christopher Columbus in 1493, Puerto Rico's indigenous population was composed of highly spiritual individuals who worshipped multiple gods believed to reside in nature. It was a common belief that these

An Island Christmas

The Twelve Days of Christmas have nothing on Puerto Rico. Here, Las Navidades (the Christmas holidays) start the day after Thanksgiving and end in mid-January with the San Sebastián Street Festival. On any given day during the Christmas holiday period (usually after 10pm), a roving band of *parranderos* — like carolers but dressed in straw hats and playing guitars and maracas — will wake an unsuspecting friend with Christmas songs and raucous demands for food and drink. After the visitors have emptied the pantry and the refrigerator, the owners of the home close up the house and join the *parranderos* at the next house, and the next house, and so on, until dawn, when the last house serves everyone the traditional *asopao de pollo* (chicken and rice stew).

Nochebuena (Christmas Eve) is an official half-day holiday when friends and family come together over a large meal, followed by midnight Mass. Many Puerto Ricans have adopted the tradition of Santa Claus on Christmas Day, called **Navidad.** In addition to presents from St. Nick, the highlight is a daylong party that usually involves roasting a whole pig over wood charcoal.

On December 28, the north coast town of Hatillo commemorates Herod's slaughter of innocents in Bethlehem with **Día de los Inocentes,** a celebration featuring costumed parades throughout the countryside where tricks are played on friends and family.

At the stroke of midnight on New Year's Eve or **Año Viejo** (Old Year), tradition dictates that locals eat 12 grapes, sprinkle sugar outside the house for good luck, and throw a bucket of water out the window to get rid of the old and make room for the new. Fireworks light up the sky at the Puerto Rico Convention Center in San Juan at midnight.

Puerto Rico's traditional Christian holiday is **Día de los Reyes** (Three Kings Day) on January 6. Festivities begin the night before with **Víspera de los Reyes** (Eve of the Epiphany of the Kings), when children fill drinking glasses with water for thirsty Wise Men and fill shoeboxes with grass for their camels. The next morning children discover that the water and grass have been consumed and find gifts that have been left beneath their beds.

The **San Sebastián Street Festival** in Old San Juan originated as a day to honor Saint Sebastian. It takes place mid-January, which makes it a natural bookend to the island's holiday season. The four-day festival is likened to Mardi Gras without the beads when hundreds of thousands of people descend on Old San Juan for parades, concerts, artisan booths, and lots of eating and drinking.

gods controlled everything from the success or failure of crops to one's choice of a spouse.

All that began to change when Ponce de León arrived in 1508, bringing with him several Roman Catholic priests who ministered to the new colony and set about converting the Taíno Indians to the faith, beginning with baptisms. In 1511, Pope Julius II created a diocese in Caparra, the island's first settlement.

Today, depending on the source, Puerto Rico's population is between 75 and 85 percent Roman Catholic. Although weekly church attendance is far below that figure, the Catholic Church has great influence on Puerto Rican life. Each town has a Catholic church at its center and celebrates its patron saint with an annual festival. Although many patron-saint festivals have become much more secular over time, they typically include a religious procession and special Mass to mark the day. Images of saints are common items in traditional households, and you can't enter a church without seeing clusters of women lighting candles, praying, or kissing the hem of the dress worn by a statue of Mary.

Some Puerto Ricans practice a hybrid form of religion called *espiritismo,* which combines elements of the Catholic religion and Indian beliefs in nature-dwelling spirits that can be called on to effect change in one's life. Similarly, some Puerto Ricans of African descent practice Santería, introduced to the island by Yoruba slaves from West Africa. It also observes multiple gods and combines elements of Catholicism. Practitioners of both religions patronize the island's *botanicas,* stores

Fiestas Patronales

The most elaborate and renowned *fiestas patronales* take place in San Juan and Loíza, but all of the municipalities' celebrations honoring their patron saints offer visitors a unique opportunity to get a concentrated dose of local culture. Here is a list of some of the island's *fiestas patronales*.

FEBRUARY

- **Manatí:** La Virgen de la Candelaria, February 2
- **Mayagüez:** La Virgen de la Candelaria, February 2
- **Coamo:** La Virgen de la Candelaria and San Blas, February 3

MARCH

- **Loíza:** San Patricio, March 17
- **Lares:** San José, March 19
- **Luquillo:** San José, March 19

MAY

- **Arecibo:** Apóstol San Felipe, May 1
- **Maunabo:** San Isidro, May 15
- **Toa Alta:** San Fernando, May 30

JUNE

- **Barranquitas:** San Antonio de Padua, June 13
- **Dorado:** San Antonio de Padua, June 13
- **Isabela:** San Antonio de Padua, June 13
- **San Juan:** San Juan Bautista, June 23
- **Orocovis:** San Juan Bautista, June 24
- **Toa Baja:** San Pedro Apóstol, June 30

JULY

- **Culebra:** Virgen del Carmen, July 16
- **Hatillo:** Virgen del Carmen, July 16
- **Morovis:** Virgen del Carmen, July 16
- **Aibonito:** Santiago Apóstol, July 25

- **Fajardo:** Santiago Apóstol, July 25
- **Guánica:** Santiago Apóstol, July 25
- **Loíza:** Santiago Apóstol, July 25
- **San Germán:** San Germán, July 31

AUGUST

- **Cayey:** Nuestra Señora de la Asunción, August 15
- **Adjuntas:** San Joaquín and Santa Ana, August 21
- **Rincón:** Santa Rosa de Lima, August 30

SEPTEMBER

- **Jayuya:** Nuestra Señora de la Monserrate, September 8
- **Moca:** Nuestra Señora de la Monserrate, September 8
- **Salinas:** Nuestra Señora de la Monserrate, September 8
- **Cabo Rojo:** San Miguel Arcangel, September 29
- **Utuado:** San Miguel Arcangel, September 29

OCTOBER

- **Yabucoa:** Los Angeles Custodios, October 2
- **Naguabo:** Nuestra Señora del Rosario, October 7
- **Vega Baja:** Nuestra Señora del Rosario, October 7
- **Quebradillas:** San Rafael Arcangel, October 24

NOVEMBER

- **Aguadilla:** San Carlos Borromeo, November 4

DECEMBER

- **Vega Alta:** La Inmaculada Concepción de María, December 8
- **Vieques:** La Inmaculada Concepción de María, December 8
- **Ponce:** Nuestra Señora de la Guadalupe, December 12

that sell roots, herbs, candles, soaps, and amulets that are employed to sway the spirits to help individuals achieve success, whether it be in business, love, or starting a family.

Once the United States arrived in Puerto Rico in 1898, Protestantism began to grow on the island, and all major sects are represented. Pentecostal fundamentalism has developed in recent decades, and there is a small Jewish community on the island as well.

HOLIDAYS AND FESTIVALS

No matter when you visit Puerto Rico, there's a good chance there's a holiday or festival going on somewhere on the island. Among the biggest festivals are Ponce's **Carnaval** in February; Hatillo's **Festival de Máscaras** and **Día de los Inocentes** in December; and **Festival Nacional Indígena** in Jayuya in November.

Being a U.S. commonwealth, Puerto Rico has adopted an American-style celebration of Christmas, but it also celebrates the more traditional **Día de los Reyes,** also known as **Three Kings Day,** on January 6. On January 5, children fill shoeboxes with grass to feed the Wise Men's camels and place them under their beds. In the morning, the grass is gone and in its place is a present.

But most notably, all 78 municipalities in Puerto Rico honor their patron saints with annual festivals called ***fiestas patronales.*** Although special Masses and religious processions may be a part of the celebrations, secular festivities such as musical performances, dancing, traditional foods, artisan booths, and games often take precedence. The festivals typically take place in the main plaza.

LANGUAGE

Puerto Rico has two official languages: Spanish and English. Many Puerto Ricans living in metropolitan areas are bilingual, but by far the majority of the population uses primarily Spanish. Spanish is spoken in the public school system, and English is taught as a foreign language.

In recent years, the designation of Puerto Rico's official language has been caught in a political volley between the pro-statehood and pro-commonwealth factions. In 1991, Governor Rafael Hernández Colón, a proponent of commonwealth status, declared Spanish as the sole official language. He was preceded by Governor Pedro Rosselló, a proponent of statehood who changed the official language to English. But for now, both languages enjoy official status.

EDUCATION

Puerto Rico has a 94 percent literacy rate, and its educational system is structured the same as in the United States—kindergarten through 12th grade. In addition to the public school system, the Catholic Church operates a private school system. Both systems teach in Spanish. There are also several English-language private schools on the island.

There are several institutions of higher learning in Puerto Rico, the largest one being the Universidad de Puerto Rico, with campuses in Mayagüez, San Juan, Río Piedras, and Humacao. Other schools include Universidad Polytechnica de Puerto Rico, Universidad Intermericana de Puerto Rico, Universidad Carlos Albizu, and Universidad del Sagrado Corazón. There are also two arts schools—Escuela de Artes Plásticas de Puerto Rico and Conservatorio de Música de Puerto Rico.

The Arts

Puerto Rico is a melting pot of indigenous, Spanish, and African influences, and nowhere is that more apparent than in the island's rich cultural life. Food, music, art, dance—they all reflect different aspects of the cultures that came together over time to create *la vida criolla* (the Creole life).

MUSIC

Music is a huge part of Puerto Rican life. Sometimes it seems as though the whole island reverberates to a syncopated beat, thanks to the strains of music that waft from outdoor concerts, open windows, barrooms, passing cars, and boom boxes. Nearly every weekend there is a holiday or festival in Puerto Rico, and at the core of its celebration is always music. During a recent stay in Old San Juan, each morning began with the sound of a lone elderly man walking up the deserted street singing a heartbreaking lament that echoed off the 18th-century buildings.

The island has made many significant contributions to the world of music at large, starting with the birth of a couple of uniquely Puerto Rican instruments. The national instrument of Puerto Rico is the *cuatro,* an adaptation of the Spanish guitar that features 10 strings arranged in five pairs and is typically carved from solid blocks of laurel. Several classic Puerto Rican instruments date to the indigenous people, including the popular *güiro.* Similar in principle to the washboard, the *güiro* is a hollowed gourd with ridges cut into its surface, which is scraped rhythmically with a comblike object. Other prevalent local instruments that reflect African influence are the *barril,* a large drum originally made by stretching animal skin over the top of a barrel; the *tambour,* a handheld drum similar to a tambourine but without the cymbals; and the maraca, made from gourds and seeds.

Some of Puerto Rico's earliest known musical styles are *bomba* and *plena,* which have roots in the African slave culture. They're both heavy on percussion and lightning-fast rhythms. *Bomba* features call-and-response vocals and is accompanied by frenzied dancing in which the dancers match their steps to every beat of the drum. In *plena,* the emphasis is on the vocals, which are more European in origin and retell current events or local scandals. Local *bomba* masters include Los Hermanos Ayala (traditionalists from Loíza) and the more contemporary Cepedas (based in Santurce, San Juan). Reviving interest in *plena* is the band Plena Libre.

Akin in philosophy to the origins of American country music, *música jíbara* is the folk sound of Puerto Rico's rural mountain dwellers, called *jíbaros.* Performed by small ensembles on *cuatro, güiro,* bongos, and occasionally clarinets and trumpets, *música jíbara* is more Spanish in origin than *bomba* or *plena,* although the Caribbean influence is unmistakable. Vocals, which play an important part in *música jíbara,* are usually about the virtues of a simpler way of life. There are two types of *música jíbara—seis* and *aguinalda. Seis* is typically named after a particular town, and the lyrics are often improvised and sung in 10-syllable couplets. *Aguinaldos* are performed around Christmas by roaming carolers. Ramito (1915-1990) is considered Puerto Rico's quintessential *jíbaro* artist.

While Puerto Rican slaves grooved to *bomba* and the farmers played their folk tunes, Puerto Rico's moneyed Europeans turned their attentions to classical music, eventually giving birth around 1900 to *danza,* a romantic classical style of music often described as Afro-Caribbean waltz. Originating in Ponce, *danza* was performed on piano, cello, violin, and *bombardino* (similar to a trombone) for dancers who performed structured, ballroom-style steps. The form is celebrated in Ponce with the annual Semana de la Danza in May. The most famous composers of *danza* were

Manuel Gregorio Tavarez (1843-1883) and his pupil, Juan Morel Campos (1857-1896).

In 1956, renowned Catalan cellist and composer Pablo Casals moved to Puerto Rico, and a year later Festival Casals was born. The international celebration of classical music continues today in concert halls in San Juan, Ponce, and Mayagüez every June and July. In Old San Juan there is a museum dedicated to Casals, featuring his music manuscripts, instruments, and recordings.

Of course, salsa is the music most associated with Puerto Rico today. A lively, highly danceable fusion of jazz, African polyrhythms, and Caribbean flair, salsa is performed by large ensembles on drums, keyboards, and horns. When people refer to Latin music, they usually mean salsa. It is the predominant form of music heard on the island, so just stop in almost any bar or restaurant advertising live music and you're likely to hear it. Watching expert salsa dancers move to the music is as entertaining as listening to the music. Born in New York City but Puerto Rican by heritage, percussionist and composer Tito Puente (1923-2000) was a major influence on salsa music. Other masters include Celia Cruz (1924-2003) and Willie Colón, but there are scores of popular Puerto Rican salsa artists who perform today.

Reggaetón, a blend of American hip-hop, *bomba, plena,* and Jamaican dancehall, is the musical form born and bred in Puerto Rica. The first big breakout artist was Daddy Yankee, who grew up in the public housing projects of San Juan and managed to cross over into the American market. Reggaetón festivals have become a popular pastime in Puerto Rico, but you can also hear it in nightclubs and blasting from car windows. Other popular reggaetón artists include Don Omar, Tego Calderón, Ivy Queen, and Calle 13.

VISUAL ARTS

The visual arts have been a thriving art form in Puerto Rico for centuries, and its artists' output runs the gamut from baroque European-influenced paintings to contemporary conceptual pieces that challenge the definition of art.

Puerto Rico's best-known early artists were José Campeche (1751-1809) and Francisco Oller (1833-1917). Campeche was of mixed race, born in San Juan to a freed slave, Tomás Campeche, and a native of the Canary Islands, María Jordán Marqué. He was primarily a self-taught artist, first learning the skill from his father, but he studied for a time with Luis Paret, an exiled Spanish painter who lived in Puerto Rico for awhile. As was common at the time, Campeche primarily painted portraits of wealthy landowners and religious scenes in heavily ornamented detail, which was in keeping with the rococo style of the day. He painted more than 400 paintings during his lifetime, the majority of them commissions. Campeche's *Virgen de la Soledad de la Victoria* was the first acquisition of the Museo de Arte de Puerto Rico, where you can see many other examples of his work.

Oller was born in Bayamón and studied art at the Academia de Bellas Artes in Madrid from 1851 to 1853. He also studied in Paris from 1858 to 1863, where he was a contemporary of Pissarro, Cézanne, and Guillaumins and exhibited at several Paris salons. Influenced by realist and impressionist styles, his work encompassed portraits, landscapes, and still lifes. But once he returned for good to Puerto Rico in 1884, his work became primarily realist in nature, typically rendered in somber colors. His subjects tended to focus on traditional Puerto Rican ways of life. One of his most famous paintings is *El Velorio (The Wake),* which depicts a rural family gathered in a home for an infant's wake and which can be seen in a gallery at the Universidad de Puerto Rico in Río Piedras. Oller's work has been acquired by many important museums, including the Musée d'Orsay in Paris.

Two other important early artists were Miguel Pou (1880-1968) and Ramón Frade (1875-1954), whose paintings celebrated the dignity of *jíbaro* (peasant) life.

Another internationally recognized artist was island transplant Jack Delano (1914-1997), a significant photographer who chronicled the Puerto Rican people and way of life from 1941 until his death. Born in Kiev, Ukraine, he first came to Puerto Rico in 1941 on assignment for the U.S. Farm Security Administration in conjunction with President Franklin D. Roosevelt's New Deal programs. The program sent many famous photographers throughout the United States to document rural life. In addition to Delano, they included Walker Evans, Dorothea Lange, Marjory Collins, and Gordon Parks, among others. After the war, Delano returned to Puerto Rico in 1946, settled there permanently, and continued to photograph the island's changing culture. His work is journalistic in nature but is deeply imbued with a respect for the human condition. In addition to his photography, Delano was a musical composer of sonatas.

Beginning in the 1940s, a radical new art form exploded in Puerto Rico that reflected growing concern among artists and writers that the island's native culture was being subsumed by American influence. That sentiment was expressed in visually striking representations of graphic poster art, called *cartels*. Originally funded by the local government, artists produced colorful illustrations of important books, plays, songs, and poems, as well as political slogans and quotations. Eventually the art form evolved away from its boosterish origins. Some artists used the form to criticize the government and social issues, while others celebrated the island's natural and architectural beauty. Today it's most commonly seen advertising festivals. Among its most celebrated artists is Lorenzo Homar (1913-2004), who was a recipient of the National Medal of Honor and cofounder of the Centro de Arte de Puertorriqueño, which played an important role in advancing the graphic art form. The Museo de Arte de Puerto Rico has a gallery devoted to an excellent collection of *cartels*.

Another significant artist was Rafael Tufiño (1922-2008), whose somber paintings captured the island's people and customs, as well as its pockets of squalor. Tufiño was also a cofounder of the Centro de Arte de Puertorriqueña and a faculty member for the Puerto Rico Institute of Culture's art school, Escuela de Artes Plásticas.

Puerto Rico's arts scene continues to evolve. Recognizing the positive impact art can have on the economy, in 2001 Governor Sila M. Calderón initiated a $25 million program to fund the **Puerto Rico Public Art Project,** which put in place scores of contemporary site-specific public art installations throughout the island. Many works are meant to be functional, in the form of bus stops, park benches, and vendor kiosks, or to enliven the roadways of major thoroughfares and stops along the new commuter rail service (Tren Urbano). Pieces vary from murals to conceptual multimedia installations to earthworks, and 20 percent of the works were created by Puerto Rican artists. Among the local and international artists involved were Ana Rosa Rivera, Víctor Vázquez, Ramón Berríos, Lourdes Correa Carlo, Charles Juhasz, and Liliana Porter.

For details on the project, including maps and descriptions of the pieces, visit www.artepublicopr.com, in English and Spanish.

CRAFTS

Puerto Rican artisans produce a variety of crafts unique to the island's culture. The most distinctive craft is the ***vejigante* mask,** a brilliantly colored object made from coconut shells or papier-mâché featuring large protruding horns. The masks represent the Moors in annual festivals revolving around street pageants that reenact Spain's defeat of the Moors in the 13th century. Although there are several artists who create the masks, the Ayala family artists in Loíza are considered the masters of the form. Prices range $30-250. *Vejigante* figurines made from a variety of materials, including ceramic, glass, and metal, are also popular collectible items made by local artisans and come in all price ranges.

Puerto Rico's oldest and most traditional craft form is the **santo,** primitive-looking woodcarvings of Catholic saints. Santos originated with low-income families who wanted representations of their favorite saints to display in their homes but couldn't afford the expensive plaster ones available for purchase. Today, santos are highly collectible, and many museums, including Museo de las Americas in Old San Juan, exhibit priceless collections of vintage santos. New santos can be found in the island's finer crafts and gift shops and cost $80-500.

Mundillo is a delicate, handmade lace created by tying fine threads using bobbins, which facilitate weaving the threads into an intricate pattern. The lace is used to embellish tablecloths, handkerchiefs, and christening gowns, among other things. The art form has roots in Spain, but the *mundillo* pattern is specific to Puerto Rico. It's primarily produced in and around the tiny town of Moca near Aguadilla on the west coast, where several artisans live. *Mundillo* can be purchased at finer gift shops around the island and at some festivals. Because it is so labor-intensive, *mundillo* is somewhat pricey. A handkerchief rimmed with a small amount of *mundillo* starts around $30, but a handkerchief made entirely of *mundillo* can cost more than $100.

The crafting of woven cotton **hammocks** is an art form that continues a tradition started by the Taíno Indians, who used them not only to sleep on but also for food storage and other utilitarian purposes. The town of San Sebastián in the western fringe of the Cordillera Central is the best known source of the hammock, but they're available at most crafts and gift shops throughout the island starting at about $30.

Other popular low-priced craft items include **seed jewelry,** colorful earrings, bracelets, and necklaces made from the seeds of trees and plants on the island; ***güiros,*** percussion instruments made from gourds; and landscape paintings on pieces of rough-hewn wood.

LITERATURE

Literature in Puerto Rico has historically revolved around national identity and the tension of being U.S. citizens in a Latino culture. Its literary heritage began to emerge in the mid-1800s, and among its earliest notable works was *El Gibaro* (1849) by Manuel Alonso y Pacheco. Part prose, part poetry, *El Gibaro* celebrated the simple life of Puerto Rico's farmers, called *jíbaros.*

But the first writer to receive literary prominence was Alejandro Tapia y Rivera (1826-1882) of San Juan, a playwright and abolitionist who wrote many works, including biographical pieces on important Puerto Ricans such as Spanish admiral Ramón Power y Giralt, artist José Campeche, and the pirate Roberto Cofresí.

One of Puerto Rico's early writers who was revered throughout the Caribbean and South America was Eugenio María de Hostos (1839-1903), a writer and educator who led civic-reform movements throughout Latin America. His seminal work is *Peregrinación de Bayoán* (1863), a work of fiction that illustrated injustices under the Spanish regime and called for independence from Spain.

After Puerto Rico came under control of the United States, a new crop of writers, called the Generation of 1998, began to flourish. Fueled primarily by politics, several writers of this era combined the art of poetry with the craft of journalism. José de Diego (1867-1918) of Aguadilla and Luís Muñoz Rivera (1859-1916) of Barranquitas were significant poets and journalists who fueled the island's independence movement with their words. Diego, considered a precursor of the modernist movement in Puerto Rico, produced several books of poetry, including *Pomarrosas, Jovillos, Cantos de Rebeldia,* and *Cantos del Pitirre.* Rivera's most significant work was a book of poems called *Tropicales.*

One of the most important writers of this era was Antonio S. Pedriera (1899-1939), whose work *Insularismo* examined how U.S. political control had affected Puerto Rican culture in the first 35 years.

In the 1940s, there was a mass migration of Puerto Ricans to the United States—primarily New York City—and the island's literature took a significant shift reflecting that phenomenon. Suddenly there was an output of work by Puerto Rican immigrants who found themselves grappling with issues of dual identity. In 1951, playwright René Marqués (1919-1974) of Arecibo wrote his most critically acclaimed play, *The Oxcart,* which chronicled the mass exodus of Puerto Ricans to New York City. Also noteworthy is *A Puerto Rican in New York* (1961), by Jesús Colón (1918-1974), who was born in Cayey but grew up in the United States.

The 1960s and 1970s saw the birth of a literary movement called Nuyorican literature. Nuyorican is the name given to New Yorkers of Puerto Rican heritage. Some of the most notable writers of this movement were Piri Thomas, author of *Down These Mean Streets* (1967), and Nicholasa Mohr, who wrote *Nilda* (1973), both of which dealt with life in the urban barrios of New York City. By the 1980s, the Nuyorican movement exploded on the spoken-word scene with work that had a strong political message. New York's Nuyorican Poets Café was and still is the epicenter of this movement, providing a forum for such celebrated poets as Ponce-born Pedro Pietri (1944-2004), for whom a street in New York City was recently named, and New York-born Felipe Luciano, founder of the Young Lords activist group. Also once a regular at Nuyorican Poets Café was Gurabo-born Miguel Piñero (1946-1988), who was a playwright and actor. His play *Short Eyes,* about life in prison, won the New York Drama Critics Award for Best American Play in 1974. His life was depicted in a film starring Benjamin Bratt called *Piñero.*

Puerto Rican literature continues to flourish today thanks to many contemporary writers living on the island and in the United States, including poet Victor Hernández Cruz and authors Esmeralda Santiago and Ernesto Quiñonez. Santiago wrote *Conquistador* (2011), a historical novel about a sugar plantation owner in 19th-century Puerto Rico, and *When I Was Puerto Rican* (1993), a memoir about growing up on the island. Quiñonez wrote *Bodega Dreams* (2000) and *Chango's Fire* (2004).

For an excellent survey of Puerto Rican literature, read *Boricuas: The Influential Puerto Rican Writings, an Anthology* (Ballantine, 1995), featuring excerpts of works by some of the writers mentioned here, as well as many others.

DANCE

Dance plays an important role in Puerto Rican culture because it goes hand in hand with the island's rich musical heritage. But for the most part, dance is about moving to the groove of live music or DJs, whether it's at a nightclub, an outdoor concert in the town plaza, or at one of the island's countless festivals. Dance is integral to *bomba, plena,* salsa, and reggaetón music, and the thing all those forms of movement have in common is this: It's all in the hips! The exception is the ballroom style of *danza.*

When it comes to dance performance, the island leader is Guateque, the folkloric ballet of Puerto Rico. For more than 20 years this 40-member dance company and school based on Corozal has been preserving and performing the island's traditional dances, as well as adapting them into new productions. Past productions include *Los Taínos de Borkén* and *Los Dioses (The Gods),* which depict daily life and spirituality of the island's indigenous Indians.

Essentials

Transportation

GETTING THERE

Air

Puerto Rico has two international airports, **Luis Muñoz Marín International Airport** (Aeropuerto Internacional Luis Muñoz Marín, SJU) in Isla Verde, San Juan, and **Rafael Hernández International Airport** (Aeropuerto Internacional Rafael Hernández, BQN) in Aguadilla on the west coast. The only other airport to service flights from the United States is **Mercedita International Airport** (Aeropuerto Internacional Mercedita, PSE) in Ponce on the south coast.

Regional airports serving commercial travel are Isla Grande Airport (SIG) near Old San Juan; José Aponte de la Torre Airport (RVR) in Ceiba; Eugenio María de Hostos Airport (MAZ) in Mayagüez; Vieques Airport (VQS) in Isabel Segunda; and Culebra Airport (CPX) in Culebra. Airports in Fajardo and Humacao have been closed to commercial service.

Airfares to Puerto Rico fluctuate in price throughout the year, but the cheapest rates can typically be secured during the off-season, May-October, which is also hurricane season.

FROM NORTH AMERICA

Direct flights to San Juan are available from Atlanta, Boston, Chicago, Dallas/Fort Worth, Fort Lauderdale, Miami, New York City, Newark, Orlando, Philadelphia, and Washington DC.

These airlines offer flights to San Juan, Aguadilla, and Ponce from the United States:

- **American Airlines** (800/433-7300, www.aa.com)
- **Continental Airlines** (800/231-0856 or 800/523-3273, www.continental.com)
- **Delta Air Lines** (800/221-1212 or 800/325-1999, www.delta.com)
- **JetBlue Airways** (800/538-2583, www.jetblue.com)
- **Spirit Airlines** (800/772-7117, www.spiritairlines.com)
- **United Airlines** (800/864-8331, www.united.com)
- **U.S. Airways** (800/428-4322, www.usairways.com)

In Canada, direct flights to San Juan are operated by **Air Canada** (888/247-2262, www.aircanada.com) from Montréal and Toronto.

FROM EUROPE

British Airways (www.britishairways.com) offers connecting flights from the United Kingdom to San Juan via New York City or Miami. **Iberia** (www.iberia.com) offers direct flights to San Juan from Madrid.

FROM AUSTRALIA

Connecting flights from Australia are operated by **United** (through Los Angeles and Chicago) and **American Airlines** (through New York City).

FROM THE CARIBBEAN

Several small airlines offer flights to San Juan from throughout the Caribbean. They include **Air Sunshine** (888/879-8900, www.airsunshine.com) from St. Croix, St. Thomas, Tortola, Virgin Gorda, and Vieques; **Cape Air** (800/352-0714, www.flycapeair.com) from St. Croix, St. Thomas, and Tortola; and **Liat Airline** (888/844-5428, www.liatairline.com) from 22 destinations in the eastern Caribbean.

Previous: ferry to Cataño; Vieques Airlink plane

Cruise Ship

San Juan is the largest port in the Caribbean, and it is a port of call or point of origin for nearly two dozen cruise lines. The cruise ship docks lie along Calle La Marina in Old San Juan.

A few of the most popular cruise lines serving San Juan include:

- **Carnival Cruise Lines** (866/299-5698, www.carnival.com)
- **Celebrity Cruises** (800/647-2251, www.celebritycruises.com)
- **Holland America Line** (877/724-5425, www.hollandamerica.com)
- **Norwegian Cruise Line** (800/327-7030, www.ncl.com)
- **Princess Cruises** (800/774-6237, www.princess.com)
- **Radisson Seven Seas Cruises** (877/505-5370, www.rssc.com)

GETTING AROUND

Puerto Rico's easy accessibility from the States and the compact lay of the land make it a great place to go for a long weekend. Many visitors simply fly into San Juan and stay there. There are plenty of great restaurants, nightclubs, shops, beaches, and historical sights within walking or taxi distance. A reliable bus transit system and a new rail line called Tren Urbano provide inexpensive transportation throughout the city. It's understandable why some visitors are hesitant to leave behind the capital city's charms.

But escaping the bustle of the city and experiencing the island's unique natural beauty is highly recommended and easily achieved. Car-rental agencies are plentiful, and the roads are well marked and maintained. Because the island is so small, it's possible to make a day trip to any sight on the island. Just keep in mind that Puerto Rico has a high volume of traffic, which can slow your progress. Travel through the central mountain region especially can take longer than might be expected because of the narrow winding roads. Always figure in extra travel time when planning a road trip.

Car

Visitors who plan to venture outside of San Juan should plan to rent a car. This is by far the best way to explore the island. Most of the major American car-rental agencies have locations throughout the island, and there are several local agencies as well. For the most part, roads are well maintained and well marked. Gasoline is sold by the liter, speed limits are measured in miles per hour, and distance is measured in kilometers. And all road signs are in Spanish. International driving licenses are required for drivers from countries other than the United States.

Driving around San Juan can be nerve-racking for those not accustomed to inner-city driving. The sheer number of cars on the island guarantees congested roadways, so be sure to schedule extra time for road trips. Drivers tend to speed and don't leave much space between cars. They also can be creative when it comes to navigating traffic—rolling through stops and driving on the shoulder of the highway is not uncommon. Ponce has, hands-down, the worst drivers. It's practically a free-for-all, and they blow their car horns constantly.

Take extra precautions when driving in the mountains. Fortunately the traffic is light, but the roads are narrow and winding. Drivers who travel these roads every day tend to proceed at a perilously fast clip. If the driver behind you appears impatient or tailgates, pull over and let him or her pass. On roads with a lot of blind curves, it is common practice to blow the car horn to alert oncoming traffic you're approaching. If it's raining, beware of small mudslides and overflowing riverbanks, which sometimes close roads. And whatever you do, don't look down! But really, it's not as bad as it sounds. Driving through Puerto Rico's majestic mountains is well worth a few shattered nerves.

There is an excellent, major, limited-access highway system called ***autopista*** that

Highways and Driving Distances

MAJOR HIGHWAYS

- **PR 26:** East-west, San Juan airport to Condado; also known as Baldorioty de Castro Avenue
- **PR 18:** North-south, connecting PR 22 and PR 52, San Juan
- **PR 66:** Northwest-southeast, Canovanas to San Juan
- **PR 22:** East-west, San Juan to Arecibo (toll); also known as Jose de Diego Expressway
- **PR 52:** North-southwest, San Juan to Ponce (partially toll); also known as Luis A. Ferré Expressway
- **PR 30:** Northwest-southeast, Caguas to Humacao
- **PR 53:** North-south, Fajardo to Yabucoa

DRIVING DISTANCES FROM SAN JUAN

- **Aguadilla:** 81 miles (130 kilometers)
- **Arecibo:** 48 miles (77 kilometers)
- **Barranquitas:** 34 miles (55 kilometers)
- **Cabo Rojo:** 111 miles (179 kilometers)
- **Cayey:** 30 miles (48 kilometers)
- **Dorado:** 17 miles (27 kilometers)
- **Fajardo:** 32 miles (52 kilometers)
- **Guánica:** 94 miles (151 kilometers)
- **Humacao:** 34 miles (55 kilometers)
- **Jayuya:** 58 miles (93 kilometers)
- **La Parguera:** 107 miles (172 kilometers)
- **Luquillo:** 28 miles (45 kilometers)
- **Mayagüez:** 98 miles (158 kilometers)
- **Ponce:** 70 miles (113 kilometers)
- **Rincón:** 93 miles (150 kilometers)
- **Salinas:** 46 miles (74 kilometers)
- **Utuado:** 65 miles (105 kilometers)

dissects and nearly encircles the island, parts of which are toll roads ($0.25-1.25 per toll). The speed limits range 50-65 miles per hour.

The rest of the island's numbered roads are called ***carreteras,*** typically written as the abbreviation *carr.*, followed by a number, such as Carr. 193. Major *carreteras* often have spur routes that go either into a town's center or along its beachfront. A road number followed by the letter R or the word *ramal* indicates a spur route that goes through a town's commercial district. Beachfront routes are often indicated by the abbreviation *int.* or an addition of the numeral 3 after a road number.

Addresses are typically identified by road and kilometer numbers, for instance: Carr. 193, km 2. Look for the white numbered kilometer posts alongside the road to identify your location. In towns, streets are called ***avenidas*** (abbreviated as Ave.) and ***calles.***

Taxi

Most towns in Puerto Rico are served by at least one taxi service. San Juan has several reliable tourist-taxi services that serve the areas where visitors congregate. It's possible to flag one down day or night in Isla Verde and Condado, and in Old San Juan, there are two taxi stands—on Plaza de Colón and Plaza de Armas. You can also call one.

Operators include **Metro Taxi** (787/725-2870), **Major Taxi** (787/723-2460), **Rochdale Radio Taxi** (787/721-1900), and **Capetillo Taxi** (787/758-7000).

Fares between the airport and the piers in Old San Juan are fixed rates. From the airport, the rates are $10 to Isla Verde, $15 to Condado, $19 to Old San Juan, and $15 to Isla Grande Airport and the Puerto Rico Convention Center. From the piers, the rates are $12 to Condado and $19 to Isla Verde. There is a $1.50 gas surcharge, and each piece of luggage is $1. Metered fares are $3 minimum, $1.75 initial charge, and $0.10 every 19th of a mile. Customers pay all road tolls.

Público

Públicos, also known as *guaguas* or *carros públicos,* are privately owned transport services that operate communal van routes throughout specific regions of the island. In addition, most towns are served by local *públicos.* *Público* stops are usually found on a town's main plaza. This is a very inexpensive but slow way to travel because as riders get off at their appointed stops, the van will wait indefinitely until it fills up with new riders before heading to the next stop.

Público transportation from San Juan to outlying areas is provided by **Blue Line** (787/765-7733) to Río Piedras, Aguadilla, Aguada, Moca, Isabela, and other areas; **Choferes Unidos de Ponce** (787/764-0540) to Ponce and other areas; **Lina Boricua** (787/765-1908) to Lares, Ponce, Jayuya, Utuado, San Sebastián, and other areas; **Linea Caborrojeña** (787/723-9155) to Cabo Rojo, San Germán, and other areas; **Linea Sultana** (787/765-9377) to Mayagüez and other areas; and **Terminal de Transportación Publica** (787/250-0717) to Fajardo and other areas.

Bus

Autoridad Metropolitana de Autobuses (787/250-6064 or 787/294-0500, ext. 514, www.dtop.gov.pr/ama/mapaindex.htm) is an excellent public bus system that serves the entire metropolitan San Juan area until about 9pm. It's serviced by large, air-conditioned vehicles with wheelchair access, and the cost is typically a low $0.75 per fare (exact change required). Bus stops are clearly marked along the routes with green signs that say "Parada," except in Old San Juan, where you have to catch the bus at **Covadonga Bus and Trolley Terminal,** the large terminal near the cruise-ship piers at the corner of Calle la Marina and Calle J. A. Corretjer. When waiting for a bus at a *parada,* it is necessary to wave to get the driver to stop.

Rail

In 2005, San Juan launched **Tren Urbano** (866/900-1284, www.ati.gobierno.pr), its first long-awaited commuter train service. The system runs mostly aboveground and has 15 stations, many of which house a terrific collection of specially commissioned public art. The train connects the communities of Bayamón, the Universidad de Puerto Rico in Río Piedras, Hato Rey, and Santurce at Universidad del Sagrado Corazón. The train runs daily 5:30am-11:30pm. Fares are $1.50.

Air

Local air service within Puerto Rico, including Vieques and Culebra, is provided by

Driving Vocabulary

USEFUL WORDS

al centro: downtown
autopista: limited access toll road
calle: street
carr. or *carretera:* highway
cruce: crossroads
cruzar: to cross
cuadras: blocks
esquina: corner
estacionamiento: parking
derecha: right
derecho: straight ahead
doble: turn
izquierda: left
lejos: far
luces: traffic lights
luz: traffic light
vaya: go

ROAD SIGNS

alto: stop
calle sin salida: dead-end street
cuidado: be careful
despacio: slow
desvio: detour
este: east
hacia: to
int.: approaching intersection, or interior route
norte: north
oeste: west
ramal: business route
salida: exit
sur: south

several airlines, including **Vieques Air Link** (787/741-8331 or 888/901-9247, www.viequesairlink.com); **M&N Aviation** (787/791-7008, www.mnaviation.com); and **Air Flamenco** (787/724-1818, www.airflamenco.net).

Ferry

The **Puerto Rico Port Authority** (in Vieques 787/741-4761, 787/863-0705, or 800/981-2005; in Culebra 787/742-3161, 787/741-4761, 787/863-0705, or 800/981-2005; in Fajardo 787/863-0705 or 787/863-4560) operates daily passenger ferry service and weekday cargo and car ferry service between Fajardo on the east coast to the islands of Vieques and Culebra. Reservations are not accepted, but you can buy tickets in advance.

The operation has been plagued in recent years with scheduling irregularities and overcrowding due to ferries being out of commission for repairs. Arrive no later than one hour before departure; sometimes the ferry cannot accommodate everyone who wants to ride.

The passenger ferry takes about 1 hour to get from Fajardo to Vieques and 1.5 hours from Fajardo to Culebra. The fare is $4.50 round-trip per person. The cargo/car ferry trip takes about 2 hours to get from Fajardo to Vieques and about 2.5 hours from Fajardo to Culebra. The cost is $15 for small vehicles and $19 for large vehicles. Note that car-rental agencies in Puerto Rico prohibit taking rental cars off the main island.

Visas and Officialdom

No passports or visas are required for U.S. citizens entering Puerto Rico. Those visiting the island from other countries must have the same documentation required to enter the United States. Visitors from the United Kingdom are required to have a British passport but do not need a visa unless their passports are endorsed with British Subject, British Dependent Territories Citizen, British Protected Person, British Overseas Citizen, or British National (Overseas) Citizen. A return ticket or proof of onward travel is necessary. Australian visitors must have a passport and can stay up to 90 days without a visa.

CUSTOMS

Travelers must pass through customs at the airport in Puerto Rico before leaving the island to make sure no prohibited plants or fruits are taken off the island. Permitted items include avocados, coconuts, papayas, and plantains. Mangoes, passion fruits, and plants potted in soil are not permitted. Pre-Columbian items or items from Afghanistan, Cuba, Iran, Iraq, Libya, Serbia, Montenegro, and Sudan may not be brought into the United States. There are no customs duties on items brought into the United States from Puerto Rico.

EMBASSIES

Because Puerto Rico is a commonwealth, there are no U.S. embassies or consulates here. Several countries are represented locally by consulates, though, including the United Kingdom (Torre Chardon, Ste. 1236, 350 Ave. Chardon, San Juan, PR 00918, 787/758-9828, fax 787/758-9809, btoprl@coqui.net) and Canada (33 Calle Bolivia, 7th Floor, Hato Rey, San Juan, PR 00917-2010, 787/759-6629, fax 787/294-1205).

Recreation

Puerto Ricans are rabid sports enthusiasts, and their three biggest passions can be described as the three B's: baseball, basketball, and boxing,

BASEBALL

With origins dating back to the late 19th century, baseball was the first team sport to emerge in Puerto Rico's modern times. Currently the island is home to a winter league featuring four regional teams. Each year the winning team competes in the Caribbean Series in February, playing against winning teams from Dominican Republic, Mexico, and Venezuela.

For the first time in history, opening day for Major League baseball was held in San Juan in 2001 with a game between the Toronto Blue Jays and the Texas Rangers. The game was appropriately held in San Juan's Hiram Bithorn Stadium, named after the Chicago Cubs pitcher and the first Puerto Rican to play in the Major Leagues.

Today more than 100 Major League players are from Puerto Rico, but the island's most famous player is undoubtedly Hall of Famer Roberto Clemente, who played 18 seasons with the Pittsburgh Pirates. Clemente died in an airplane crash off the coast of San Juan on New Year's Eve in 1972 on his way to deliver aid to earthquake victims in Nicaragua.

BASKETBALL

Although once extremely popular, basketball has seen a decline in interest in recent years, which has put the future of the National Superior Basketball League in jeopardy. Established in 1932, it currently consists of 12 regional teams. The island is also home to the Puerto Rican National Basketball Team, which competes in international events. The team made history in the 2004 when it defeated the U.S. Dream Team in the Olympics in Greece.

Puerto Rican athletes who have gone on to play for the NBA include Carlos Arroyo (Orlando Magic) and Jose Barea (Dallas Mavericks).

BOXING

Puerto Rico has produced many world-class boxers, starting with the island's first National Boxing Association world champion in the bantamweight class, Barceloneta native Sixto Escobar, who first won the title in 1934. In 1948, bantamweight boxer Juan Evangelista Venegas became the first Puerto Rican to win an Olympic medal. To date, Puerto Rico has won six Olympic medals in boxing. Isabela native Juan Ruíz made history by becoming the first Latino World Boxing Association heavyweight champion by beating Evander Holyfield in 2001.

Félix "Tito" Trinidad is considered by

many to be Puerto Rico's best all-time boxer. A champion in both welterweight and middleweight divisions, Trinidad announced his retirement in 2002 with a record of 42 wins (35 by knockout) and only two losses. Since then he has come out of retirement twice to compete three more times, losing his last match in 2008 to Roy Jones. Trinidad's most celebrated win was the defeat of welterweight champion Oscar de la Hoya in an event called The Fight of the Millennium held at Mandalay Bay in Las Vegas in 1999. His victorious return to the island was marked by a jubilant turnout of thousands of fans who greeted him at the Luis Muñoz Marín International Airport in San Juan.

GOLF

Because of its verdant natural beauty, Puerto Rico has become something of a golf mecca for travelers. There are more than 20 courses on the island, most of them resort courses that tend to be upgraded and improved on a regular basis. The majority of courses are located on the eastern side of the island, from Dorado in the north to Humacao on the southeast coast.

Puerto Rico hosted its first PGA tour event, the Puerto Rico Open, in 2008 at the Trump International Golf Club in Rio Grande. The island's best-known professional golfer is Juan "Chi Chi" Rodriguez. The story has it that the PGA Hall of Famer was first introduced to the game when he was a child working as a water carrier on a sugar plantation and discovered golf caddies were better paid.

HORSE RACING AND RIDING

The development of the Paso Fino breed of horse is closely intertwined with the history of Puerto Rico, starting with the arrival of Juan Ponce de León in 1508. Among the explorer's cargo were 50 horses from which the birth of the breed can be traced.

Horse races were once held in the streets of Old San Juan as far back as 1610. Today gamblers can bet on winners at the big modern Hipódromo Camarero in Canóvanas, about 10 miles east of San Juan. Races are held Wednesday-Sunday.

Horses are still used as a mode of transportation in rural parts of the main island and throughout Vieques and Culebra. There are several stables that offer trail rides, including **Pintos R Us** (787/361-3639, www.pintosrus.com) in Rincón, **Hacienda Carabalí** (787/889-5820 or 787/889-4954, www.haciendacarabalipuertorico.com) in Luquillo, and **Tropical Trail Rides** (787/872-9256, www.tropicaltrailrides.com) in Isabela.

COCKFIGHTS

Pitting spur-wearing gamecocks against each other in a battle for the finish is a legal and a popular sport with gamblers—so much so that it's televised. Although birds do sometimes fight to the death, efforts have been made to make the sport more humane. Spurs have been shortened from 2.5 inches to 1.5 inches in length, and injured cocks may be removed from a fight.

There are more than 100 licensed cockfighting arenas in Puerto Rico. Arenas are typically found in barnlike structures in rural areas of the island, but San Juan has a modern facility in Isla Verde, Club Gallistico de Puerto Rico, which caters to a more urban crowd with food and beverage service.

WATER SPORTS

As noted throughout this book, water sports are a huge draw in Puerto Rico. Visitors come from all over the world to surf its western shores, where regional and national competitions are held. Diving and snorkeling are popular on the southwest coast and around the smaller islands off the east coast. Sailing, big game fishing, and kite-boarding are other popular sports.

TOURS

Puerto Rico has a slew of tour operators offering a variety of adventures that span the spectrum from guided city walks to deep-sea dives to mountain-climbing hikes. All tour companies require reservations.

Adventure Nature Tours

Acampa (1211 Ave. Piñero, San Juan, 787/706-0695, www.acampapr.com) offers a large selection of hiking, rappelling, ziplining, and rock-climbing adventure tours throughout the island. Sights include San Cristóbal Cañon, Río Tanamá, El Yunque, Bosque Estatal de Toro Negro, Mona Island, and Caja de Muerto Island. Acampa also sells and rents camping, hiking, and mountaineering gear at its store in San Juan. Rates are $80-170.

Aventuras Tierra Adentro (268-A Ave. Jesus T. Piñero, San Juan, 787/766-0470, fax 787/754-7543, www.aventuraspr.com, Tues.-Fri. 10am-6pm, Sat. 10am-4pm) leads cave and canyon tours that include rappelling, rock climbing, and ziplining for adventure seekers of all experience levels, including beginners. Reservations are required. Participants must be 15 or older. Cave tours take place Friday and Sunday for $170 per person. Canyon tours are on Saturday and cost $160 per person.

ToroVerde (Carr. 155, km 32.9, Orocovis, 787/944-1196, 787/944-1195, or 787/867-6606, fax 787/867-7022, www.toroverde-transportation.com, www.toroverdepr.com, Thurs.-Sun. 8am-5pm) offers zipline canopy tours, hanging bridge tours, mountain bike tours, and rappelling. Packages are $65-200. Reservations are required. Participants must be at least four feet tall. Hotel pickup can be arranged.

Diving, Snorkeling, and Boating Tours

Abe's Snorkeling & Bio-Bay Tours (787/741-2134 or 787/436-2686, www.abessnorkeling.com, reservations required) offers a variety of kayak tours, ideal for exploring beaches, mangrove bays, the bioluminescent bay (bio-bay), or undersea life in Vieques. A two-hour bio-bay tour in a double kayak is $40 adults, $20 children.

Aqua Adventure (Copamarina Beach Resort, Carr. 333, km 6.5, 800/468-4553 or 877/348-3267, www.aquaadventurepr.com, daily 9am-6pm) runs day and night dive excursions ($65-119) to sites including the 22-mile-long Guánica Wall, the Aquarium, and the Parthenon, a coral formation featuring a variety of sponges. Daily snorkeling excursions go to Gilligan's Island, Cayo Coral Reef, and Bahía de la Ballerna ($55 including equipment). Certification courses are offered. Also available are kayak, catamaran, and paddleboat rentals.

Blue Caribe Kayaks (149 Calle Flamboyan, Esperanza, Vieques, 787/741-2522) provides kayak tours of Mosquito Bay for $30 per person. Kayak rentals are also available for $10-15 per hour, $25-35 for four hours, and $45-55 all day.

Cancel Boats (Carr. 3304, on the waterfront in La Parguera, 787/899-5891 or 787/899-2972) and **Johnny Boats** (Carr. 3304, on the waterfront in La Parguera, 787/299-2212) offer on-demand tours of the La Parguera mangrove canals for $25 per person (less if you have a group) and nighttime tours of the phosphorescent bay for about $6.

Capt. Suarez Electric Boat (Carr. 987, Las Croabas dock, Fajardo, 787/655-2739 or 787/472-3128, captainsuarezbiobaypr@gmail.com) offers electric boat rides into the Laguna Grande bio-bay in Fajardo ($45 adults, $35 children).

Caribbean School of Aquatics (1 Calle Taft, Santurce, San Juan, 787/728-6606 or 787/383-5700, www.saildiveparty.com) offers full- and half-day sail, scuba, snorkel, and fishing trips from San Juan and Fajardo on a luxury catamaran with Captain Greg Korwek. Snorkel trips start at $69 per person; scuba trips start at $119 per person.

Day & Night Boat Tours (Dewey boatyard, 787/435-4498) offers a daylong snorkeling trip from Culebra to Culebrita. Cost (including drinks, snacks, and gear) is $75 per person. Custom fishing, snorkeling, and sightseeing tours can be arranged.

East Island Excursions (Puerto Del Rey Marina, Fajardo, 787/860-3434 or 877/937-4386, fax 787/860-1656, www.eastwindcats.com) offers sailing and snorkeling trips to Culebrita ($69 adults, $49 children ages 2-9).

Eco Adventures (787/206-0290, www.

ecoadventurespr.com) offers bio-bay tours of Laguna Grande in Fajardo ($45 per person) and sailing snorkel tours ($65 per person). Transportation from San Juan to Las Croabas costs $20.

Flying Fish Parasail (Black Eagle Marina, Carr. 413, Rincón, Barrio Ensenada, 787/823-2359, www.parasailpr.com, daily 9am-5pm) offers single and tandem parasail rides ($60), glass-bottom boat rides ($30), sunset and whale-watching tours ($45), and reef snorkel tours ($55-85). Reservations are required, and there's a 12-passenger maximum.

Island Adventures (Carr. 996, km 4.5, Esperanza, 787/741-0720, www.biobay.com) operates a tour of Mosquito Bay in Vieques on an electric pontoon boat that tools around the electric-blue water ($25 per person). Guides are friendly and informative.

Island Kayaking Adventures (787/444-0059 or 787/225-1808, www.ikapr.com) offers bio-bay kayak tours to Laguna Grande ($45 per person, six-person minimum). Rainforest and bio-bay combo tours cost $100 per person.

Katrina Sail Charters (Black Eagle Marina, Carr. 413, Rincón, Barrio Ensenada, 787/823-7245, www.sailrinconpuertorico.com) takes guests on snorkeling ($75 adults, $37.50 under age 12), sunset ($55, $27.50 under age 12), and full-moon sails ($55 adults only) aboard a 32-foot catamaran.

Kayaking Puerto Rico (787/435-1665 or 787/564-5629, www.kayakingpuertorico.com) offers bio-bay tours in Laguna Grande ($45 per person). Combination kayak and snorkel expeditions are also available.

Paradise Puerto Rico Watersports (Combate Beach, Cabo Rojo, 787/567-4386 or 888/787-4386, www.pprwatersports.com) offers Jet Ski rentals ($85 per hour, $45 per half hour) and tours ($30 an hour, $55 for two hours, three-person minimum).

Paradise Scuba Snorkeling and Kayaks (Carr. 304, km 3.2, La Parguera, 787/899-7611, paradisescubapr@yahoo.com) offers dive tours ($70-80), night dives ($60), snorkeling tours ($50), sunset snorkeling tours ($50-65), phosphorescent bay tours ($25), gear rental, and dive instruction. Dive sites include El Pared, Enrique, El Mario, Chimney, and Old Buoy.

Parguera Watersports (Carr. 3304, on the waterfront in La Parguera, 787/646-6777, www.prkbc.com) guides visitors in La Parguera on bio-bay or full moon kayaking adventures ($45 per person). Kiteboard instruction is $95 for the first session, $75 for additional sessions, including equipment. Rent kayaks by the hour for $20 double, $15 single, or paddleboards for $20 an hour. Day rates are available.

Sail Vieques (Carr. 200, on the waterfront in Isabel Segunda, Vieques, 787/508-7245, billwillo@yahoo.com) offers a half-day snorkeling tour ($50) and a daylong snorkel trip to the southern tip of the Bermuda Triangle ($110). Captain Bill also offers a two-hour sunset cruise for $30.

Salty Dog (1 Calle 1, El Batey, Fajardo, 787/717-6378 or 787/717-7259, www.salty-dreams.com) offers catamaran snorkeling tours including all-you-can-eat lunch buffet and unlimited rum drinks ($60 per person). A sunset cruise includes cocktails and light snacks ($50 per person).

Scuba Dogs (Balneario El Escambrón, Ave. Muñoz Rivera, 787/783-6377 or 787/977-0000, www.scubadogs.net, Mon.-Thurs. 8am-4pm, Fri.-Sun. 8am-5pm) offers snorkel tours ($55 adults, $45 kids), scuba tours ($75 for certified divers, $95 for instructional tours for first-timers), and kayak tours ($65 adults, $55 children).

Sea Ventures Dive Center (Marina Puerto del Rey, Carr. 3, km 51.2, Fajardo, 787/863-3483 or 800/739-3483, www.dive-puertorico.com) offers dive and snorkel trips to local reefs. A two-tank dive for certified divers is $120. A two-tank dive for beginners is $150. Snorkel tours cost $60. Prices include gear.

Taíno Divers (Black Eagle Marina, Carr. 413, Barrio Ensenada, 787/823-6429, www.tainodivers.com, daily 9am-6pm) offers daily snorkeling and dive trips to various dive sites, including Desecheo Island. Snorkeling trips are $50-95, scuba trips are $65-129, and Discovery scuba dives for first-timers are $119-170. Taíno also offers whale-watching cruises (late Jan.-mid-Mar.), as well as fishing charters and sunset cruises. Private excursions to Desecheo Island can be arranged. There is also equipment for rent or sale.

West Divers (Carr. 304, km 3.1, La Parguera, 787/899-3223 or 787/899-4171, www.westdiverspr.com) specializes in scuba trips to La Pared, an underwater wall and world-class dive site. Snorkel trips, sunset cruises, kayak tours, and equipment rental are also offered. A one-day, two-tank dive is $100 per person. Kayak tours cost $20-30 per hour; kayak rentals are $10-15 per hour.

Yokahu Kayaks (Carr. 987, km 6.2, Las Croabas, Fajardo, 787/604-7375, yokahukayaks@hotmail.com) offers kayak tours to Laguna Grande in Las Cabezas de San Juan with licensed guides and equipment included ($45 per person).

Fishing Tours

Bill Wraps Fishing Charters PR (Marina Puerta Real, Fajardo, 787/364-4216, 787/347-9668, or 787/278-2729, www.billwrapsfishingpr.com) offers half-day charters for $650 and full-day charters for $950, including tackle, bait, and snacks. Lunch is included with a full-day charter.

Light Tackle Adventure (Boquerón pier, 787/849-1430 or 787/547-7380, www.lighttackleadventure.8k.com) specializes in light tackle and fly-fishing excursions. Excursions for two people are $340 for four hours, $425 for six hours, $550 for eight hours. A $100 reservation deposit is required. This company also provides kayak trips to the Cabo Rojo salt flats, Boquerón Bay, Joyuda, and La Parguera. Bird-watching tours in Cabo Rojo salt flats are also available.

Light Tackle Paradise (Marina Puerto Chico, Carr. 987, km 2.4, Fajardo, 787/347-4464, $350-450 half day for four or six people) offers fishing excursions on 22-foot and 26-foot catamarans or 17-foot skiffs.

Magic Tarpon (Cangrejos Yacht Club, 787/644-1444, www.puertoricomagictarpon.com) offers half-day fishing charters for $330-460 for 1-4 people.

Makaira Fishing Charters (Black Eagle Marina, Rincón, 787/299-7374) offers half-day ($575) and full-day ($850) fishing charters aboard a 34-foot 2006 Contender. Rates include tackle and refreshments; there's a six-passenger maximum.

Parguera Fishing Charters (Carr. 304, La Parguera, 787/382-4698, www.puertoricofishingcharters.com) offers half-day ($500) and full-day ($850) charters to fish for dorado, tuna, blue marlin, and wahoo on a 31-foot, twin diesel Bertram Sportfisherman. Trips include bait, tackle, beverages, snacks, and lunch. It also offers light-tackle reef fishing, half-day snorkeling trips, and customized charters.

Taíno Divers (Black Eagle Marina, Carr. 413, Barrio Ensenada, 787/823-6429, www.tainodivers.com, daily 9am-6pm) offers half-day offshore fishing charters including tackle, bait, lunch, and soft drinks for $1,200.

Historical Walking Tours

ArqueoTours Coabey (787/342-9317 or 787/470-1862, arqueotourscoabey@gmail.com) offers family-friendly hiking tours to Taíno archaeological sites around Jayuya, including La Piedra Escrita. Rates are $65 adults, $20 ages 5-12, free for children 4 and younger. The tours are guided by a historian and archaeologist.

Legends of Puerto Rico (Old San Juan, 787/605-9060, fax 787/764-2354, www.legendsofpr.com) offers daytime and nighttime walking tours of Old San Juan that revolve around topics from history, pirate legends, and crafts. It also offers a Modern San Juan tour and hiking tours of the karst region, El Yunque, and mangrove forests. Tours range $35-85 per person.

Paddleboarding

Las Palmas Paddle (508/237-9652) offers paddleboard tours around Culebra starting at $40 per person. Introductory tours for beginners as well as adventure packages for experienced paddlers are available.

Velauno (2430 Calle Loíza, Isla Verde, 787/982-0543, www.velauno.com, Mon.-Fri. 10am-7pm, Sat. 11am-7pm) offers paddleboarding lessons ($100 first hour, $50 each subsequent hour) and tours ($75 for two hours, $25 subsequent hours).

Vieques Paddleboarding (787/366-5202, www.viequespaddleboarding.com) offers tours on stand-up paddleboards, a great way to explore the island. The four-hour downwind tour travels 2-4 miles, depending on wind conditions, along the north and south shores ($85). Or take a three-hour tour across the bay, through a mangrove forest, ending at a beach with a snorkel ($65). Kids 11 and younger can ride with adults for $20.

Surfing

Surf 787 Summer Camp (Carr. 115, behind Angelo's Restaurant, 787/448-0968 or 949/547-6340, www.surf787.com) offers year-round surfing instruction.

Located on the beach at The Ritz Carlton San Juan and El San Juan Resort & Casino in Isla Verde, **Wow Surfing School & Water Sports** (787/955-6059, www.wowsurfingschool.com, daily 9am-5pm) gives two-hour surf lessons for $85, including board. Group rates are available. Equipment rentals include surfboards ($25 an hour), paddleboards ($30), kayaks ($25), and snorkel equipment ($15 and up). Jet Ski rentals and tours are available from La Concha Resort in Condado and San Juan Bay Marina. Call for prices.

Accommodations and Food

Accommodations in Puerto Rico run the gamut from world-class luxury resorts to rustic self-serve guesthouses, which offer little more than a bed to crash on and a help-yourself attitude when it comes to getting clean linens, ice, and other items you might need. In between are a variety of American hotel chains in all price ranges and a number of small, independent hotels and inns. There are also some unique hotels of historic significance, such as **Hotel El Convento** in San Juan, a former Carmelite convent built in 1651, and **Hacienda Gripiñas,** a former coffee plantation in Jayuya located high up in the Cordillera Central.

Outside San Juan there are accommodations designated by the Puerto Rico Tourism Co. as *paradores* (www.gotoparadores.com), independently owned and operated country inns. There are 18 properties in all, with the largest concentration located on the western half of the island. Note, though, that the designation of *parador* is not a recommendation, and the quality of the properties is wildly divergent between the superior and the inferior. For details, visit the website.

ACCOMMODATION RATES

Overnight stays in Puerto Rico can range from $39 at Hotel Colonial in Mayagüez to $1,070 for a Cliffside suite at the **Horned Dorset Primavera** in Rincón. Generally, however, room rates fall between $100 and $250. There are no traditional all-inclusive resorts in Puerto Rico, where meals are included with the price of the room, although Copamarina Resort in Guánica and the Horned Dorset Primavera in Rincón offer all-inclusive packages.

A tax is applied to all accommodations, but many properties include the tax in the rate, so ask to be sure. Typically the tax is 9 percent of the rate, but hotels with casinos charge 11 percent tax. Resorts usually add on a resort service fee, which is typically an additional 9 percent.

Many accommodations offer two rates—the most expensive is during high season (typically Jan.-Apr.), the least expensive is during low season (May-Dec.). If you're traveling during high season, be sure to book your room early or you may find your options limited. Note that the high season for destinations and accommodations catering to Puerto Rican travelers may be during the summer months. Some accommodations have a third rate charged during the Christmas holiday season, which may be even more pricey than the high-season rates. Most accommodations may be booked online.

CUISINE

Puerto Rican cuisine is a hearty fare called *cocina criolla,* which means creole cooking. A typical *criolla* dish contains fried or stewed meat, chicken, or seafood, combined with or accompanied by rice and beans. Stewed dishes usually begin with a seasoning mix called ***sofrito,*** which includes salt pork, ham, lard, onions, green peppers, chili peppers, cilantro, and garlic. ***Adobo,*** a seasoning mix comprising peppercorn, oregano, garlic, salt, olive oil, and vinegar or fresh lime juice, is rubbed into meats and poultry before frying or grilling. Tomato sauce, capers, pimento-stuffed olives, and raisins are also common ingredients in Puerto Rican cuisine. Two items are integral to the preparation of *cocina criolla:* a *caldero* (a cast-iron or cast-aluminum cauldron with a round base, straight sides, and a lid) and a mortar and pestle (used to grind herbs and seeds).

The **plantain** is a major staple of the Puerto Rican diet. Similar to a banana but larger, firmer, and less sweet, it is prepared in a variety of ways. *Tostones* are a popular plantain dish. The fruit is sliced into rounds, fried until soft, mashed flat, and fried again until crisp. They're typically eaten like bread, as a starchy accompaniment to a meal. They're sometimes served with a tomato-garlic dipping sauce or something akin to Thousand Island dressing.

But probably the most popular way plantain is served is in *mofongo,* a mashed mound of fried, unripe plantain, garlic, olive oil, and *chicharrón* (pork crackling). *Mofongo relleno* is *mofongo* stuffed with meat, poultry, or seafood, and *piononos* are appetizer-size stuffed *mofongo. Amarillos,* which translates as "yellows," is the same thing as the Cuban *maduras* and is made from overripe plantains that have been sliced lengthwise and fried in oil until soft and sweetly caramelized. Bananas are also popular in *cocina criolla,* especially *guineitos en escabeche,* a green-banana salad marinated with pimento-stuffed olives in vinegar and lime juice.

Rice also figures prominently in Puerto Rican food. Most restaurants serving *comida criolla* will list several *arroz* (rice) dishes, such as *arroz con habichuelas* (beans), *arroz con pollo* (chicken), *arroz con juyeyes* (crab), *arroz con camarones* (shrimp), and *arroz con gandules* (pigeon peas). Typically in this dish the ingredients have been stewed until damp and sticky in a mixture of tomatoes and *sofrito.* A similar dish is paella, a Spanish import featuring an assortment of seafood. *Asopao,* a thick stew, is another popular rice dish, and *arroz con leche* (milk) is a favorite dessert similar to rice pudding.

Pork is very popular in Puerto Rico, and it has a variety of names: *lechón, pernil, cerdo.* But chicken and beef are common, and occasionally you'll come across *cabro* (goat) and guinea hen. Popular meat dishes include *carne guisada* (beef stew), *chuletas fritas* (fried pork chops), *carne empanado* (breaded and fried steak), *carne encebollado* (fried steak smothered in cooked onions), and *churrasco,* an Argentine-style grilled skirt steak. Restaurants along the coast usually specialize in a wide range of seafood, including *camarones* (shrimp), *langosta* (lobster), *pulpo* (octopus), and *carrucho* (conch). Fish—typically fried whole—can be found on nearly every menu, the choices usually being *chillo* (red snapper), dorado (mahimahi), or occasionally *bacalao* (dried salted cod).

Interestingly, you'll usually find the exact same dessert options at most restaurants.

They will include flan (a baked caramel custard), *helados* (ice cream), and *dulce de guayaba* (guava in syrup) or *dulce de lechosa* (papaya in syrup) served with *queso del país,* a soft white cheese. Occasionally restaurants will offer *tembleque,* a coconut custard, particularly around the Christmas holidays.

An American-style breakfast is fairly commonly found, although Puerto Ricans often eat their eggs and ham in toasted sandwiches called *bocadillos.* American coffee can sometimes be found, but the traditional *café con leche,* a strong brew with steamed milk, is highly recommended. *Bocadillos* are often eaten for lunch, particularly the *cubano,* a toasted sandwich with ham, roasted pork, and cheese. The *media noche* is similar to the *cubano,* but it's served on a softer, sweeter bread.

Although American fast-food restaurant chains can be found in Puerto Rico, the island has its own traditional style of fast-food fare often sold from roadside kiosks. Offerings usually include fried savory pies and fritters made from various combinations of plantain, meat, chicken, cheese, crab, potato, and fish.

DRINKING

The legal drinking age in Puerto Rico is 18. Although all types of alcoholic beverages are available, rum is the number one seller. There are three types of rum: white or silver, which is dry, pale, and light-bodied; gold, which is amber-colored and aged in charred oak casks; and black, a strong, 151-proof variety often used in flambés. Favorite rum drinks are the Cuba libre, a simple mix of rum and Coke with a wedge of lime; the piña colada, a frozen blended combination of rum, cream of coco, and pineapple juice; and the mojito, a Cuban import made from rum, simple syrup, club soda, fresh lime juice, and tons of fresh muddled mint. *Chichaito* is a rum and anise flavored shot often served after a Puerto Rican meal, and a *coquito* is an eggnog like cocktail made with rum and served during the Christmas holidays.

When it comes to beer, Puerto Ricans prefer a light pilsner, and you can't go wrong with Medalla. It's brewed in Mayagüez and won the bronze in its class at the World Beer Cup 1999. Presidente beer, made in the Dominican Republic, is also popular.

Conduct and Customs

ETIQUETTE

A certain formality permeates life in Puerto Rico. It's customary to acknowledge one another, including shop owners, with a greeting: *buenas dias* for good day, *buenas tardes* for good afternoon, and *buenas noches* for good evening. If you approach someone to ask the time or for directions, preface your question with *perdóneme* (excuse me). When a waiter delivers your meal, he or she will say *buen provecho,* and it's customary to say the same to diners already eating when you enter a restaurant.

Traditionally Puerto Ricans are exceedingly cordial. Even in San Juan, rudeness is rarely encountered. If you're lost or need help, they will cheerfully point you in the right direction. But Puerto Ricans don't typically display much interest in fraternizing with tourists. Americans who venture into bars catering primarily to the local dating scene may get a chilly reception if they're perceived as romantic rivals. The exception is bars that depend on the tourist dollar or that are in towns with a large U.S. expatriate population, such as Rincón or Vieques, where you're likely to know everybody's name by the time you leave.

Dress appropriately for the occasion. Although most upscale restaurants don't necessarily require a coat and tie, some do, so inquire. Otherwise, a well-groomed, nicely attired appearance is expected. And never wear beach attire, skimpy halter tops, or

Popular *Criolla Cocina* Dishes

Traditional Puerto Rican cuisine is called *criolla cocina*. Like the people of Puerto Rico, the cuisine's roots can be found at the intersection of the Taíno, Spanish, and African cultures. Most dishes are either slowly stewed throughout the day or quickly fried just before eating.

Many Puerto Rican dishes start with *sofrito*. Similar to a roux in Cajun cooking, it is a reduction of tomatoes, green bell pepper, onion, garlic, and cilantro. And plantains, both ripe and green, are eaten at just about every meal.

Here are some dishes commonly served in homes and restaurants throughout Puerto Rico.

- ***a la criolla:*** a cut of meat or fish served in a sauce made from tomatoes, green bell pepper, onion, garlic, and cilantro
- ***amarillos:*** a side dish of ripe plantains sliced lengthwise and slowly fried in oil until caramelized
- ***arañitas:*** fried balls of shredded plantain; often served as a snack or appetizer
- ***arroz con gandules:*** a thick pigeon peas and rice dish seasoned with *sofrito*
- ***arroz con jueyes:*** a thick land crab and rice dish seasoned with *sofrito*
- ***arroz con pollo:*** a thick chicken and rice dish seasoned with *sofrito*
- ***asopao:*** a thick rice stew made with chicken, pork, beef, or seafood
- ***bacalao:*** dried salt cod
- ***carne guisado:*** beef stew
- ***chicharrones:*** fried pork skins
- ***chicharrones de pollo:*** fried chunks of chicken
- ***chillo entero frito:*** whole fried snapper with the head on
- ***chuleta can can:*** a thick, deep-fried pork chop specially cut to retain a thick rind of fat and a strip of ribs
- ***churrasco* with *chimichurri* sauce:** an Argentine-style grilled skirt steak served with a piquant green sauce made from olive oil, garlic, and parsley
- ***empanado bifstec:*** a slice of steak pounded thin, breaded, and fried
- ***encebollado bifstec:*** a slice of steak pounded thin and served with caramelized onions

short shorts anywhere but the beach or pool. Although young fashionable Puerto Rican women may sometimes dress provocatively, visiting American women are advised to use some modesty or risk attracting unwanted male attention.

To the relief of nonsmokers, smoking has been banned in all restaurants, lounges, clubs, and bars in Puerto Rico, with the exception of establishments with outdoor seating. Public drinking has also been banned.

MACHISMO

Machismo appears to be becoming somewhat a thing of the past, particularly in San Juan, where mainland American influence is heaviest. The days of men verbally harassing or flashing young women is no longer a common occurrence, although vestiges of it remain around some wilderness beaches where perpetrators are far from the eyes of the *policía*. Nevertheless, it is interesting that *cabron* is a favored, mock-aggressive greeting

- **flan:** caramel custard
- ***frituras:*** fritters, such as *alcapurrias, empanadillas,* and *bacalaito,* typically sold from street-side kiosks, trucks, tents, and vans
- ***guineitos en escabeche:*** pickled green banana salad with onions and green olives
- ***lechón asado:*** whole roasted pig
- ***longaniza:*** spicy sausage usually made from pork and seasoned with annatto
- ***mallorca:*** a slightly sweet knot of bread dough, baked and dusted with powdered sugar—served split, buttered, and toasted or stuffed with hot ham and cheese for breakfast
- ***mofongo:*** a cone-shaped dish of mashed fried plantain seasoned with olive oil and garlic and fried bits of pork skin, bacon, or ham
- ***mofongo rellenas:*** *mofongo* stuffed with chicken, meat, or seafood
- ***morcilla:*** black blood sausage
- **paella:** Spanish dish similar to *arroz con pollo* but with saffron and filled with a variety of seafood instead of chicken
- ***panapén:*** breadfruit
- ***Pasteleon:*** similar to lasagna but instead of pasta, it's layered with ripe plaintains
- ***pasteles:*** like tamales; mashed plantain or cassava stuffed with pork or chicken and steamed in banana leaves, typically served around the Christmas holidays—don't eat the leaf!
- ***pescado in escabeche:*** pickled fish served cold; raw fillets are marinated in seasoned vinegar, similar to ceviche
- ***pique:*** hot sauce made from vinegar, lime juice, and hot peppers
- ***quesito:*** a sweet, sticky twist of puff pastry with a dab of cream cheese inside
- ***salmorejo de jueyes:*** stewed land crabmeat served over rice
- ***tembleque:*** coconut custard; often served around Christmas
- ***tostones:*** slices of green plantain fried twice and smashed; served like bread as an accompaniment to other dishes

among many men in Puerto Rico. Technically it means "goat," but its idiomatic translation is a man who's cuckolded by a cheating wife. There was a time when calling a man a *cabron* was a sure way to get a black eye, and used in the heat of an argument, it still is. But today it's more commonly used as a term of affection between male friends.

Meanwhile, the flip side of machismo—Old World chivalry—is still very much alive and well in Puerto Rico, especially among older men who appear to take pride in their gestures of kindness toward women.

CONCEPTS OF TIME

San Juan operates much like any big American city. The pace of life is fast, service is expedient, and everybody's in a hurry. But the farther you get away from San Juan, and most markedly in Culebra and Vieques, things tend to operate on "island time"—that is, at an extremely leisurely pace. You may be the only person in the restaurant, but it may still take 30 minutes or longer to receive your meal. Posted hours of operation are more suggestion than reality. Visitors are best advised to chill out and accept that this is just the way things are in Puerto Rico. If fawning service is required to have a good time, then stick with the resorts.

Health and Safety

Dengue fever, which is spread to humans by mosquito bites, is endemic in Puerto Rico. During non-outbreak years, there are typically between 3,000 and 9,000 suspected dengue cases reported in Puerto Rico. During epidemic years, the most recent of which ended in July 2014, the numbers can reach the tens of thousands. Symptoms of dengue include fever, headache, sore joints, nausea, vomiting, rash, bleeding. It is typically treatable at home with ibuprofen and liquids, but advanced cases may require hospitalization for treatment of dehydration.

Chikungunya virus shares many of the same symptoms of dengue; it is also spread by mosquitos. But Chikungunya has more serious lingering effects, and it has been on the rise in Puerto Rico. There were about 4,000 confirmed cases in 2014.

To prevent exposure to dengue and Chikungunya, use bug repellant containing DEET, Picaridin, IR3535, oil of lemon eucalyptus, or para-methane-diol.

Visitors should also take precaution against **sunstroke.** Summer can be brutally hot, especially in urban areas. It's important to drink lots of water, especially if you're doing a lot of walking or other physical activity. A hat and sunscreen are recommended. Or you could do as some of the local women do and use umbrellas to keep the beating rays at bay.

The quality of health care in Puerto Rico is comparable to that in the United States, and all major towns have at least one hospital and pharmacy, including Walgreens. The water is as safe to drink as it is in the United States, as are raw fruits and vegetables.

CRIME

Most of the crime in Puerto Rico revolves around the drug trade. The island is on a drug-transportation route that begins in Venezuela and passes through the Dominican Republic and into Puerto Rico on the way to the U.S. mainland. Add to that a poverty level of 44 percent, and you have a certain level of desperation. Ponce and Loíza have experienced high rates of murder, but most crimes are of the petty street variety—especially theft from automobiles or snatched purses. The street drug trade in San Juan operates out of La Perla, a former squatter's village outside the city wall beside Old San Juan.

Prostitution is illegal in Puerto Rico, although there's at least one strip club in San Juan that's reputed to be a bordello. Prostitutes do sometimes work the streets—even in quiet towns such as Mayagüez—and they're often more likely to be transgendered men than women.

The most common threat to visitors is having their possessions stolen from a rental car. Never leave anything of value visible in your car and always keep it locked. There are also occasional reports of carjackings and stolen vehicles. The police patrol San Juan regularly, and they keep their blue lights flashing all night long to announce their presence. For any emergency—crime, fire, wreck, injury—dial 911 for help.

Travel Tips

WHAT TO PACK

The activities you plan to pursue in Puerto Rico will dictate what you will need to pack. If you plan to sunbathe by day and hit the discos by night, pack your swimsuit and trendiest club wear. If a shopping marathon is on the agenda, pack comfortable walking shoes and an empty duffel bag for carrying back your loot. If you want to go hiking in the mountains, long lightweight pants and hiking boots are in order. If you stay in the mountains overnight, bring a light jacket.

No matter what you do, bring **sunscreen, bug spray, a wide-brimmed hat, an umbrella,** and some **bottled water.** You'll need protection from the sun and the occasional sand-flea attack while you're on the beach. And if you're traveling during the rainy season, expect a brief shower every day. You'll be grateful for some **light raingear,** such as a poncho and waterproof shoes or sandals.

Light cotton fabrics are always recommended. Puerto Rico's temperatures fluctuate 76-88°F on the coastal plains and 73-78°F in the mountain region. The humidity hovers around a steady 80 percent. Note that wearing bathing suits or short shorts is inappropriate anyplace other than the pool or beach, and a few restaurants require a jacket and tie.

If you plan to navigate the island by car, bring a **Spanish-English dictionary** and a current, detailed **road map.** Just about every business on the island accepts credit cards and debit cards, and virtually every town has at least one ATM. The only time you'll need cash is if you plan to shop or buy food from roadside vendors, which you definitely should do.

MONEY

Puerto Rico's form of currency is the U.S. dollar, which is sometimes referred to as *peso.* Full-service banks with ATMs are plentiful, the most common one being Banco Popular. Banking hours are Monday-Friday 9am-3:30pm. Credit cards and debit cards are accepted virtually everywhere. The only time cash is required is when buying items from roadside vendors and occasionally even they will accept plastic.

A sales tax, between 5.5 percent and 6.7 percent depending on the municipality, has recently been instituted in Puerto Rico, and hotel taxes can vary depending on the type of property. Hotels with casinos charge 11 percent tax, and hotels without casinos charge 9 percent tax. There may also be resort fees, energy surcharge fees, and other charges. When determining the price of a hotel room, ask whether or not the tax is included in the stated price.

Tipping practices are the same as in the United States—15-20 percent of the bill, unless a gratuity has already been added.

COMMUNICATIONS

Published five days a week, the ***San Juan Star*** (www.sanjuanweeklypr.com) is San Juan's only English language newspaper, featuring locally produced content and wire stories from the *New York Times.* ***El Nuevo Día*** (www.endi.com) is the island-wide Spanish-language daily newspaper. ***La Perla del Sur*** (www.periodicolaperla.com) is a daily paper serving Ponce. ***The New York Times*** and ***The Miami Herald*** can be commonly found in hotels and newsstands in San Juan.

The free bimonthly ***Qué Pasa?*** (www.qpsm.com) is an English language travel magazine published by Travel and Sports (www.travelandsports.com) for the Puerto Rico Tourism Company. The magazine's current issue is available online, and the publishing company's website is an exhaustive source of information about the entire island.

Television broadcasting is regulated by the U.S. Federal Communications Commission. There are three commercial channels:

Telemundo (channel 2), **Televicentro** (channel 4), and **Univision** (channel 11), and one public channel—**TUTV** (channel 6). Local programming features sitcoms, talk shows, news, and soap operas, all in Spanish. Multichannel cable and satellite TV is also available.

Phones and Cell Phones

Puerto Rico has one area code—787—and it must always be dialed when placing a call. Nevertheless, all calls are not local, so long-distance rates may apply. U.S. cell phones with nationwide service should function fine in Puerto Rico.

Shipping and Postal Service

Mail service is provided by the U.S. Postal Service. Although mailing letters and post-cards to and from the island costs the same as in the United States, international rates apply when shipping items to the island. United Parcel Service and overnight shipping companies such as Federal Express also operate on the island.

TIME ZONE

Puerto Rico observes **Atlantic standard time** and does not practice daylight saving time. Therefore, time in Puerto Rico is one hour later than eastern standard time November-March and the same as eastern daylight time from the second Sunday in March until the first Sunday in November.

WEIGHTS AND MEASURES

Puerto Rico uses the metric system. Gasoline is bought in liters (1 gallon = 3.7 liters), and distance is measured in kilometers (1 mile = 1.61 kilometers). The exception is speed, which is measured in miles per hour.

STUDY AND VOLUNTEER OPPORTUNITIES

Spanish Abroad (5112 N. 40th St., Ste. 203, Phoenix, AZ 85018, 888/722-7623 or 602/778-6791, www.spanishabroad.com) offers Spanish-language immersion classes with homestays in Hato Rey, San Juan.

ACCESS FOR TRAVELERS WITH DISABILITIES

As a territory of the United States, Puerto Rico must adhere to the Americans with Disabilities Act, which ensures access to public buildings for all. While some historic buildings may be exempt, most have been adapted for access with ramps, elevators, and wheelchair-accessible restrooms. The majority of hotels have at least one accessible hotel room. Most sidewalks have curb cuts at crosswalks to accommodate wheelchairs, scooters, and walkers, and traffic lights have audible signals to assist visitors with sight impairments with street crossings.

TRAVELING WITH CHILDREN

San Juan offers lots to do for families with children of all ages. The historic forts and museums hold plenty of interest for youngsters, and many water sports are suitable as well, including fishing, boating, and swimming. And with a few exceptions, most restaurants welcome young diners. As in any urban center, parents should keep a close watch on their children at the pool and beach, especially if there is no lifeguard on duty, and along busy sidewalks where there is car traffic. It is advisable to keep sunscreen, bug spray, and bottled water on hand at all times.

WOMEN TRAVELING ALONE

Puerto Rico is safe for women traveling alone or in groups. But precautions should be taken. Dressing provocatively can attract catcalls and other forms of unwanted attention, and bathing suits should never be worn anywhere but at the beach or pool. Women traveling solo should avoid remote wilderness beaches and late-night bars that cater primarily to locals. Safety in numbers is a good rule to follow when going out at night.

GAY AND LESBIAN TRAVELERS

Despite Puerto Rico's strong patriarchal society in which a traditional sense of manhood is highly prized, homosexuality is generally accepted, especially in San Juan, which is something of a destination for the LGBT traveler. There are a number of nightclubs that cater specifically to a gay and lesbian clientele, and certain beaches are known to attract a gay crowd. San Juan is also a popular port of call for gay cruises.

Tourist Information

TOURIST OFFICES

Located across the street from Pier 1, **Puerto Rico Tourism Company** (500 Ochoa Bldg., Calle Tanca, Old San Juan, 787/721-2400 ext. 3901, www.seepuertorico.com, daily 9am-5:30pm) is a wealth of tourist information. Some of the island's towns have their own tourist offices, usually on or near the plaza and often in the *alcaldía* (city hall) building. Unfortunately, many of them tend to be open sporadically, despite posted hours of operation.

MAPS

There are free maps and travel publications, such as ***Places to Go, Bienvenidos,*** and ***Qué Pasa!*** magazines, available at many stores, restaurants, and hotels. For a detailed road map of the island, **International Travel Maps of Canada** (www.itmb.com) is your best option, but you'll have to order online before you go. National Geographic's excellent illustrated map of the Caribbean National Forest is available from its website (www.nationalgeographic.com/maps).

Resources

Glossary

ajillo: garlic
a la criolla: a cut of meat or fish served in a sauce made from tomatoes, green bell pepper, onion, garlic, and cilantro
alcapurria: fritter of mashed yautia, yuca, and green banana stuffed with meat or crab and deep fried
al centro: downtown
alto: stop
amarillos: fried ripe plantains
appertivos: appetizers
arañitas: fried balls of shredded plantain; often served as a snack or appetizer
arepa: a small, round patty of corn meal batter fried, split open on one side, and stuffed with meat or seafood
arroz: rice
arroz con gandules: a thick pigeon peas and rice dish seasoned with *sofrito*
arroz con jueyes: a thick land crab and rice dish seasoned with *sofrito*
arroz con pollo: a thick chicken and rice dish seasoned with *sofrito*
asado: roasted
asopao: rice stew
autopista: divided limited-access highway
avenida: avenue
azúcar: sugar
bacalaito: codfish fritter
bahía: bay
balneario: publicly maintained beach
barbacoa: meat grilled over a fire or charcoal; also the name of the grill
barcazas: whole plantains sliced lengthwise, stuffed with ground beef, and topped with cheese
barrio: neighborhood
batata: white yam
batey: ceremonial ball field used by Taíno people
bebida: beverage
bio-bay: shorthand for bioluminescent bay, one of three mangrove lagoons in Puerto Rico that contain microorganisms called dinoflagellates that glow in the dark
bocadillo: sandwich, typically toasted
bohique: Taíno spiritual leader
Borinquen: Taíno name for Puerto Rico
bosque estatal: public forest
botánica: shop that sells herbs, scents, and candles used by practitioners of *espiritismo* or Santería
brazo gitano: translates as "gypsy arm," but it refers to a jellyroll cake filled with fruit traditional to Mayagüez
cabro: goat
cacique: Taíno chief
café: coffee
calle: street
camarones: shrimp
capilla: chapel
carbón: grilled
carne: beef
carne guisado: beef stew
carretera: road
carrucho: conch
cayos: cays, islets
cebollado: onion
cemí: Taíno amulet
cerdo: pork
chicharrones: fried pork skins
chicharrones de pollo: fried chunks of chicken
chillo: red snapper

chillo entero frito: whole fried snapper with the head on
chorizo: spicy pork sausage
chuleta can can: a thick, deep-fried pork chop specially cut to retain a thick rind of fat and a strip of ribs
chuletas: chops, typically pork
churrasco: grilled, marinated skirt steak
criolla cocina: Puerto Rican cuisine
coco: coconut
coco dulce: an immensely sweet confection of fresh, coarsely grated coconut and caramelized sugar
coco frio: chilled coconuts still in their green husks served with a hole cut in the top and a straw stuck through it; inside is refreshing thin coconut milk
conejo: rabbit
coqui: tiny tree frog that emits an eponymous chirp
cordero: lamb
criolla: creole; means "Puerto Rican-style"
cruce: crossroads
cruzar: to cross
cuadras: blocks
cubano: toasted sandwich with pork, ham, cheese, and pickles
derecha: right
derecho: straight
doble: turn
dorado: mahimahi
empanadilla: savory turnover stuffed with meat, chicken, seafood, or cheese
empanado: breaded and fried meat
encebollado bifstec: a slice of steak pounded thin and served with caramelized onions
ensalada: salad
espiritismo: Taíno-based religion that believes deities reside in nature
esquina: corner
estacionamiento: parking
este: east
faro: lighthouse
fiestas patronales: festivals that celebrate the patron saints of towns
flan: caramel custard
frito: fried
frituras: fritters
gandules: pigeon peas
guayaba: guava
guineitos en escabeche: pickled green banana salad with onions and green olives
habichuelas: beans
helado: ice cream
hielo: ice
horno: baked
izquierda: left
jámon: ham
jíbaro: rural resident, hillbilly
juevos: eggs
juyeyes: land crab
laguna: lagoon
lancha: ferry
langosta: rock lobster
leche: milk
lechón: pork
lechonera: restaurant serving pit-roasted pork and other local delicacies
lechosa: papaya
lejos: far
luces: traffic lights
luz: traffic light
malécon: seawall promenade
mallorca: a slightly sweet knot of bread dough, baked and dusted with powdered sugar—served split, buttered, and toasted or stuffed with hot ham and cheese for breakfast
mantequilla: butter
mariscos: seafood
máscaras: masks
mavi: a fermented Taíno beverage made from the bark of the *mavi* tree
media noche: sandwich similar to a *cubano,* but on a softer, sweeter bread
mercardo: market
mofongo: cooked unripe plantain mashed with garlic and olive oil
mofongo rellenas: *mofongo* stuffed with chicken, meat, or seafood
mogote: conical, haystack-shaped hill
mondongo: beef tripe stew
mundillo: handmade lace that's created with bobbins
muralla: wall
ñame: yam
norte: north

Nuyorican: a Puerto Rican person who migrated to New York

oeste: west

paella: Spanish dish similar to *arroz con pollo* but with saffron and filled with a variety of seafood instead of chicken

pan: bread

panadería: bakery

panapén: breadfruit

papas: potatoes

papas rellenas: a big lump of mashed potatoes stuffed with meat and deep-fried

parador: privately owned inn in a rural area

parque: park

pasteles: like tamales; mashed plantain or cassava stuffed with pork or chicken and steamed in banana leaves, typically served around the Christmas holidays—don't eat the leaf!

pastelillos: savory turnover stuffed with meat, chicken, seafood, or cheese

pechuga de pollo: chicken breast

pernil: pork

pescado: fish

pescado in escabeche: pickled fish served cold; raw fillets are marinated in seasoned vinegar, similar to ceviche

picadillo: seasoned ground beef used to stuff *empanadillas*

pimento: pepper

piña: pineapple

pinchos: chunks of chicken, pork, or fish threaded on a skewer and grilled shish-kebab style

pionono: seasoned ground beef wrapped mummy style in slices of plantain and deep-fried

pique: hot sauce made from vinegar, lime juice, and hot peppers

platano: plantain

playa: beach

postre: dessert

públicos: public transportation in vans that pick up multiple riders along an established route

pueblo: town center

pulpo: octopus

quesito: a sweet, sticky twist of puff pastry with a dab of cream cheese inside

queso: cheese

queso del país: soft white cow cheese

relleno: stuffed food item, as in *mofongo relleno*

reserva forestal: forest reserve

sal: salt

salida: exit

salmorejo de jueyes: stewed land crabmeat served over rice

Santería: Afro-Caribbean-based religion that observes multiple gods

santos: small wood carvings of Catholic saints

setas: mushrooms

sopa: soup

sorullos or sorullitos: fried cheese and cornmeal sticks

sur: south

Taíno: people who were indigenous to Puerto Rico when it became a Spanish colony

taquitos: chicken, ground beef, crab, or fish rolled up in a tortilla and deep-fried

tembleque: coconut custard; often served around Christmas

tocino: bacon

tortilla española: a baked egg and potato dish

tostones: twice-fried, flattened pieces of plantain

vaya: go

vejigante: horned mask worn in festivals

yautia: taro root, similar to a potato

yuca: cassava, a root vegetable

ABBREVIATIONS

Ave.: Avenida

Bo.: Barrio

Carr.: Carretera

Int.: approaching intersection, or interior route

km: kilometer

Spanish Phrasebook

Your Puerto Rico adventure will be more fun if you use a little Spanish. Puerto Ricans, although they may smile at your funny accent, will appreciate your halting efforts to break the ice and transform yourself from a foreigner to a potential friend.

Spanish commonly uses 30 letters—the familiar English 26, plus four straightforward additions: ch, ll, ñ, and rr, which are explained in "Consonants," below.

PRONUNCIATION

Once you learn them, Spanish pronunciation rules—in contrast to English—don't change. Spanish vowels generally sound softer than in English. (Note: The capitalized syllables below receive stronger accents.)

Vowels

- **a** like ah, as in "hah": *agua* AH-gooah (water), *pan* PAHN (bread), and *casa* CAH-sah (house)
- **e** like ay, as in "may:" *mesa* MAY-sah (table), *tela* TAY-lah (cloth), and *de* DAY (of, from)
- **i** like ee, as in "need": *diez* dee-AYZ (ten), *comida* ko-MEE-dah (meal), and *fin* FEEN (end)
- **o** like oh, as in "go": *peso* PAY-soh (weight), *ocho* OH-choh (eight), and *poco* POH-koh (a bit)
- **u** like oo, as in "cool": *uno* OO-noh (one), *cuarto* KOOAHR-toh (room), and *usted* oos-TAYD (you); when it follows a "q" the **u** is silent; when it follows an "h" or has an umlaut, it's pronounced like "w"

Consonants

- **b, d, f, k, l, m, n, p, q, s, t, v, w, x, y, z,** and **ch** are pronounced almost as in English; h occurs, but is silent—not pronounced at all
- **c** like k as in "keep": *cuarto* KOOAR-toh (room), Tepic tay-PEEK (capital of Nayarit state); when it precedes "e" or "i," pronounce **c** like s, as in "sit": *cerveza* sayr-VAY-sah (beer), *encima* ayn-SEE-mah (atop)
- **g** like g as in "gift" when it precedes "a," "o," "u," or a consonant: *gato* GAH-toh (cat), *hago* AH-goh (I do, make); otherwise, pronounce **g** like h as in "hat": *giro* HEE-roh (money order), *gente* HAYN-tay (people)
- **j** like h, as in "has": *Jueves* HOOAY-vays (Thursday), *mejor* may-HOR (better)
- **ll** like y, as in "yes": *toalla* toh-AH-yah (towel), *ellos* AY-yohs (they, them)
- **ñ** like ny, as in "canyon": *año* AH-nyo (year), *señor* SAY-nyor (Mr., sir)
- **r** is lightly trilled, with tongue at the roof of your mouth like a very light English d, as in "ready": *pero* PAY-doh (but), *tres* TDAYS (three), *cuatro* KOOAH-tdoh (four)
- **rr** like a Spanish r, but with much more emphasis and trill. Let your tongue flap. Practice with *burro* (donkey), *carretera* (highway), and Carrillo (proper name), then really let go with *ferrocarril* (railroad)

Note: The single small but common exception to all of the above is the pronunciation of Spanish **y** when it's being used as the Spanish word for "and," as in "Ron y Kathy." In such case, pronounce it like the English ee, as in "keep": Ron "ee" Kathy (Ron and Kathy).

Accent

The rule for accent, the relative stress given to syllables within a given word, is straightforward. If a word ends in a vowel, an n, or an s, accent the next-to-last syllable; if not, accent the last syllable.

Pronounce *gracias* GRAH-seeahs (thank you), *orden* OHR-dayn (order), and *carretera* kah-ray-TAY-rah (highway) with stress on the next-to-last syllable.

Otherwise, accent the last syllable: *venir* vay-NEER (to come), *ferrocarril* fay-roh-cah-REEL (railroad), and *edad* ay-DAHD (age).

Exceptions to the accent rule are always marked with an accent sign: (á, é, í, ó, or ú), such as *teléfono* tay-LAY-foh-noh (telephone), *jabón* hah-BON (soap), and *rápido* RAH-pee-doh (rapid).

BASIC AND COURTEOUS EXPRESSIONS

Most Spanish-speaking people consider formalities important. Whenever approaching anyone for information or some other reason, do not forget the appropriate salutation—good morning, good evening, etc. Standing alone, the greeting *hola* (hello) can sound brusque.

Hello. *Hola.*
Good morning. *Buenos días.*
Good afternoon. *Buenas tardes.*
Good evening. *Buenas noches.*
How are you? *¿Cómo está usted?*
Very well, thank you. *Muy bien, gracias.*
Okay; good. *Bien.*
Not okay; bad. *Mal* or *feo.*
So-so. *Más o menos.*
And you? *¿Y usted?*
Thank you. *Gracias.*
Thank you very much. *Muchas gracias.*
You're very kind. *Muy amable.*
You're welcome. *De nada.*
Goodbye. *Adios.*
See you later. *Hasta luego.*
please *por favor*
yes *sí*
no *no*
I don't know. *No sé.*
Just a moment, please. *Momentito, por favor.*
Excuse me, please (when you're trying to get attention). *Disculpe* or *Con permiso.*
Excuse me (when you've made a boo-boo). *Lo siento.*
Pleased to meet you. *Mucho gusto.*
How do you say . . . in Spanish? *¿Cómo se dice . . . en español?*
What is your name? *¿Cómo se llama usted?*
Do you speak English? *¿Habla usted inglés?*
Is English spoken here? (Does anyone here speak English?) *¿Se habla inglés?*
I don't speak Spanish well. *No hablo bien el español.*
I don't understand. *No entiendo.*
How do you say . . . in Spanish? *¿Cómo se dice . . . en español?*
My name is . . . *Me llamo . . .*
Would you like . . . *¿Quisiera usted . . .*
Let's go to . . . *Vamos a . . .*

TERMS OF ADDRESS

When in doubt, use the formal *usted* (you) as a form of address.

I *yo*
you (formal) *usted*
you (familiar) *tu*
he/him *él*
she/her *ella*
we/us *nosotros*
you (plural) *ustedes*
they/them *ellos* (all males or mixed gender); *ellas* (all females)
Mr., sir *señor*
Mrs., madam *señora*
miss, young lady *señorita*
wife *esposa*
husband *esposo*
friend *amigo* (male); *amiga* (female)
sweetheart *novio* (male); *novia* (female)
son; daughter *hijo; hija*
brother; sister *hermano; hermana*
father; mother *padre; madre*
grandfather; grandmother *abuelo; abuela*

TRANSPORTATION

Where is . . . ? *¿Dónde está . . . ?*
How far is it to . . . ? *¿A cuánto está . . . ?*
from . . . to . . . *de . . . a . . .*
How many blocks? *¿Cuántas cuadras?*
Where (Which) is the way to . . . ? *¿Dónde está el camino a . . . ?*
the bus station *la terminal de autobuses*
the bus stop *la parada de autobuses*
Where is this bus going? *¿Adónde va este autobús?*
the taxi stand *la parada de taxis*

the train station *la estación de ferrocarril*
the boat *el barco*
the launch *lancha; tiburonera*
the dock *el muelle*
the airport *el aeropuerto*
I'd like a ticket to . . . *Quisiera un boleto a . . .*
first (second) class *primera (segunda) clase*
roundtrip *ida y vuelta*
reservation *reservación*
baggage *equipaje*
Stop here, please. *Pare aquí, por favor.*
the entrance *la entrada*
the exit *la salida*
the ticket office *la oficina de boletos*
(very) near; far *(muy) cerca; lejos*
to; toward *a*
by; through *por*
from *de*
the right *la derecha*
the left *la izquierda*
straight ahead *derecho; directo*
in front *en frente*
beside *al lado*
behind *atrás*
the corner *la esquina*
the stoplight *la semáforo*
a turn *una vuelta*
right here *aquí*
somewhere around here *por acá*
right there *allí*
somewhere around there *por allá*
road *el camino*
street; boulevard *calle; bulevar*
block *la cuadra*
highway *carretera*
kilometer *kilómetro*
bridge; toll *puente; cuota*
address *dirección*
north; south *norte; sur*
east; west *oriente (este); poniente (oeste)*

ACCOMMODATIONS

hotel *hotel*
Is there a room? *¿Hay cuarto?*
May I (may we) see it? *¿Puedo (podemos) verlo?*
What is the rate? *¿Cuál es el precio?*
Is that your best rate? *¿Es su mejor precio?*
Is there something cheaper? *¿Hay algo más económico?*
a single room *un cuarto sencillo*
a double room *un cuarto doble*
double bed *cama matrimonial*
twin beds *camas gemelas*
with private bath *con baño*
hot water *agua caliente*
shower *ducha*
towels *toallas*
soap *jabón*
toilet paper *papel higiénico*
blanket *frazada; manta*
sheets *sábanas*
air-conditioned *aire acondicionado*
fan *abanico; ventilador*
key *llave*
manager *gerente*

FOOD

I'm hungry *Tengo hambre.*
I'm thirsty. *Tengo sed.*
menu *carta; menú*
order *orden*
glass *vaso*
fork *tenedor*
knife *cuchillo*
spoon *cuchara*
napkin *servilleta*
soft drink *refresco*
coffee *café*
tea *té*
drinking water *agua pura; agua potable*
bottled carbonated water *agua mineral*
bottled uncarbonated water *agua sin gas*
beer *cerveza*
wine *vino*
milk *leche*
juice *jugo*
cream *crema*
sugar *azúcar*
cheese *queso*
snack *antojo; botana*
breakfast *desayuno*

lunch *almuerzo*
daily lunch special *comida corrida* (or *el menú del día* depending on region)
dinner *comida* (often eaten in late afternoon); *cena* (a late-night snack)
the check *la cuenta*
eggs *huevos*
bread *pan*
salad *ensalada*
fruit *fruta*
mango *mango*
watermelon *sandía*
papaya *papaya*
banana *plátano*
apple *manzana*
orange *naranja*
lime *limón*
fish *pescado*
shellfish *mariscos*
shrimp *camarones*
meat (without) *(sin) carne*
chicken *pollo*
pork *puerco*
beef; steak *res; bistec*
bacon; ham *tocino; jamón*
fried *frito*
roasted *asada*
barbecue; barbecued *barbacoa; al carbón*

SHOPPING

money *dinero*
money-exchange bureau *casa de cambio*
I would like to exchange traveler's checks. *Quisiera cambiar cheques de viajero.*
What is the exchange rate? *¿Cuál es el tipo de cambio?*
How much is the commission? *¿Cuánto cuesta la comisión?*
Do you accept credit cards? *¿Aceptan tarjetas de crédito?*
money order *giro*
How much does it cost? *¿Cuánto cuesta?*
What is your final price? *¿Cuál es su último precio?*
expensive *caro*
cheap *barato; económico*
more *más*
less *menos*
a little *un poco*
too much *demasiado*

HEALTH

Help me please. *Ayúdeme por favor.*
I am ill. *Estoy enfermo.*
Call a doctor. *Llame un doctor.*
Take me to . . . *Lléveme a . . .*
hospital *hospital; sanatorio*
drugstore *farmacia*
pain *dolor*
fever *fiebre*
headache *dolor de cabeza*
stomach ache *dolor de estómago*
burn *quemadura*
cramp *calambre*
nausea *náusea*
vomiting *vomitar*
medicine *medicina*
antibiotic *antibiótico*
pill; tablet *pastilla*
aspirin *aspirina*
ointment; cream *pomada; crema*
bandage *venda*
cotton *algodón*
sanitary napkins use brand name, e.g., Kotex
birth control pills *pastillas anticonceptivas*
contraceptive foam *espuma anticonceptiva*
condoms *preservativos; condones*
toothbrush *cepilla dental*
dental floss *hilo dental*
toothpaste *crema dental*
dentist *dentista*
toothache *dolor de muelas*

POST OFFICE AND COMMUNICATIONS

long-distance telephone *teléfono larga distancia*
I would like to call . . . *Quisiera llamar a . . .*

collect *por cobrar*
station to station *a quien contesta*
person to person *persona a persona*
credit card *tarjeta de crédito*
post office *correo*
general delivery *lista de correo*
letter *carta*
stamp *estampilla, timbre*
postcard *tarjeta*
aerogram *aerograma*
air mail *correo aereo*
registered *registrado*
money order *giro*
package; box *paquete; caja*
string; tape *cuerda; cinta*

CUSTOMS

border *frontera*
customs *aduana*
immigration *migración*
tourist card *tarjeta de turista*
inspection *inspección; revisión*
passport *pasaporte*
profession *profesión*
marital status *estado civil*
single *soltero*
married; divorced *casado; divorciado*
widowed *viudado*
insurance *seguros*
title *título*
driver's license *licencia de manejar*

AT THE GAS STATION

gas station *gasolinera*
gasoline *gasolina*
unleaded *sin plomo*
full, please *lleno, por favor*
tire *llanta*
tire repair shop *vulcanizadora*
air *aire*
water *agua*
oil (change) *aceite (cambio)*
grease *grasa*
My . . . doesn't work. *Mi . . . no sirve.*
battery *batería*
radiator *radiador*
alternator *alternador*
generator *generador*
tow truck *grúa*
repair shop *taller mecánico*
tune-up *afinación*
auto parts store *refaccionería*

VERBS

Verbs are the key to getting along in Spanish. They employ mostly predictable forms and come in three classes, which end in *ar*, *er*, and *ir*, respectively:

to buy *comprar*
I buy, you (he, she, it) buys *compro, compra*
we buy, you (they) buy *compramos, compran*

to eat *comer*
I eat, you (he, she, it) eats *como, come*
we eat, you (they) eat *comemos, comen*

to climb *subir*
I climb, you (he, she, it) climbs *subo, sube*
we climb, you (they) climb *subimos, suben*

Here are more (with irregularities indicated):

to do or make *hacer* (regular except for *hago*, I do or make)
to go *ir* (very irregular: *voy, va, vamos, van*)
to go (walk) *andar*
to love *amar*
to work *trabajar*
to want *desear, querer*
to need *necesitar*
to read *leer*
to write *escribir*
to repair *reparar*
to stop *parar*
to get off (the bus) *bajar*
to arrive *llegar*
to stay (remain) *quedar*
to stay (lodge) *hospedar*
to leave *salir* (regular except for *salgo*, I leave)

to look at *mirar*
to look for *buscar*
to give *dar* (regular except for *doy*, I give)
to carry *llevar*
to have *tener* (irregular but important: *tengo, tiene, tenemos, tienen*)
to come *venir* (similarly irregular: *vengo, viene, venimos, vienen*)

Spanish has two forms of "to be":

to be *estar* (regular except for *estoy*, I am)
to be *ser* (very irregular: *soy, es, somos, son*)

Use *estar* when speaking of location or a temporary state of being: "I am at home." *"Estoy en casa."* "I'm sick." *"Estoy enfermo."* Use *ser* for a permanent state of being: "I am a doctor." *"Soy doctora."*

NUMBERS

zero *cero*
one *uno*
two *dos*
three *tres*
four *cuatro*
five *cinco*
six *seis*
seven *siete*
eight *ocho*
nine *nueve*
10 *diez*
11 *once*
12 *doce*
13 *trece*
14 *catorce*
15 *quince*
16 *dieciseis*
17 *diecisiete*
18 *dieciocho*
19 *diecinueve*
20 *veinte*
21 *veinte y uno* or *veintiuno*
30 *treinta*
40 *cuarenta*
50 *cincuenta*
60 *sesenta*
70 *setenta*
80 *ochenta*
90 *noventa*
100 *ciento*
101 *ciento y uno* or *cientiuno*
200 *doscientos*
500 *quinientos*
1,000 *mil*
10,000 *diez mil*
100,000 *cien mil*
1,000,000 *millón*
one half *medio*
one third *un tercio*
one fourth *un cuarto*

TIME

What time is it? *¿Qué hora es?*
It's one o'clock. *Es la una.*
It's three in the afternoon. *Son las tres de la tarde.*
It's 4 a.m. *Son las cuatro de la mañana.*
six-thirty *seis y media*
a quarter till eleven *un cuarto para las once*
a quarter past five *las cinco y cuarto*
an hour *una hora*

DAYS AND MONTHS

Monday *lunes*
Tuesday *martes*
Wednesday *miércoles*
Thursday *jueves*
Friday *viernes*
Saturday *sábado*
Sunday *domingo*
today *hoy*
tomorrow *mañana*
yesterday *ayer*
January *enero*
February *febrero*
March *marzo*
April *abril*
May *mayo*
June *junio*
July *julio*
August *agosto*
September *septiembre*
October *octubre*

November *noviembre*
December *diciembre*
a week *una semana*
a month *un mes*
after *después*
before *antes*

(Courtesy of Bruce Whipperman, author of *Moon Pacific Mexico.*)

Suggested Reading

ARTS AND CULTURE

Delano, Jack. *Puerto Rico Mio: Four Decades of Change.* Washington: Smithsonian Books, 1990. Includes 175 duotones of former Farm Security Administration photographer Jack Delano's visual chronicle of the island and its people. Includes essays in Spanish and English by educator Arturo Morales Carrión, historian Alan Fern, and anthropologist Sidney W. Mintz.

Muckley, Robert L., and Adela Martinez-Santiago. *Stories from Puerto Rico. New* York: McGraw-Hill, 1999. A collection of legends, ghost stories, and beloved true accounts that reflect the island's folklore. In English and Spanish.

Santiago, Roberto, ed. *Boricuas: Influential Puerto Rican Writings—An Anthology.* New York: One World/Ballantine, 1995. A fantastic collection of poems, speeches, stories, and excerpts by Puerto Rico's greatest writers, past and present, including Jesús Colón, Pablo Guzman, Julia de Burgos, and many more.

CHILDREN'S BOOKS

Bernier-Grand, Carmen T. (author), and Ernesto Ramos Nieves (illustrator). *Juan Bobo: Four Folktales from Puerto Rico.* New York: HarperTrophy, 1995. Four humorous folktales about the trials and tribulations of the lovable, misguided little boy Juan Bobo.

Ramirez, Michael Rose (author), and Margaret Sanfilippo (illustrator). *The Legend of the Hummingbird: A Tale from Puerto Rico.* New York: Mondo, 1998. Learn about Puerto Rico's history, climate, and traditions in this beguiling tale of transformation.

HISTORY AND POLITICS

Carrión, Arturo Morales. *Puerto Rico: A Political and Cultural History.* New York: W. W. Norton & Co., 1984. An examination of Puerto Rico's commonwealth status and how it got there.

Monge, José Trias. *Puerto Rico: The Trials of the Oldest Colony in the World.* New Haven: Yale University Press, 1999 (paperback). An examination of Puerto Rico's political status through history and an outlook on its future.

Odishelidze, Alexander, and Arthur Laffer. *Pay to the Order of Puerto Rico: The Cost of Dependence.* Dover: Allegiance Press, 2004. A look at Puerto Rico's political status from an outsider—a Russian native. Although Puerto Rico's options for future political status are well documented, the author openly favors statehood.

Rouse, Irving. *The Taínos: Rise and Decline of the People Who Greeted Columbus.* New Haven: Yale University Press, reissue 1993. A history of the Taíno culture based on intensive study of archaeological sites.

LITERATURE

Santiago, Esmeralda. *Conquistadora.* New York: Knopf, 2012. Historical fiction about a strong-willed Spanish woman who sails to

Puerto Rico with her husband and brother-in-law in 1844 to run a sugar plantation.

Santiago, Esmeralda. *When I Was Puerto Rican.* Cambridge: Da Capo Press, 2006. A memoir about growing up in Puerto Rico and immigrating to the United States.

Santiago, Roberto. *Boricua: The Influential Puerto Rican Writings, an Anthology.* New York: Ballantine, 1995. Fifty selections of 19th- and 20th-century works by Puerto Rican writers.

NATURE AND WILDLIFE

Lee, Alfonso Silva. *Natural Puerto Rico/ Puerto Rico Natural.* Saint Paul: Pangaea, 1998. An examination of the fauna of Puerto Rico by Cuban biologist Alfonso Silva Lee. In Spanish and English.

Oberle, Mark W. *Puerto Rico's Birds in Photographs.* Bucharest: Humanitas, 2000. More than 300 color photographs document 181 species of birds found in Puerto Rico. Comes with a CD-ROM including audio clips and more photographs.

Raffaele, Herbert. *A Guide to the Birds of Puerto Rico and the Virgin Islands.* Princeton: Princeton University Press, 1989. Contains information on 284 documented species as well as 273 illustrations.

Simonsen, Steve. *Diving and Snorkeling Guide to Puerto Rico.* Deland: Pisces Books, 1996. A guide to the best diving and snorkeling sites around the island.

Internet Resources

TRAVEL INFORMATION

En Culebra Magazine
www.enculebra.com

Well-researched and well-written articles cover various aspects of life in Culebra, with lots of great travel information.

Isla Culebra
www.islaculebra.com

A terrific source for vacation rentals on Culebra. The best feature is its very active, informative travel forum. Post a question and someone will know the answer.

Puerto Rico Day Trips
www.puertoricodaytrips.com

This individually owned and operated site is well researched and updated on a regular basis. Lots of good practical information.

Puerto Rico Tourism Co.
www.seepuertorico.com

Produced by the Puerto Rico Tourism Co., this is an excellent source of well-researched information on history, culture, events, and sights with a promotional slant.

Tourism Association of Rincón
www.rincon.org

In addition to a plethora of general tourist information on Rincón, this site provides info services of interest to residents, including locations for churches, hair salons, and cleaners. Plus, there's some great photography.

Vieques Travel Guide
www.viequestravelguide.com

A reliable source of vacation rentals, tourist sights, shops, transportation, and more on Vieques.

Welcome to Puerto Rico
www.topuertorico.org

Individually owned and operated site offering extensive information on the history, government, and geography of all 78 municipalities.

HISTORY, POLITICS, AND CULTURE

Historic Places in Puerto Rico

www.nps.gov/history/nr/travel/prvi

The National Park Service site provides details on all the historic sites that fall under its purview.

Music of Puerto Rico

www.musicofpuertorico.com

Excellent source for information on Puerto Rican music, from folk and *danza* to *bomba* and salsa to reggaetón. Also contains audio clips, biographies of native musicians, lyrics, and musical history.

Public Art

www.artepublicopr.com/english

Official source for Puerto Rico's $25 million public art project, including project proposals, artists' biographies, and maps to the sites.

Puerto Rican Painter

www.puertoricanpainter.com

An all-inclusive look at local artists currently working in Puerto Rico, the site includes a list of galleries, artist biographies, and galleries of artwork.

Puerto Rico and the Dream

www.prdream.com

An intelligent and discriminating site about the history, culture, and politics of Puerto Rico that includes audio files of oral histories, galleries of select art exhibitions, historical timelines, archival photos, and discussion forums. The site really has its finger on the pulse of all matters important to Puerto Ricans.

Taíno Cyber Culture Center

www.indio.net/taino

A clearinghouse for links to articles on Taíno history, news, research, and culture.

NATURE AND WILDLIFE

The Conservation Trust of Puerto Rico

www.fideicomiso.org

In addition to working to preserve the island's natural beauty, the Conservation Trust of Puerto Rico offers a variety of educational nature and culture tours.

U.S. Fish and Wildlife Service

www.fws.gov/caribbean

The U.S. Fish and Wildlife Service operates this site featuring information on the island's wildlife refuges, geographic regions, and efforts to restore the population of Puerto Rican parrots.

Index

AB

C

DE

F

G

HI

JKL

M

NO

P

QRS

T

UV

WXYZ

List of Maps

Acknowledgments

I want to thank my parents, Ted and Jo Teagle, who instilled in me a passion for travel. Had they not been adventurous enough to move our family to Puerto Rico in the early 1970s, this book would never have happened. I also want to thank my sons, Derrick and Drew, who bring so much joy to my life and inspire me to be my best every day.

Very special thanks go to Jennifer Bhagia-Lewis and Evelyn Amaya Ortega for their expert fact-checking skills and to photographers Anne Murray Mozingo, John Thompson, Omar Vega, and Frederick Noble for allowing me to use their images.

I owe much gratitude to my dear friends and traveling companions, Shelly Williams, Scottie Williams, and Amy Tinaglia. Thanks for coming along for the ride. I will always treasure our friendship.

And special thanks go to my lifelong friend Caryl Altman Howard for introducing me to this beguiling island and for playing a major role in some of my fondest memories of life in Puerto Rico.

Photo Credits

Title page photo: © Steven Gaertner/123rf.com

All photos © Suzanne Van Atten except page 4 © Sorin Colac/123rf.com; page 5 © Maciej Maksymowicz/123rf.com; page 9 (top) © Daniel Alvarez/123rf.com, (bottom left) © Todd Arena/123rf.com, (bottom right) © Mark Franco/123rf.com; page 10 © Wangkun Jia/123rf.com; page 12 © Victor Moussa/123rf.com; page 14 © pyzata/123rf.com; page 15 © Todd Arena/123rf.com; page 17 © Todd Arena/123rf.com; page 18 (bottom) © Omar Vega; page 28 © Omar Vega; page 113 © John Thompson

Also Available

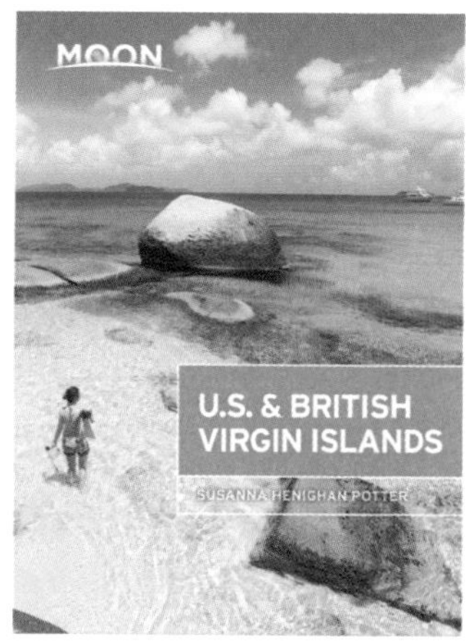

MAP SYMBOLS

Expressway	City/Town	Airport	Golf Course
Primary Road	State Capital	Airfield	Parking Area
Secondary Road	National Capital	Mountain	Archaeological Site
Unpaved Road	Point of Interest	Unique Natural Feature	Church
Feature Trail	Accommodation	Waterfall	Gas Station
Other Trail	Restaurant/Bar	Park	Glacier
Ferry	Other Location	Trailhead	Mangrove
Pedestrian Walkway	Campground	Skiing Area	Reef
Stairs			Swamp

CONVERSION TABLES

°C = (°F - 32) / 1.8
°F = (°C x 1.8) + 32
1 inch = 2.54 centimeters (cm)
1 foot = 0.304 meters (m)
1 yard = 0.914 meters
1 mile = 1.6093 kilometers (km)
1 km = 0.6214 miles
1 fathom = 1.8288 m
1 chain = 20.1168 m
1 furlong = 201.168 m
1 acre = 0.4047 hectares
1 sq km = 100 hectares
1 sq mile = 2.59 square km
1 ounce = 28.35 grams
1 pound = 0.4536 kilograms
1 short ton = 0.90718 metric ton
1 short ton = 2,000 pounds
1 long ton = 1.016 metric tons
1 long ton = 2,240 pounds
1 metric ton = 1,000 kilograms
1 quart = 0.94635 liters
1 US gallon = 3.7854 liters
1 Imperial gallon = 4.5459 liters
1 nautical mile = 1.852 km

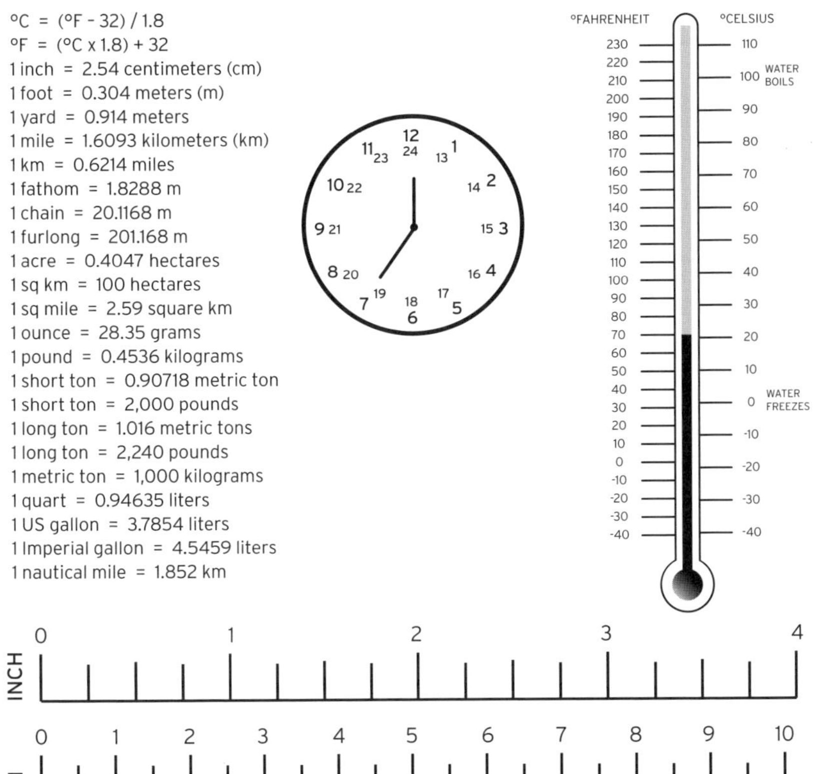

MOON SAN JUAN, VIEQUES & CULEBRA
Avalon Travel
a member of the Perseus Books Group
1700 Fourth Street
Berkeley, CA 94710, USA
www.moon.com

Editor: Sabrina Young
Series Manager: Kathryn Ettinger
Copy Editor: Naomi Adler Dancis
Production and Graphics Coordinator: Darren Alessi
Cover Design: Faceout Studios, Charles Brock
Moon Logo: Tim McGrath
Map Editor: Kat Bennett
Cartographers: Kat Bennett, Brian Shotwell
Proofreader: Alissa Cyphers
Indexer: Greg Jewett

ISBN-13: 978-1-63121-227-7
ISSN: 2325-5706

Printing History
1st Edition — 2013
2nd Edition — November 2015
5 4 3 2 1

Front cover photo: Sun Bay, South Coast Vieques, Puerto Rico © Thomas R. Fletcher / Alamy
Back cover photo: © Todd Arena/123rf.com

Printed in Canada by Friesens